## LINDA ELLERBEE

### *And So It Goes*

"Funny, Acerbic and, Most of All, Informed. Ellerbee writes deliciously and on target."
—**Mike Wallace**

"Turning These Pages is More Fun Than Flipping Channels. Linda Ellerbee, a serious journalist, has written a funny book about TV news that serious people should tune in to."
—**Leslie Stahl**

"Freewheeling ... Funny and Candid ... Ellerbee has bucked the odds and contributed something quite special to the canon of media nonfiction. *'And So It Goes'* is a book about TV, written by someone on TV, that is more entertaining than the TV being written about. Ellerbee's book is a riot."
***—Philadelphia Inquirer***

"On screen, Linda Ellerbee is that startling thing, a network person with edge. In print she is even sharper and funnier, a natural writer with good stories and an unnerving message: TV is human."
—**Roy Blount, Jr.**

"Literate, Witty and Lots of Fun to Read. As the old saying goes, I wish I had written this book. Linda Ellerbee captures all the zaniness, as well as seriousness, of our business."
—**Sam Donaldson**

"Linda has always been a great writer but in television news her words were lost in the fleeting airwaves. Now her irreverent wit is with us for posterity! Don't Miss It."
—**Connie Chung**

***MORE...***

"Ms. Ellerbee Has Lots to Say ... incisive and witty!"
—*Wall Street Journal*

"An Unsparingly Honest Account of the world of TV news, jammed with juicy anecdotes and written with Ellerbee's unmistakably dry wit." —*Us*

"A Real Treasure ... wonderful, hilarious, informative ... Linda Ellerbee's book makes me want to stop total strangers on the street and quote from it ... Nobody in television can be as intelligent or witty as she is."
—**Dan Jenkins**

"Wryly talkative, a little on the profane side, and often very funny." —*Washington Post*

"Ellerbee Drags the Skeletons Out of the Closet, names names, and tells all—from the 'old' days when women were a rarity on television news programs, to the present, when they're less rare but still endangered ... This is Probably the Best Book on Television to Come Along in Years, and It's Definitely the Most Entertaining." —*Ms.*

"Wonderfully Funny ... This book could become the *I Ching* of the TV news business ... Ellerbee writes in the lean, wry style that has been her hallmark ... She is an original." —*Village Voice*

"Candid ... Vivid and Witty ... Her Vibrant humor, candor and inability to take herself too seriously make this book worth the admission price." —*L.A. Daily News*

"A Good, Brisk, Entertaining Read for anybody with a morbid curiosity about what television journalism is like from the inside ... breezy, blowzy, raffish, flip, and funny."
—*Columbia Journalism Review*

"One of the Funniest and Frankest Television Memoirs Ever Written ... full of tragi-comic anecdotes about her business and wise observations about how television news programs really work ... wonderful!" —*Vogue*

"Ellerbee Talks Tough about the shortcomings of her profession and salty about sex and sexism at the office ... *'And So It Goes'* is a breezy collection of anecdotes about covering the news both soft and hard..." —*Time*

"Linda Ellerbee is that rare bird among television journalists whose pluck, sense of humor and inquisitive intelligence inject a welcome note of originality into TV news' pleasantly soporific conformism. In her unabashed memoir, *'And So It Goes,'* she evokes highlights of her career, offering incisive anecdotes, inside dope, and assertive opinion on the state of the world."
—*Back Stage*

"Breezy and Flip and Very Good ... Ellerbee gives us style and plenty of substance, such as her admission that underestimating the viewer's intelligence is a 'condition of the trade.'" —**UPI**

"On TV, Linda Ellerbee is acerbic, smart, laugh-out-loud funny. In this book she's just the same—only longer and free to tell the off-camera truth. She believes viewers are smarter than almost anything on TV. We *know* she is."
—**Gloria Steinem**

"Wonderful ... Funny ... Always on Target." —*Variety*

# "And So It Goes"

## Adventures in Television

Linda Ellerbee

BERKLEY BOOKS, NEW YORK

This Berkley book contains the complete
text of the original hardcover edition.
It has been completely reset in a typeface
designed for easy reading and was printed
from new film.

"AND SO IT GOES"

A Berkley Book / published by arrangement with
G. P. Putnam's Sons

PRINTING HISTORY
G. P. Putnam's Sons edition / April 1986
Berkley edition / June 1987



ISBN: 0-425-10237-8

A BERKLEY BOOK ® TM 757,375
Berkley Books are published by The Berkley Publishing Group,
200 Madison Avenue, New York, New York 10016.
The name "BERKLEY" and the stylized "B" with design
are trademarks belonging to Berkley Publishing Corporation.
PRINTED IN THE UNITED STATES OF AMERICA

# *Acknowledgments*

It was Deni Auclair's idea that I write a book, even though I'd never written one before and might have nothing to say, for all I knew. However, Ms. Auclair and Putnam's mentioned a figure large enough to render me momentarily insane. Giddily, I promised to find something to say. That was July, 1983. By July, 1984, I'd spent the money, written nothing and stopped returning Deni Auclair's phone calls. There was nothing to do but give back the money. Putnam's, however, didn't want the money; Putnam's wanted a book. It remains an accurate observation that the lack of alternatives clears the mind wonderfully.

I want to thank the people who helped, beginning with those who sheltered me. Pete Simmons lent me his house at Spofford Lake, New Hampshire. David Berg invited me to stay at his house in Houston in July, 1984, because, he said, Houston was so miserable in July I would not be tempted to do anything *but* write. Kit and Billy Wohl lent me their wonderful, haunted apartment in New Orleans's French Quarter for the month of August—anyone who will spend July in Houston will not flinch at August in New Orleans. Beth and Chuck Dudley fed and otherwise sustained me during that time, and proved how old friends get to be old friends.

I am indebted to Susan Hennessy and Leslie Lovell for typing and thinking at the same time, and to Nadine Stewart, for being a friend and for researching and checking over what I wrote, in spite of my protests that too many facts could really drag a story down.

I'm grateful to Esther Newberg, my agent, who encouraged me before she'd seen a word of this and continued to encourage me after she had; and to Ralph Mann, who has represented me in television all these years and who must try to find me work after the book comes out. I especially want to thank Neil Nyren, my editor, who helped to pare away the dreck and showed me a thing or two.

Joshua, my son, took the time to read everything as it was written, and gave me unbiased, solid advice. ("Mother, the whole chapter stinks. Start over.") Vanessa, my daughter, forced me to see myself and my work more clearly, even if the view wasn't always as pretty that way. And Jerry Paul did his best to make an honest writer out of me.

Finally, I would like to thank James Mangan of the Associated Press, who fired me fifteen years ago—and all five presidents of NBC News for whom I've worked so far—without whom this book would not have been possible.

LINDA ELLERBEE
September, 1985
New York

*This book is dedicated*
*to the Unaccompanied Minors,*
*the Lawyer Criminal*
*and the plumber in Albuquerque.*

# CONSIDER THIS

Reality has come to seem more and more like what we are shown by cameras.
SUSAN SONTAG

I wouldn't mind writing one of those books about the good old days—how I went out into the land and committed journalism, covering the important stories, every one of them, everywhere, better than anyone—but the thing about lying is that unless you're a political candidate or a network vice president, you've got to set yourself some limits and hold fast. Anyway, the only people in my business worth a damn are those who haven't written a book about television news. I would prefer to be counted with that group, so let me say right now that this isn't a book about television news.

That is, it's not a book about how television news failed to keep its promise, leaving the global village stranded in the wings; nor is it a book about this altogether swell human being who rose to unparalleled heights in television news, despite being female, brunette, uneducated, Texan, Pisces or wrong. Or right.

All I mean to do here is tell a few good stories. What kinds of stories and why I tell them, apart from obvious and perfectly true reasons having to do with ready cash, can be explained by telling one story now, which is sure to disappoint my family. I was raised by and have raised people who regard telling one story when two would do as a sign someone is not really trying. Around my place, brevity is an acquired taste.

The story is about the day my son, Josh, was brief. He was fourteen years old. It was summer. He stood on the Mall in Washington, D.C., and watched me make a fool of myself. He wasn't alone; I did it on national television. The program did not, as we are fond of putting it, sing, and Josh's mom did not rise above it. She was not wonderful. She was not a bright note in an otherwise dim hour. She was not, she wished, there.

Later that same night, a group of us who had worked on the show gathered for some serious second-guessing, with emphasis on whether the program should have been aired live, as it was, or taped earlier and fixed in time for air. It's become a generic argument in television news, with one side insisting the spontaneity of live television, including the risks involved, is the medium's greatest charm—and its future—while the other side argues that good television is better than live television. Tape the show. Edit the show. Air the result. We wring plenty from that rag, and on the night I'm talking about we were just warming to our subject when Josh decided to explain things.

Didn't we understand anything? Tape. *Live?* We had it all wrong. He gestured toward the group of us.

"This is live. You, me, everybody in this room. *This* is live." He pointed to the inevitable box in the corner of the room.

"That, Mom—*that's television.*"

What this is, I guess, is a book without a hero or a moral, a reminder to myself that live is not life, that mine is a craft and not a calling, and most important: it's not brain surgery. It's not nuclear physics. It's television. It's *only* television.

It's nice to know.

Josh knew it all the time, but then he does not work in television. Consider this a hint.

While this book probably ought not to be looked at as journalism in the strict sense of the word, it does attempt to answer the five basic questions of journalism: Who? What? Where? When? Why? *Who,* for example, said, "Remember, the First Amendment is only an amendment"? *When* did the Salvadoran refugee appear on national television disguised as a hubcap? *What* is the I.T.P. factor and must it always be higher for goats? *Where* did the television producer tell the president to shut up and stick to the TelePrompTer? *Why* do you get the news you get?

Regarding the last question, you have to read the whole book, or be content with the answer I gave my mom. As a woman who stopped taking her only child to see Walt Disney movies after they killed off Bambi's mother, she found the news and the news programs too depressingly absurd to contemplate, until I told her we made it all up.

A final note to any of my colleagues—or employers—who read this book: I made it all up. Consider this a hint, too.

# WELCOME TO THE HOUSE OF TELEVISION

If you're going to play
the game properly,
you'd better know every rule.
BARBARA JORDAN

We call them Twinkies. You've seen them on television acting the news, modeling and fracturing the news while you wonder whether they've read the news—or if they've blow-dried their brains, too. I make my living as a reporter and sometimes-anchorwoman on network television and, like almost everyone in my business, I've an overdeveloped ego and a case of galloping ambition. Some of my colleagues want to be The Anchorman on the Mount. Others see themselves as the Ace Reporter. Because of *60 Minutes,* there's a whole herd of them determined to be The Grand Inquisitor, and because of the way ratings affect our jobs, a heady number want only to be The Friendliest Anchor on the Block. At least one wants to be Jesus. Me, I just didn't want to be thought of as a Twinkie.

By 1978, I was sure I'd escaped, that I was a rare breed of television journalist, that I was known for my, um, skill. After all, wasn't I in New York City about to coanchor the NBC News magazine *Weekend* and didn't everybody say *Weekend* was a writers' program? I must be a hell of a writer. And didn't everybody say *Weekend* was a program where eloquent use of pictures counted as much as words? I must be a visual genius. It was clear: using nothing but my little words and pictures, I would push the frontiers of television news. The only trouble, as I saw it, was that too many people failed to spot how special I was. They seemed to think that because I was a television anchorwoman I must be a Twinkie.

Take what happened with my neighbor. I'd just found a place to live in Greenwich Village. The day I moved in, she introduced herself and asked what I did. I told her about *Weekend,* how fine it was, how smart I was, and when I was done, she said, "Oh, I see. You mean you're a television anchorwoman. That's nice, dear."

She said I must meet a certain tenant in her building because the tenant and I would have so much to talk about. I asked what the tenant did and was told that at the moment the tenant was cutting hair. (A hairdresser? This woman wasn't paying attention.) I declined, explaining I couldn't see how the tenant and I had much to say to each other, not that I had anything against cutting hair but I was, I hinted, into more important stuff. My hair was not a concern; I was a journalist.

I never did meet the tenant, but a year or so later, when the children and I went to the movies one day, there was a terrible commotion in our part of the theater when the credits rolled, because there on the screen after the words "edited by," was the name of the tenant I had passed up meeting. The name of the movie? *Hair.* The tenant wasn't cutting hair. The tenant was cutting *Hair.* I was a Twinkie.

You can be assured a good deal of dedication and hard work had gone into making me a self-absorbed jerk. It didn't happen overnight, but it does happen rather often in this business. It's easy to be smug, doing what I do. Television news is the candy store. They pay me to read. They pay me to travel around the world. They pay me to watch things happen, to go to parades, fires, conventions, wars, circuses, coronations and police stations—all in the name of journalism—and they pay me well. Walter Mitty, had he known, should have taken my job. As a matter of fact, Walter Mitty *could* have taken my job; I got it by accident.

There were no journalists in my family in Texas. They all worked for a living. I did not see *The Front Page* as a child; nobody I knew wanted to grow up to be Hildy Johnson, although several people I knew wanted to grow up to be Lyndon Johnson. My family read and I cannot remember being unable to read, but reading was something you did in school or for fun; it wasn't something you got paid to do. Writing was what you did when Aunt Rose sent a birthday gift or Mrs. Scott asked for a paper about what was important in *Silas Marner* and you hadn't read it. (Later I read it and the answer is, "Nothing.") Travel was what you did for two weeks in August. Reading, writing and traveling were good things to do but they weren't serious. Getting married was serious. That's what they told me.

I certainly didn't learn about journalism at college, although I did draw a few cartoons for the student magazine at Vanderbilt University, but I can't think they made much of an editorial statement, because the only one I can remember showed an ugly woman standing in front of one of those machines which gives you quarters in exchange for dollar bills and has printed across its front: "CHANGE—ONE DOLLAR." In the little balloon coming out of the ugly young woman's head, I had written, "I've spent $18 and I haven't changed yet." Garry Trudeau was not threatened.

We weren't given to making strong editorial statements, those of us who were freshmen at Vanderbilt in 1962. Events that would change a nation were going on all over the South, but on campus in Nashville the watchword was "apathy." It was the year parodied a decade and a half later by the National Lampoon movie *Animal House.* There really were toga parties. Students dressed in bed sheets to get drunk and lunge at other students. Fraternities threw the parties, the same fraternities that wouldn't let Jews join because they were afraid everybody who wasn't Jewish might quit. They were probably right. Those who were not members of fraternities or sororities, or were not members of the *right* fraternities or sororities, we called "nubs." Anyone who wrote for the school newspaper was a communist, we figured. Anyone who had anything to do with the school theater department was a queer, of course. The largest organization on campus was the Young Republican Club. The second largest was the group made up of students who gave blood once a year for four years in order to get free blood transfusions for life. I belonged. We didn't have nasty names for black people on campus. We didn't have to. At Vanderbilt, in 1962, the only black people I saw on campus were raking leaves or washing dishes.

Someone at *Newsweek* magazine, writing fondly of

that time, said college students in 1962 were just a bunch of fun-loving, "apolitical anarchists." If "apolitical" means we did not do our own thinking and did not care that we didn't, then we were apolitical. If "anarchist" means someone who dresses just like everybody else at all times and tries to act just like everybody else at all times, then we were anarchists, right down to our madras wraparound skirts, Bass Weejun loafers, white blouses with Peter Pan collars and our circle pins.

Ah, the circle pins. The myth was, you wore the pin on one side of your collar if you were a virgin, on the other side if you were not. This required a young woman to remind herself which she was while getting dressed every morning—and whatever the answer, it was an uncomfortable way to start the day. It also required a young woman to keep straight about which side of the collar meant what, or, like some of us, to pin the damn thing on whichever side was easiest and know you had a fifty percent chance of being right.

We used the same code words, the same group-speak that hid more than it revealed, and we followed most of the rules, no matter how silly. For example, women were not allowed to wear slacks to class in 1962, and were permitted to wear slacks while walking around the Vanderbilt campus only if they were worn under a full-length raincoat. A real anarchist would have burned the dorm. An apprentice anarchist would have burned the raincoat. Instead, I went around for a year and a half feeling like a flasher. And I joined a sorority, and did not study very hard, and wasted my parents' money, my teachers' time and my chance for a college education. I am as nostalgic for the good old days at Vanderbilt as I am for the Cuban missile crisis, which also took place in 1962.

In 1964 I quit school. I was nineteen, an age at which I regularly found it difficult to locate my backside with both hands. There followed some years during which what happened to me can be of little interest to anyone outside my immediate family and is of interest to them only when I insist. I moved around some, married some, had two babies, worked for three radio stations, one of which hired me to read the news because I sounded black—my Texas heritage—and the black woman it had hired did not. Since it was an all-black radio station, the all-white management thought sounding black was as good as being black—maybe better. In radio I learned about keeping logs, editing audiotape, writing copy, selling air time, announcing and "running a board," which sounds one hell of a lot more sporting than it is. It means turning dials, spinning turntables and pushing buttons so that everything does what it is supposed to, when it is supposed to, so that sounds do not trespass on each other and, at the same time, so there is no dead air. In radio silence is usually regarded as a gaffe, an indiscretion not to be committed in public.

Those years, many of them, coincided with what we sometimes call "the sixties" and other times call "the last children's crusade." Some people get religion. I got politics, let my hair grow, took off my shoes, put on an old army jacket, marched, sang, lived in a commune, learned how to kill and dress deer, learned I didn't want to do that, talked revolution, walked the woods in Alaska, walked the river between Texas and Mexico and bored absolutely everybody with my answers to everything. May I never eat another bowl of brown rice as long as I live.

Yes, it was an important time in this country's history, but I was not an important part of it. Mostly I just talked a good game. Still, I believed. Oh, did I believe. I believed until the day I found myself in Juneau, Alaska, without a job, without a husband, without an education—but *with* a three-year-old daughter and a two-year-old son to raise. Then I became a journalist.

It was as simple as could be: I needed the money. No dream. No vision. No ambition. I needed the money to raise my children. Recently, I'd been fired from my job at radio station KJNO in Juneau, Alaska, over what you might call a personality conflict. Mine conflicted with that of the man who owned the station. We disagreed about one or two little things, like how his station ought to be run. He pointed out that I might be right but only one of us owned the station, so it would be real interesting to see how fast I could pack. I learned something valuable from the experience; I learned I could pack very fast. It has come in handy. Once an editor explained to me that a journalist was just an out-of-work reporter. If that's so, then I have been—from time to time—one hell of a journalist. Never trust anyone in this business who hasn't been fired at least once. I have been fired more than once, and always for cause. I am trustworthy.

For a while I got work writing speeches and radio and television programs for Terry Miller, majority leader of the Alaska state senate, who managed to stay in politics in spite of my help. During that time I wrote letters to dozens of radio stations and newspapers in the Southwest; I wanted to go home. I was tired of looking at gray, green, and silver. I wanted to look at yellow, red, and brown; I was tired of mountains, I wanted sky. My family, good people that they were, wanted the children and me to move in with them, in Houston, but with more strings attached than my pride was going to allow. Still, they wanted me, and no news organization did, with the exception of one.

The Dallas bureau of the Associated Press answered my letter. It said it had tests I could take, and if I passed them, *maybe* I could have a job, even though I had no degree and little experience. Three radio stations, two small newspapers and a state senator's speeches did not count for much under the heading EXPERIENCE. But I had to take the tests *in Dallas*—the Associated Press was not going to send tests to another city, state or country. The children went to a neighbor, I went to Dallas and to the bookstore at Southern Methodist University, where it was possible to get a copy of the reading list for the basic journalism course offered there. Then, for not too much money, it was possible to buy second-hand copies of those books and also possible to stay up for two days and nights in a motel room reading the books, which is how I happened to go to work for the Associated Press, a fine news-gathering organization and one for which I might still be working, were it not for the Letter.

Other people have written about the Letter but I have not; for years I didn't even want to think about it. That can happen when you humiliate yourself. The Associated Press was exactly right to fire me. The mistake it made was hiring me in the first place, which, I believe, is how they still feel about it over there.

I was hired to write stories for the broadcast wire that could be read on radio and television newscasts. It was December, 1972, and the AP had recently purchased word processors for its Dallas bureau. Some of us used the word processors more intelligently than others. Some of us who are low-tech now were low-tech then.

But only one of us wrote on her word processor a long, chatty letter to a friend in Alaska. In it I maligned a couple of Texas newspapers, the Dallas city council, the Vietnam war, and a fellow I was dating, topping it off with a little something about a mutual friend who was leaving the AP in Dallas. I believe I suggested that when she left, the bureau chief, who (in fine AP fashion) I named, might rid himself of any discriminatory guilt by hiring a half-black Chicano lesbian who could handle the AP stylebook.

I was no fool; I hit the keys on the word processor that would give me a printed copy of the letter—and would *not* send the letter out on the AP wire. The letter was mailed and I went home, unaware I had also hit the key that put the letter on hold in the computer. The following morning there was a space shot. The AP had invited people from member newspapers and radio and television stations to come to NASA, in Houston, so they could all see how well the new word processors worked.

They saw. Something in the computer keyed my letter, which was immediately sent out over the AP wire in four states. I was fired only because the AP's legal department told them it absolutely was against the law to shoot me, no matter how good an idea it might be. Once again I had no money, no job and two children to support, and this time everybody was laughing but me and the Associated Press.

I got lucky. What was an embarrassment to me was funny to many other people, and some of them had jobs to offer. One ran a newspaper, one of the newspapers I had mocked in the Letter. Another ran a radio station. Even UPI called to talk, but the call that mattered, eventually, was the call from Dick John, news director at KHOU-TV, the CBS affiliate in Houston. He said I wrote funny. He asked if I'd ever considered working in television news. I had rarely considered watching television news, I told him. I didn't own a television. What's more, I'd recently moved to Texas from Alaska, a state that in a way didn't own a television. When I lived in Alaska, television news was accomplished this way: every day, when the Pan Am over-the-pole flight stopped in Anchorage to refuel, it dropped off a cassette of the *CBS Evening News*. The cassette was picked up, taken to the television station and broadcast that night, one day late—probably the best way to watch the stuff.

The television reporters I'd seen on the street since my return were always asking some poor soul how he *felt* about something. No, thank you, I was neither interested nor qualified to work for television. After all, I'd seen it. Dick John said the pay was twice what the AP paid; I said I believed I could learn television. Just before we hung up, he asked me was I three feet tall with warts and if so, how big were the warts? I told him I had had the warts burned off, but I had a face like a moon-pie and was that okay? He said it was, he guessed, what with lighting and all. I went to work in television news. Do they do these things on the telephone anymore?

What is the lesson here? Why should a woman fired for plain stupidity be rewarded for being stupid with years and years of being well-if-not-overpaid to perform interesting work? If it helps, remember that Lizzie Borden was acquitted.

Local television news is where you ride the elephant. I mean that. When the circus comes to town, any town, the elephants must be walked from the train to wherever the circus will perform. It's called, unoriginally but accurately, "the elephant walk," and it is always scheduled early in the morning, often early on Sunday morning so it doesn't interfere with traffic, but late enough in the day so that the sun is up. There is a reason for this. Television needs light. Circuses know television will cover the elephant walk every year, and every year some idiot television reporter will ride the elephant for his story, usually only once, but ride it he will one day, because local television news is the place where you invariably wind up doing something you just know you're going to regret later, and you do regret it. After you've done it. I have ridden the elephant. Between January, 1973, and November, 1975, I worked as a local television news reporter, first for KHOU and then for WCBS, the CBS-owned station in New York City.

It seems the Associated Press had fired me at just the right time—actually, a day sooner would have been just the right time as far as the AP was concerned—but I'm talking about time as far as it concerned me. KHOU had hired its first woman reporter in 1971; she'd done so well she'd left Houston for a better job. KHOU thought maybe it would try hiring another woman—and see.

The woman I replaced was Jessica Savitch. Blonde, beautiful and poised, Jessica had become sort of beloved in Houston. In fact, she had been one big hit, and, as you would expect, one hard act to follow. I would go out on stories, fumbling tape recorders, microphone cords and light stands, muttering to myself, trying to keep in mind what little television "stuff" I knew, trying not to get in the cameraman's way, and I would approach some member of the city council to ask him what he thought about gun control (in Houston, never very much), only to be asked by the councilman, "Whar's Jessica? Whar's that cute little thang? And who're you, gal?" It was enough to depress a less dedicated journalist with fewer mouths to feed.

When I tell that story, I'm not making fun of how Texans talk, even though we talk funny. I had an uncle who used to tell people he'd just met how he was in the "awl bidness." They all do that. In his case, it was true. He worked in a "fillunstayshun." And not for "playzhure." I know the reason I cannot speak French is that I first learned it from a teacher who began each lesson by making us say after her, "Bone jewer." Now, people *practice* talking Texas, even Texans—if they want to get along in Texas. My pal David Berg is a criminal lawyer in Houston. David was raised in Houston but says his success with Texas juries started to increase the day Richard "Racehorse" Haynes, another Texas criminal lawyer, taught him how to say "Gawd," while wearing a six-hundred-dollar suit. (Racehorse says that's not true; he says nobody can say "Gawd" right in a suit that costs more than two hundred fifty. He says that dawg won't hunt, which may be where Dan Rather got it.)

However, what is useful in Texas is not always useful in television, as I found out years later when NBC News sent me back to Texas for a few weeks to cover some stories there. When I returned, I was asked to rerecord all my narration for the stories because on the tapes I sounded like a Texan. I didn't know, right then, that they meant I was afflicted. It turned out it was okay with them that I was Texan, what with the card I carried that said I could read and all. What wasn't okay was *sounding* like a Texan. I explained to them that Iowa corn and Louisiana crayfish cause people to speak differently. A man from Boston is not to be confused with a man from North Carolina. Why, in North Carolina, you have to listen very carefully to understand anything anyone is saying to you, and still it is chancy. It's how we are, though, and that's good.

My bosses said that was nice, but it didn't have anything to do with television, although one of them confessed to having heard of Iowa. My bosses said we should all sound alike. They said we should all sound as if we'd grown up in the same place. I asked them what place that was. One executive thought his office would be appropriate, and the others soon agreed since they hadn't been to Iowa or North Carolina but they'd all been to his office. It became clear: people on television were meant to sound like they'd grown up in a network vice president's office. In some cases, it may be true. If you're on television, you can't be from Texas, or Brooklyn, Oregon, Nebraska or New Jersey. Especially New Jersey. You can't be from anyplace because the people who run television news aren't. After I understood, I practiced sounding as if I were from nowhere. Now they say I can go home again. As long as I don't talk to anybody.

Luckily, none of this mattered in Houston, in 1973. Everybody else talked like me so I didn't have to worry about my accent. That made one thing I didn't have to worry about, and just about the only one. Television was hard work. Who figured it would be such hard work? Somebody handed me a microphone, pointed a camera at me, and said, "You're on television, kid. Do something." Do what? I knew nothing about television news, nothing about how it should be put together, and there is no training program for that, not at a local station and not at a network.

I learned that, in television, you had to do what a print reporter did, and then you had to do things a print reporter didn't. The print reporter didn't have to read his reports out loud. He didn't have to care about light, or the absence of it. He didn't worry about planes flying overhead, tools breaking—*or getting the shot.* You are supposed to be *there* and not somewhere else when whatever is going to happen happens, because they can *say* it over for you, but they can't *do* it over for you—at least they're not supposed to and you're not supposed to let them. That is called "staging" the news. Also, the print reporter doesn't have to mess with trying to match words with picture, trying not to speak of oranges when the picture is of apples, trying to choose the best pictures, regretting the picture he forgot to make, discarding the picture not needed. All the print reporter has to worry about are the damn facts and the damn words.

I did the only possible thing under the circumstances. I threw myself upon the mercy of the cameramen, who were also the editors of the film. They taught me. Bit by bit. I remember one of them explaining to me, and explaining it gently, that when chasing a politician down the steps of the courthouse, I would be better off if I got *in front of* the politician and tried to stop him, since the cameraman wasn't getting too good a picture when all he could see was my back and the back of the politician, both retreating from his lens. I kept forgetting the mike cord was attached to the cameraman—to his equipment, anyway. The third time I tripped politician, cameraman, and myself, I remembered. I did worse things, but I don't have to confess to those and so I'm not. I had all the prejudice of a print reporter where television was concerned. Print reporters like to look down on TV and TV reporters, at least until they are offered jobs in TV. I'm not sure why this is; after all, in 1983, the year that TV gave the country *Vietnam: A Television History,* a thirteen-part series on public television and an outstanding piece of journalism, print gave the country *USA Today,* a newspaper for people who find television news too complex.

Houston was what is known as a good "news" town. They had a lot of murders in Houston, some politician or another was always under indictment (generally with reason), the space center at NASA could be counted on for stories and every autumn there was weather. A hurricane hits or threatens to hit that part of the Gulf Coast every September.

At KHOU each reporter covered one to four stories a day. Most of what we put on the air was short on production and long on wire-service–style reporting. We set a lot of store by action, too. There was one cameraman who never felt he had the complete story unless he got a shot of the bullet from head on. This man had trouble finding reporters to go with him on stories where there might be bullets. High-speed chases were standard fare; we had police radios in our cars, and the robber seldom got two blocks from the bank before we were in hot pursuit. That was all fine and thrilling except when we would accidentally get between the cops and whomever it was they, at high speed, were chasing. It happened more than once. I objected for reasons of cowardice. The police objected on empiric grounds. The robbers liked it a lot. However, most of the time we got along well with the cops, and for a time reporters were allowed to read police files. The practice stopped after what happened with the twenty-seven bodies, the reporters from New York City, and the snake.

It began when two teenagers, Richard Brooks and David Wayne Henley, charged with the murder of a man named Dean Corryl, confessed that, with Corryl, they had tortured and murdered twenty, maybe thirty young people, most of them runaway boys. (It was twenty-seven by the time they stopped digging.) The two boys took Houston police officers to a boat shed. Eleven partially decomposed bodies were dug up there. At that point it became a national story. Reporters from the networks, wire services and news magazines hit town the next day—on deadline. Reporters in the national press corps can be a little disrupting: they're loud and don't care much about niceties; they're not going to be in town that long.

The Houston police chief was a down-home sort of fellow, a good ol' boy who didn't care whether he had much (or any) experience in criminology or police administration. His was an appointed position, and he was the jolly sort who said every time he saw me, "Hi, girlie. What's news? Heh. Heh." A couple of years later, ol' sport found himself in more trouble when some of his boys were convicted of throwing some Mexicans off a bridge. This was not a police chief to welcome a bunch of arrogant sons of bitches from New York, Los Angeles and *Dallas,* for Chrissakes, pushing him, sticking mikes into his face and asking him a bunch of damn-fool questions about runaway boys.

When Theo Wilson, crime reporter for the New York *Daily News,* wanted to know how twenty-two cases of runaway boys from the *same* neighborhood in his city had managed to escape the notice of his crime-stopping police force, the chief said it was time those people went home. When Theo Wilson and some of the other national reporters discovered Houston homicide detectives regularly let local reporters go through police files—and had been letting us do so on this case while the police chief stonewalled the national press—well, things began to get interesting. Theo Wilson was not a large woman, nor a young one. She was an average-looking, disheveled little lady who would tap-dance up one side of you and back down the other if you happened to get in her way while she was working on a story—even if you were the police chief. He must have known that, somehow. He never called Theo "girlie." If he had, he wouldn't have done it again. And Theo was only one of a group of hardworking, everyday, nonglamorous national reporters who didn't know the chief and didn't care about his opinion of them. They were on the job. He was in the way.

First, the chief yelled at us, the local reporters. Then he decided to let all reporters, even the ones from Dallas, follow along the next day, when Brooks and Henley had promised to show the police more graves, this time in the Sam Houston National Forest, about sixty miles north of Houston.

It was a grand procession. There were cars of city cops, cars of cops from the county where the procession began, cars of cops from the county where we were going, cars of state troopers, cars of Texas Rangers—and the local and national press. Somewhere in this long line of cars heading up the highway to the woods were two young men carrying internal maps of past horrors. With so many cars, it was nearly dark when we got to where people were supposed to be buried. It had rained and we walked into a forest that was damp, dripping, smelly and more than a little scary, considering the kind of picnic it was. For maybe half an hour, thirty or forty strangers followed Henley and Brooks in what may have been circles, for all I knew. Some of us began to think the boys were having a bit of fun, according to what they thought was funny. Henley stopped. The spot looked no different from any other spot in the forest.

"Dig here," he said.

Two feet under the earth were Masonite boards and under those, mutilated bodies of young boys, boys you might have known, boys you might have been kin to. It was dark now. They dug by the light of television cameras. Finally, Henley said there was nothing else in that hole and turned, walking deeper into the night woods. There was no trail, none that we could see. We followed Henley.

"Dig here."

The television lights were turned on. The cameras were not. Digging began and you could hear the sound of shovels scraping, trees dripping, the sound of your heart beating—which is why the noise the rattlesnake made when the shovel hit it caused such a stir. People went every which way. One scream encouraged another. Veteran homicide detectives hit notes generally reserved for the castrati, and a Texas Ranger, making his way to safety, up a tree, was seen using—as rungs—the heads and shoulders of an entire ABC crew.

Well, now, don't you know the national reporters wrote stories about Texas cops and Texas *Rangers* yelling and climbing trees, which made the Houston police chief madder than ever. Local reporters wrote stories about what happened in the forest, too, but the only people who read or saw those stories already knew about the police chief, so we should have been safe.

We weren't. The chief said it was *our* fault; we'd had too much liberty. Look what it had led to. It had led to people like that Theo Wilson woman wanting to know about runaway boys. It had led to people who didn't *understand* Houston asking him about Houston.

After that, the Houston Police Department started to lie to us the same way it lied to outsiders, which was regularly and impersonally. The files were closed.

The prejudice of the police chief reflected the feelings of most Texans, and likely most reporters. I've heard it said that the first law of journalism is to confirm existing prejudice, rather than contradict it. For example, in 1973 television news in Houston covered murders only if white people were involved, or—if it had to do with blacks or Mexicans—only if there were more than three bodies. It shouldn't have been that way, but it was, and I've seen the same reasoning used in New York City, Chicago and Los Angeles. It was not a Texan, but an executive of *Time* magazine who said, "We report the world as we see it, intelligently and thoughtfully, from a moderately conservative point of view. Though, mind you, we've often been quite liberal—in the 1930s we suggested that Negroes weren't really being treated as equal."

In defense of all of us—journalists and real people—I would like to say we've gotten smarter. I would like to say that. However, I can't. I see some improvement. For example, on a visit to Texas in 1983, I happened to go to the town of Goliad, site of a battle during what we were taught in school to call the Texas "war for independence." When I was in school it was described like this: The greasy, smelly Mexicans marched into the land of the freedom-loving Texans and kicked the shit out of all those good people until Sam Houston came along and gave them what for. Twenty years later, in 1983, the pamphlets available at the mission in Goliad, the site of the battle, actually went so far as to hint that the land the freedom-loving Texans wanted to own *did happen to belong to Mexico.* As for the "smelly" part, anyone who knows a thing about Texas weather knows that before air-conditioning, everybody smelled, most especially the Texans, since they insisted on wearing clothes more suited to Tennessee and Virginia.

To say Texas moved into the twentieth century as far as its history books are concerned is pleasant; to say Texas moved into the twentieth century in its biology books is conjecture. In the spring of 1984, NBC News sent Allison Davis—a field producer, friend and troublemaker—and me to Texas. The result would be a ten-minute story, broken into two parts on *Nightly News,* about the state that may be said to choose our textbooks. Texas, as the largest single purchaser of textbooks, has the ear of the publishers, and possibly some other parts as well, because what Texas wants printed usually gets printed. The books, of course, go to many other states, too, states that don't have the clout to dictate content. In 1974, the state of Texas said it would not buy books for biology classes unless those books presented Darwin's theory of evolution as only one theory, giving equal time to other theories—like the Bible story of creation. In the ten years that followed, the teaching of evolution in high-school textbooks dropped anywhere from thirty to eighty percent across the nation. There were biology textbooks in which the word evolution could not even be found in the index, and now, in 1984, the state of Texas was writing new rules; now it was dropping the requirement that evolution be taught at all, as long as "creationism" *was* taught. Allison and I talked to Joe Kelly Butler, president of the Texas School Board. Wasn't Texas being a bit high-handed? Said Butler: "We feel no responsibility to the other states."

This was just the kind of statement that made Allison think all Texans were crazy. Being a woman of uncommon sense, she has no patience with anyone she feels has none or at least isn't showing any at the moment, and she is seldom if ever able to keep her mouth shut about it, which is why, when we are on the road together, I occasionally find myself starting sentences with, "What Allison really meant to say was . . ."

The day I met Allison, her first day on the job, I'd been assigned to take her out on a story and check her out; she was, after all, a black woman, and management is never sure about that sort of thing. We were going to do a story about the number of people who had begun sending their children to private schools, and why. Allison came into my office, strode into it, actually, sat down all firm-like, fixed me with a look designed to intimidate the correspondent, and informed me we would not use the term "busing" because the correct term was "court-ordered desegregation." She went on for ten minutes, and when she was done ranting, I told her we would use the term "busing" because this was network television, where seconds counted, and "busing" might not suit her sensibilities, but "busing," by God, was *short.* She understood immediately. We became good working partners and we became good friends, and sometimes I use the term "court-ordered desegregation."

But before she decided to tell the Texas School Board president how absurd his position was, I thought I'd deflect her by reminding her it wasn't only Texans: If the state of Texas believed that its view of the world should prevail, no matter how peculiar the view—it was no more curious than the Vatican deciding, as it had the year before, that after a closer look, Galileo was still wrong. In that case, said Allison, the Vatican was crazy, too, at least as far as Galileo went. She was going to explain to Joe Kelly Butler the error of his and his state's ways. I told her she didn't understand Texas, that's all. She thought it meant something that a few years before—in the heat of a summer night—the Texas Legislature had voted to round off pi to three. And she was all for rushing over to San Jacinto County to cover the story of Humpy Parker, the sheriff there. Humpy was in hot water because some dumb ol' deputy had leaked to the press Sheriff Humpy's rules concerning cars passing through his county. The deputies, it seems, had been told to stop and check cars carrying black people, cars carrying people who looked like hippies—and all cars with Louisiana license plates. Allison got excited and said *that* said something about Texans, too. I'm pleased to say it did; Humpy got ten years.

Later, the Texas School Board changed its mind and struck its 1984 rule concerning evolution. Allison has never changed her mind about Texans. To her, we're still crazy. Who knows? If I'd had Allison along to help me make friends around Texas eleven years before, I probably wouldn't have lasted in the state or at KHOU very long. Without her help I lasted eight months.

In late summer of 1973, a fellow telephoned me, said his name was Eric Ober, he was assistant news director at WCBS-TV in New York City, he'd seen some of my work on the story of the runaway boys and their murderers (I don't know how) and was I interested in working in New York? I was not. I told him I was too old. New York City was for the twenty-two-year-olds, and I was twenty-eight. I did not tell him that in two years I'd lost two jobs, one husband, my first battle with a computer and considerable hide off my ego. I also did not tell him that I'd gained a new last name; I had married again. I had been Linda Veselka; now I was Linda Ellerbee, and I thought it would be a nice touch if I were able to stay in one place, on one job, with one last name, for a year, for a change. None of that was any of his business since I wasn't going to move to New York, anyway. He asked if I would come to New York and talk to them about the job. That I would do. I hadn't been in New York in years, and the last time my accommodations had been a sleeping bag for one. I figured WCBS could do better.

When I told my husband about the telephone call, he didn't laugh. He said I should think it over, go to New York and pay attention to what was said by those people. Meanwhile, in New York, "those people" were getting confused and one of them was getting angry—all before I'd worked a day there. Seems Eric Ober had called KHOU and asked for a tape of more stories of mine. KHOU had asked me to put three stories on a tape and send it to New York, which I did. Ober saw the tape, then called the news director at KHOU to find out why he (Ober) had asked for a tape of one reporter's work and gotten a tape of another reporter's work instead—*a reporter who wasn't as good.* He didn't want to hire Linda Ellerbee. He wanted to hire Linda Veselka. What was going on and, by the way, exactly how many Lindas did KHOU have on staff? (Apparently we do not, in fact, *all* look alike to management.)

Nobody told me about any of this. I went to New York almost sure I didn't want the job and most sure I didn't want to live in New York City. I retained my certainty until the taxi from the airport neared the approach to the Triboro Bridge. File this away somewhere: If you don't want to live in New York, don't take that road into the city, at sunset, on a clear day when the city skyline is backlit with the sun and the promises they made us in every corny old movie about New York we ever saw. I felt like Gene Kelly. I wanted to tap-dance in the backseat of the taxi. I think I did try a simple time step outside the door at WCBS. Inside the door, I was met with baffled looks. Was I sure I was Linda Veselka and not Linda Ellerbee? They wanted to make sure they'd gotten the right one, even if I didn't want to work in New York. I took the job. It was sweet of them to offer me money, but then they didn't know they'd already hired me on the ride into town.

My assignment at WCBS was to be "hard-news" reporter for the eleven o'clock broadcast. That meant I spent most of my time covering strikes, murders, fires, riots and strikes. In New York City, every union strikes every few years, whether it needs to or not. Being reporter for the late newscast also meant I had to deal with the new toy—the minicam—and the live news report. The station wanted, or thought it wanted, a live news report every night. I recall broadcasting a live report from a blood-donor clinic in Queens. My assignment editor told me the clinic would be packed with people rushing to give blood for an eleven-year-old paraplegic who, before the accident on the ramp, sang at street fairs to raise money for blind children. The broadcast would have been stronger if I hadn't been the only person in the clinic, except for the nurse. I telephoned the assignment editor and argued vehemently about the validity of reporting live from an empty clinic, and from such a glaring absence of a story. Then, when that didn't work, I did what they paid me for. After all, what's a pint of blood among cowards?

Once the crew and I rushed to the East River, where a New York City fireboat was sinking. The firemen had the boat lashed to another boat. The crew and I climbed on board, set up for our live report, a precarious, chancy operation in those days, then waited until we were on the air. I asked the fireman why his boat was sinking. He said *his* wasn't; ours was. Turned out he was right.

The first time I ever covered a demonstration, live, was one afternoon outside the Israeli consulate. We arrived and assembled the cumbersome equipment, but by the time we were ready to go on the air, the demonstration had moved around the corner, so we hauled the cables around the corner, but by the time we got there, the demonstration had moved around the next corner. A fight broke out. Many people clubbed one man. I ran back to the crew. We must hustle. We shouldn't miss this. We hustled, but when we moved the truck around the first corner so we could move the cable around the next corner, the man and the people who were clubbing him had pushed their way into the lobby of a midtown office building. We never got the story. You can do a lot with cables, but you cannot take them through a revolving door.

Later the equipment was less unwieldy, which came in handy the night the angry people took the Statue of Liberty hostage. I forget what it was they wanted; they let her go after two hours. What the producer of the eleven o'clock news wanted was a live report from the island—Liberty Island—never mind it was ten o'clock already, never mind that if we got there it would be too dark to see anything. He wanted a live report—and a live picture.

I rented a tugboat because the tugboat was there and, never having rented a tugboat in my life, I thought it would be worth it to see if I could. We got to the island. We went on the air. Watching television, you couldn't see a blasted thing—as I said, it was dark—but the entire time we were on the air you could hear the cameraman throwing up.

"What the hell," said the producer. It was live.

Local television news is often accused of going for the showy over the serious. "Are there flames?" People who say that about local news do not understand about November. Pick any November. Pay attention to what too many local news operations choose to air and promote during that month.

*Decadence in the 80s: A Five-Part Report:*
1. Is There a Pregnancy Crisis in Our Nursery Schools?
2. You Do So Get Warts.
3. Playing Doctor Causes Communism.
4. Herpes and How to Tell If Your Daughter Has It.
5. Is Your Babysitter Gay?

*Another Special Feature from the News Team That Cares What You Tell Your Child About Sex—And Why You'll Never Get It Right.*

Children, if they've watched *Dallas,* already have a working familiarity with lust. They learned about impotence from *Donahue. Love, Sidney* taught them about homosexuality, and, one hopes, tolerance. *Kojak* told them all the street names for prostitution and prostitutes. Soap operas offer daily classes in frigidity, menopause, abortion, infidelity and loss of appetite. If they've watched more than one made-for-television movie, they know about rape. Johnny Carson gives graduate courses in divorce and Jerry Falwell has already spoiled all of it with his class—"An Overview of Sin 101." Parents should probably view television as a blessing; after all, it took television to finally get sex education out of the schools and back in the home, where it belongs. Call it educational TV.

But in November, as well as May and February, local television news thinks you need to be told even more about sex, violence and communicable diseases. Those are "sweeps" months, as in rating sweeps. The ratings of television news programs taken during those months count more than ratings taken during other months, because the "sweeps" ratings are ones that will be used to set what a station—or network—may charge advertisers; therefore, during November, May and February, the viewer will be fed a high-calorie dose of what television news operations believe the viewer really wants to see, or at least will not want to miss. And television news says to itself, "Give 'em sex and violence, because we know that's what they want."

It's the Shetland pony theory of problem solving, a theory that embraces both sex *and* violence. During World War Two, a committee of British military psychiatrists had this swell idea for ending the war quickly. It seems Hitler had what amounted to a phobia concerning pornography and Aryan purity: pornography did not exist in the Third Reich, not to Hitler, because no real Aryan would do dirty things or want to look at pictures of dirty things being done. Therefore, if confronted with irrefutable evidence that Aryan people *did so* do dirty things, Hitler might go over the edge, collapse and take the German army with him. The psychiatrists' plan involved the RAF, a brave group of men who were willing to give their lives for their country. What they were not willing to do was to fly over Berlin, dropping thousands of photographs of young German women copulating with Shetland ponies. The RAF said the war would have to be won some other way. It was, but it took longer. (I stole this story from *The People's Almanac,* and if it's not true, please don't tell me.)

In television news, when the ratings aren't so good, we tend to send out for a dozen Shetland ponies and take our chances. Long wars are for those with long contracts and the independently wealthy. In television news, you stand a better chance at being independently wealthy than at getting the long contract. Shetland ponies: what a great idea! It's so, so prurient! The newscast is saved.

Local news has no lock on the sensational. When I was a local reporter, working for KHOU in Houston, I put on the air a three-part series on "Home Safety—And Why Your Home Isn't Safe." The point of the thing was to scare the viewers. Many years later, when I was a national correspondent for NBC News, I was assigned to a five-part series of reports on the increase of violent crime in America. The series would air on *Nightly News,* with each night's five minutes on violence done by a different reporter. It was a big deal, this series. The fact that it would air during a "sweeps" month was mere coincidence, as it was mere coincidence that the subject of violent crime had been the cover story on both *Time* and *Newsweek* the week before, as it was mere coincidence that the week before *that* the Justice Department had released a study saying what a violent nation we had become. Journalism is filled with coincidence.

My assignment for the five-part series at NBC News

was to kick off the week by making sure everyone understood what terrible trouble the country was in—go on the air, read the Justice Department figures, interview the experts, turn a phrase or two, arouse the viewers, and shut up, which would have been fine except for Allison Davis. Most people have to work at it, but Allison has a natural talent for making trouble. She is one of those truly dangerous journalists comfortable in courthouse basements, staring at deeds, poring over records and columns of numbers until she finds the place where the numbers don't add up as they should. So, when NBC assigned her to work with me on Part I of the violence series, the first thing Allison did was to check the Justice Department figures, to make sure they were accurate. They weren't. That is, there were two sets of statistics on violent crime, only one of which was considered reliable. The more reliable study showed that the rate of violent crime had not risen in seven years. The Justice Department chose to use the other study. To be more accurate, the brand-new attorney general chose to use the other study, the one that showed an increase in violent crime, even though his own department rated it less accurate. Allison and I went to Washington to talk with Reagan's new attorney general, William French Smith. We asked him why he decided to base his "war on violent crime" on statistics that were frightening, but questionable. He asked us where we studied law. We asked him why he was trying to scare people. He said, rather incautiously, that the figures didn't matter as much as the polls mattered, and all the national polls showed that violent crime was the number one concern of most Americans. Why were we making such a fuss about numbers? He said he knew, and the president knew, that if reducing violent crime was a major concern of the American people, it would be the first priority of the new Justice Department.

That it might have occurred to the White House that an epidemic of violent crime was a sexier issue than, say, organized crime or white-collar crime—and a much easier problem to solve, since the epidemic of violent crime didn't exist—is something nobody but a nasty old journalist would suggest. Allison suggested it. The attorney general said he had other appointments and would we please excuse him. Too bad. We were hoping he might break down on camera and confess all about the politics of violent crime.

We returned to New York to tell NBC we'd shot hell out of the premise of the five-part series on violence. We hoped NBC News would see the humor of it all. We hoped even more that NBC News would believe us and not the Justice Department. NBC News did. It did not, however, cancel the series. Instead, it allowed us to begin the week with a report on an epidemic of—not violence—but fear of violence. Allison and I took a camera crew to Glenwood Springs, Colorado, a town of fewer than six thousand people, a town that hadn't had a murder in eleven years or a rape in fourteen years, but taught martial arts as a required course in its junior high school, and where Girl Scouts were no longer allowed to walk home alone after dark, neighborhoods formed "watch groups," and one police officer told people that if somebody broke into your home and was shooting at you, shoot back. It was a town where, as in other towns and cities, old people had begun to live in their houses as prisoners, afraid to go out because fear had become more real than fact. And we reported that the Justice Department had its figures wrong, sort of.

That was early in 1981. In 1984, the Reagan administration announced that its war on violent crime was over. Crime had lost; statistics from the Justice Department showed a drop in the rate of violent crime. Public opinion polls showed that people credited Ronald Reagan and his policies. This time, arriving at the statistics on violent crime, the Justice Department used the other statistics, therefore, the violent crime rate fell. None of this should surprise anyone in television. It was almost November and November is "sweeps" month. In their business it's called election day.

Network reporters and producers like to think they are much better than local television reporters and producers. At the network, we know we are the keepers of the flame and those people in local news are the bozos. We like to hint that what they lack in substance they make up for in shallow. Consider the questions they ask. It is said that in journalism there is no such thing as a dumb question, only dumb answers. That is wrong. I worked for local news. There are dumb questions.

Once, on assignment in Alabama, I watched a reporter for local news there cover a story about a trampoline tournament. The winner of the tournament was a college student who had only one leg. He'd lost his other leg a year before in an automobile accident. Came the interview. The camera stayed on the face of the student as the reporter asked the following: "Gee, fellow, you won that contest good, but I heard you *used to* play football and run track. Does it ever, ever bother you that you'll *never* be able to do any of those things again?"

That is what you call your dumb question, one more variation of the all-time dumb television news question: "How do you feel about . . . ?" Fill in the blank. How do you feel, Mr. Arevir, about eight of your nine children dying in that fire? How does it feel, Cindy Lou, to be the only little blind girl pitching in the major leagues? How do you feel, Mr. President, about peace?

In Chicago, a television reporter once asked a bystander how she felt when she saw the scaffolding start to fall. The scaffolding had three men on it; they were working on a building under construction. All three were killed.

"I didn't feel anything," said the woman. "I didn't see the scaffolding fall."

"Well," said the reporter, "how would you have felt if you *had* seen it?"

In defense of us all, that reporter was fired.

A stupid question almost always means the reporter does not understand enough to ask any other kind of question. In Alaska, following the crash of an airplane into the side of a mountain in which 111 people died, the medical examiner held a news conference. One reporter, not content with facts, wanting something "grabbing," kept at the medical examiner, demanding to know precisely what had killed the 111 people. Finally, the medical examiner, fed up with the reporter's nonsense, said, "Son, let me put it this way. The plane stopped and the people didn't."

In 1975, in New York City, the mayor held a news conference, yet one more news conference to discuss that city's impressive financial difficulties. As simply as was possible, considering it was not a simple situation, the mayor explained what was going on. It took a while, and when he was done the first question was asked—by a reporter from a local television station.

"Tell me, Mr. Mayor, does this mean curtains for the Big Apple?"

The mayor had no answer, of course; that was okay

because the reporter had no question. In local television news it's important to have a question, because in local television news, questions are used on the air, right along with the answers. Print reporters don't do that, but television reporters—most of them—are constantly auditioning to be television reporters someplace else, and for that, they need—or think they need—to be frequently seen and heard in their news reports. So even if they ask stupid questions, they use the stupid questions on the air. In television, local or network, there are exceptions; there are reporters who need never be ashamed of their questions, reporters like Ted Koppel, who happens to be the best interviewer on television. Most of us are not Ted Koppel, however. Most of our questions do not deserve to be heard. Sometimes this is true of the answers, too, but we're talking about questions here.

Shortly after Lyndon Johnson died, Mrs. Johnson held an auction at the LBJ ranch. She wanted to get rid of some cattle. What the television reporter from Houston meant to ask, I think, was whether the cattle really were worth the price they were commanding. What he *did* ask—and did include in his report—was this question: "Mrs. Johnson, are people bidding so much money just so they can own a Lyndon Baines Johnson memorial cow?"

So you see, the dumb question does exist in journalism. The old rule is wrong. Or is it? When Betty Ford was First Lady, she held a news conference. What needed to be asked was asked and answered. No news was made. Everyone there was ready for the thing to end. But there was this one reporter who kept asking useless questions, the final useless question being, "Mrs. Ford, have your children used marijuana?"

Jeez, what a dumb, dumb question. You could hear the murmurs all over the room. Everybody exchanged looks. They were right. It would have been a dumb question—if the president's wife had not answered, "Yes."

I don't remember, but I like to think that question was asked by a reporter from some local television station, God bless 'em all.

Almost everybody who works in television news liked the *Mary Tyler Moore Show*, and what most of us liked best was the abcessed brain of Ted Baxter, anchorman extraordinaire. The pompous, near-illiterate, egomaniacal anchorman was the lovely, absurd combination of the worst parts of everyone who has ever anchored a local television newscast. There is a little Ted Baxter in all of us. During the time I worked for local television, I anchored only once. It was in New York City, and I substituted for Rolland Smith on WCBS's eleven o'clock newscast. The mind protects its own; I cannot recall if it was for one night or one week. I was awful. The station did not repeat its mistake. However, I remember, quite clearly, that for one night—or one week—people wanted to bring me coffee, comb my hair, write my scripts, make the room warmer or colder, fetch me a sandwich, offer me cigarettes and tell me I was wonderful. For a short time, people wanted to make me happy. That was nice. People don't do that for mere reporters. This anchoring stuff was okay, and boy, were the hours better. A person could get to like this. How do I look?

That's how it happens and it is to the credit of the men and women who anchor local newscasts—or network newscasts—that there are not more Ted Baxters. The local anchormen with whom I worked—

there were no anchorwomen at either station during my time—were professional, thoughtful men who knew their cities and their trade. At WCBS, that man was, and is, Jim Jensen. He's anchored the six o'clock news there for twenty-five years, and you don't last that long in New York or anywhere else without being good at what you do, which Jensen is. You also don't last if you don't know how to protect yourself, which Jensen does.

Once upon a time someone at WCBS decided Jensen should have a partner, a coanchor, in this case a fellow from another town, fresh to the big city, fresh to big-city ways. Your basic new gun in town. Jensen behaved graciously to the new gun, whose name also was Jim. Naturally, the new Jim had to change his name, but I guess he didn't mind much because Jim, the real Jim, had been so gosh-darned nice about it. That's what the new Jim said. Everything seemed to be going smoothly, but from time to time the new Jim seemed to slip, to bobble and generally to look foolish on the air. The truth was, the new Jim was not as good as the old Jim. Someone at WCBS had made a mistake. Of course, nobody at WCBS wanted to admit that, so they told the two Jims to be more friendly-like on the air, to chat with each other, like pals. They should ask each other about the news stories. Right.

There was this one night. The Jims were on the air. Jensen read a story. The next story was to be read by the new Jim. All he had to do was to read the words from the TelePrompTer, and what was written on the TelePrompTer was all the new *or* the old Jim knew about this particular story. There was no tape. The script on the TelePrompTer went something like this:

> "There was a five-alarm fire this afternoon in the South Bronx. Three people were killed. Firemen say they suspect arson."

There was no more information available. Here's what happened. Jim Jensen finished reading the story which came before. They shared a prompter—each man could see what the other was to read. When Jensen finished his story, he turned to the new kid and did exactly what management had told him to do; he talked to the new Jim about the news.

"Well, I see you're about to tell us about that terrible fire this afternoon up in the South Bronx. I don't know much about it but I understand it went to five alarms and that three people were killed. I hear the fire department thinks it was arson, but, gee, let me shut up now. What can you tell us about that story?"

Folks, that's how it's done downtown.

The new Jim left WCBS not too long after that; he really wasn't ready for the big leagues, although today he is a capable, well-liked anchorman—in New York City.

You see, we *can* learn; he did—but I have to say the poor man's discomfort afforded those of us in the newsroom more joy than anything else that happened there during my time, unless you count the day J. J. Gonzales punched out the assignment editor, and all you need to know about that story is that the act was long overdue and you can have your choice of reasons why.

Jim Jensen is still a star in New York City. His face is as familiar as the mayor's, and Jim has had *his* job longer. Local celebrity is a fact of local television. The celebrity even filters down to the street reporter sometimes. If you're a reporter and not an anchor, usually you are a local celebrity only if you cover theater, film, or both. Such is the case in New York City. Those people often look a little strange as well, but never mind. They are known at restaurants, theaters, parties of the rich and famous, and their dry cleaners.

On the beat I covered, the best you could hope for was immediate seating at night court. Dead people stuffed in oil drums are not glamorous; nor do they send out invitations to dinner. Furthermore, most politicians do not own restaurants, not ones you would want to eat at, anyway, and national political conventions are not, no matter what they say, parties. Finally, City Hall does not do shirts.

In all my time working in local news, the only perk I got from the job was that, for a while, I could get good seats for *A Chorus Line.* I paid for the seats, but they were terrific seats. It happened because I covered strikes. One day the local chapter of the musicians' union went on strike, or was locked out, depending on whose word you took. The strike closed all the Broadway musicals and kept one brand-new musical from opening. That was *A Chorus Line.* Negotiations were being held at the World Trade Center, in the offices of Vincent McDonnell, state labor mediator.

For the duration of the strike lockout, I was down there every night, and it was the damnedest labor dispute I ever covered. In one room were a dozen or so representatives of the musicians' union. The business of negotiation is slow and so to pass the time, some of them had brought along their instruments. They sat there in their room—and they played stuff. Broadway stuff.

Across the hall, in the other room and on the other side of the issue, were the Broadway producers, who sat around telling show business stories—funny, inside stories about Broadway and the people who make Broadway their life. Once in a while, a producer or two would begin to sing along with the music that happened to float into their room from across the hall—from the "enemy" room. It was a very merry strike and the only one where reporters hummed along.

That went on for days. As a result, I got to know some delightful folks from a part of New York City life that did not usually find itself in the news stories I covered. We had such a jolly time that most of the reporters—none of whom was used to this kind of strike—were ever so sorry when it ended. We were, however, happy that *A Chorus Line* would be able to open on Broadway, because a group of hard-news reporters who had covered this strike had made arrangements to go to the play. We may have spent most of our time in precinct houses and jails, but we were going to get fourth-row-center-aisle seats for *A Chorus Line* because—*we knew the producers*. It was all set. It would be grand, and it would have been grand if the hospital workers hadn't chosen the night we had tickets for the theater to go out on strike in Queens. So much for the celebrity beat.

In fairness, even local reporters who cover dull old hard-news stories get some share of celebrity, just because they are covering them for *television*. You can't help it. There you are, night after night, doing *something* and *doing it on television*. This is especially true if you stay at a particular television station for any length of time. Many do not. Some move from station to station like bees in search of the bigger and still bigger flower, convinced the bigger flower hides the most honey. Others, who like their jobs and like their towns, would like to stay where they are, but they must be very careful not to be blindsided.

A couple of years back, I read in the New York City newspapers that a television station in town was about to have a "major housecleaning." I only wish that meant somebody was going to sweep the newsroom and dust the TelePrompTer. It meant, naturally, that people were going to be fired. According to the newspapers, however, they weren't going to be fired without reason. No, sir. The station had a good reason for firing some of its on-the-air reporters. They were getting old. Somebody from the station management explained it in the papers. He said reporters who were over thirty-five were reporters who were over the hill, as far as television news was concerned.

I understood that. After thirty-five, too many facts rattling around inside a brain will turn any mind to mush. I'm sure it can be scientifically demonstrated that nights spent in the streets, years spent at typewriters and in edit rooms, time spent haggling with politicians—and city editors—will surely cause wrinkles. The face sags. The cheerleader smile atrophies. It gets increasingly harder to lift the corners of one's mouth when reporting what the citizens of your fine city have done to one another on a given day. However, one is supposed to smile; this is written somewhere inside the head of too many station managers and news directors, and they *know*, they are *sure* it is easier to smile if you don't know anything. (They are right.) They know this because they paid money to consultants who told them so. I cannot prove it, but I suspect consultants pay other consultants to tell them. I know that's why you seldom see station managers and news directors on the air: they are old and dried up from the work of handing over money to television news consultants.

This particular station didn't say whether consultants were the ones who told them to "clean house." The station merely said it was firing these people to improve its coverage of New York City, and in order to further that goal, it had hired new talent from Des Moines, Oklahoma City and Green Bay. That made perfect sense. The only thing better than being under thirty-five was being under thirty-five and from out of town.

No wonder so many people who work for local television stations think they would rather work for a network. I was one of them. A network seemed saner. I didn't know any better then. Besides, going to the network was considered, as a rule, a step up. Network news was more serious than local news, that was understood.

Ellen Fleysher and I talked about that very thing one night about three months after I had left WCBS to go to work for NBC News in Washington, D.C. At the time, we were sitting at the bar of the Park Lane Hotel on Central Park South in New York City, a well-mannered place to have a drink. Ellen had come to work at WCBS sometime during the two years that I had worked there; Ellen still worked there. She still worked as a local reporter. I, on the other hand, had "gone network." We talked about my new job, my future, the important stories I would cover, the important people I would meet, the places I would see. No more five-alarm fires in the South Bronx for me. This was the real thing. The big enchilada. Network. Network television news. I may have smirked a bit.

The bartender came over to where we were. We ordered. He paused.

"Excuse me, but aren't you Ellen Fleysher from Channel Two?" She said she was. He looked at me, the network journalist.

"Hey—didn't you used to be on television, too?"

# JOHN PETER ZENGER AND THE LUNCH LID

When you have an
efficient government you
have a dictatorship.
HARRY TRUMAN

When I worked in Washington I kept a saw in my office. There was a reason. Cutting notches in my bookcase may not have helped me to understand what went on in Washington, but it was cheaper than primal therapy. Finally, a senior White House official made me see what the trouble was when it came to television and government. Asked to name the White House's biggest complaint about the networks, he said, "They want to run their game shows instead of our game shows." I wish I could tell you his name. I wish he'd said it to me. He didn't; he said it to another reporter and all I can add is that it was said in November of 1983, during the first Reagan administration. You must be satisfied with an unnamed source. This chapter, you see, is about Washington, D.C., and so who said what is as important as what was said, especially if you are mildly unclear about what was said and totally ignorant about who said it. There is a gentle absurdity about Washington, D.C., and it is easy to develop affection for the place, if you can forget that the consequences of what goes on there are real, whereas what goes on there may not be. Alice, while in Wonderland, was *required* to believe six impossible things before breakfast. In Washington they do it by choice. You wake up in the morning, open the paper and read that the president, commenting on what he feels is a basic failure of the media to pay attention to detail, says, "If Lincoln were alive today, he'd roll over in his grave." Betyourass.

That was the first year I was in Washington, my first year as a network correspondent. The second year I was there, the Speaker of the House, explaining his opposition to television cameras in the House chamber, said, "We must keep the status quo just as it is." Always, always.

The third and final year I worked in Washington some members of the House of Representatives told television reporters that it was in fact possible that congressmen* were out of touch with the average working woman and man in America. It was possible, they conceded, because a recent public opinion poll regarding public trust had placed congressmen near the bottom of the list, topping no occupations but those of corporation executives and union leaders. The idea of a workingmen's caucus caught fire.

*I know. But it's laborious to write out "congressmen and congresswomen" each time, and "congressperson" is stilted. For generic use, I will stick with "congressmen." For the same reason, I will, throughout the book, use "he" as the generic pronoun. So sue me.

The idea was solid. There was already a women's caucus and a black caucus, not to mention a Democratic and a Republican caucus. Two of those were small and two of those were not, but all four made sense. Why not a workingmen's caucus? Why should workingmen elected to the Congress not gather to address the needs of their own? It was agreed; there would be but one rule for joining the workingmen's caucus. The congressman must swear that at some time or another he'd earned his keep by working with his hands. The organizers set out to enlist their distinguished colleagues and, after surveying 435 members of the House, they found *eight* who qualified, but only because they counted one congressman who'd bartended his way through law school.

Did they care that the number of elected representatives who'd worked with their hands was so small? No, they didn't; they didn't have to. The week before, another poll had shown that slightly less than forty-one percent of the population knew who their congressman was.

Regrettably, the years I spent in Washington were not the ones reporters talk about when they talk about the exciting years. What I mean is, Nixon had already left town. By the time I got there, some reporters seemed to think political reporting had lost its erection. The republic seemed in no immediate danger, and so they walked with a post-Watergate slump. These were tame times, compared to what went before and came later, and I have no stories about toppling presidents or losing wars.

Naturally, we got stirred up at the slightest hint of anything passably interesting and possibly illegal, especially if it concerned the White House or anyone connected with the White House. Remember Bert Lance?

I've always thought there was a pretty good chance Mr. Lance's financial acrobatics might have gone mostly unnoticed, if President Carter's press secretary, Jody Powell, had not whimsically (and as it turned out, foolishly) dared the Washington press corps to find anything drastically wrong with Bert Lance's finances. Also, it was August. News that happens in August does not happen in Washington. Almost everybody has left town by August, either to get out of the heat or to get back in office—remember, August comes only a short time before November. Finally, and this is the big one, Watergate was still over. Nixon was still gone. Franco was still dead. And we still had to write about something.

We settled for rhinestones. For example, I covered what happened when the sexual purity of the United States House of Representatives was dragooned by a secretary who could not type. Or spell. Or show up for work. Her name was Elizabeth Ray. His name was Wayne Hays. One of them was the Democratic congressman from the 18th district in Ohio. It is not recorded whether the congressman could type. The point is, neither of them was doing what was called for in their job descriptions, and what they were doing, they were doing on my time and my dime—and yours. This made for lively enough copy, and for a while we whooped it up daily on our networks and in our newspapers. At last someone had been paid for getting screwed by the Congress. You had to admit that was news.

The story, as bad fortune would have it, faded fast. Those kinds of stories usually fade right about the time the public servant announces to all that his extremely poor health, about which no one has heard a word until now, makes it necessary for him to leave Washington on the next plane. Many of them also find God just before they take off. Naturally, we were sorry to see the story go. Almost nothing sells as well as sex, on the Hill or the air.

Except molehills. Molehills sell very well in Washington. Any ambitious Washington journalist, which is any journalist inside the city limits at the moment, can—with minimum practice—fashion the smallest of mounds into a mountain big enough to call a news story. Look for this one in October:

"Good morning, this is the news. There is a crisis in Washington; the government is out of money!"

What's wrong with that story? Technically it's correct. Every year, about that time, the House and the Senate vote on the bill that will authorize money to pay for the *business* of government for the next year—and every year congressmen load that appropriation bill with amendments ranging from one that would cause a small dam to be constructed near the place a congressman thinks he would like to build a lake house, to one that would make abortion a federal crime punishable by public hanging. Then they have a fine long time debating it all. As early (or as late) as 1861, a New Yorker observing the Congress noted what he called the "utter inability of congressmen to understand why anyone would urge a bill from which no one could selfishly secure an advantage." Nothing has changed.

While the Congress exercises its rites of pontification, we begin newscasts by announcing the government is out of money. Please understand that during this time soldiers do not actually take off their uniforms and catch the first bus home. The mail does not go more undelivered than usual. The bureaucrats do not quit and go play golf, nor do they spend their days in the service of their country *without pay.* That is about how we report it, though, and then—at the last possible moment—when the most impossible amendments get shaved from the bill, a vote is taken on an appropriation bill and the government is back in business again. We report that as if it were news, too; it happens every year and every year we cover it as if it were the first time we'd heard of such a thing.

*"Good morning. The government is out of money."*

Call it anxiety journalism. How pleasant, instead, to turn on the breakfast news and hear the reporter say, "Good morning. Relax. You know the world did not end while you slept, if we're leading our newscast with that old chestnut about the government being out of money. If that's all the news there is, we're all in good shape." Or, if the reporter wished to tell the truth, he might consider the federal deficit for a moment and begin his newscast by saying, "Good morning. The government has been out of money for years. Take that with your Post Toasties."

However, that's not news either. That's fact, and fact that is fact every day is not news; it's truth. We report news, not truth. It's part of our unwritten code. Reporters, like lawyers, doctors and other thieves, set store by unwritten codes, which are more flexible than written ones. That's why nobody wants to write them down. For example, the unwritten code demands a reporter rot in jail before he reveals his sources.

In Washington, sources are more important than politicians, even when they are politicians. The only thing better than a source is a reliable source, or a knowledgeable source, which is a reliable source with a college degree. *All* sources, it is assumed, are informed sources, but in Washington people will assume anything. For years, during the Nixon administration, a highly placed source on board Air Force Two gave reporters information about the shuttle diplomacy of Secretary of State Henry Kissinger. Most people in Washington assumed that source was Kissinger himself. It wasn't. The reporters made it all up.

If you'll notice, highly placed sources become Washington insiders when they talk to *Newsweek*, and some are able to make the switch to Capitol observers in time for the final edition of the Washington *Post*, where they are quoted only if two of them say the same thing, or one of them says it late at night in a parking garage. Sometimes, in Washington, sources speak only for what they call "background." Background is when a public official gives off-the-record information to reporters at a news conference; deep background is when he does it in his office.

Sources are fine if you know something worth protecting. I had my sources in Washington, and I guess it's safe to reveal them now. The lady who ran the elevator in the part of the Capitol where I worked was a source. Every day she took reporters up to the third floor, where the Press Gallery and the Radio-TV Gallery were located. Every afternoon she told me who came back from lunch snockered. She was a fine source to cultivate, if only so she wouldn't tell people if I came back from lunch snockered. The Clerk of the House was another source for me. He told me when the House would meet and when it would not. That's good to know if you are the reporter assigned to cover the House, which I was. I could have gotten the information just by reading the newspaper every day, but newspapers don't count as sources—unless you are the assignment editor at a television station or network. Then newspapers are your biggest sources.

I know. That's how I got in trouble my first day on the job in Washington—and I wasn't in Washington that day. NBC News had hired me to be a Washington correspondent, then told me that in order to be a good Washington correspondent, I'd better spend a week in New York. I believe they wished me to see how the network worked. I believe they thought it actually did. One way I was going to "see how we do things here" was to watch *Nightly News* in the office and company of Mark Landsman, national assignment editor for NBC News.

One of the stories on that first night's broadcast, my first night working at NBC, concerned a Vietnamese woman who, caught in the panic of the American troop withdrawal from Vietnam in 1975, quite literally had thrust her two small children into the hands of an American serviceman who was on board one of the last U.S. helicopters to leave Saigon. The children came to America, were adopted by an Army major and his wife, and now—more than a year later—the kids were wearing Smurf tee-shirts and arguing baseball in Blackstone, Virginia; but *now*—more than a year later—the birth mother of the children had made her way to this country, and she wanted her children back. In looking for them, she had gotten as far as Dallas, where she'd found out from the army that her children were healthy and living in Virginia with a family that expected them to stay. It was a no-win situation, a sad coda to a dirty little war. A newspaper found out what was going on and wrote the story. That's how television assignment editors learned about it. When the assignment editor at NBC News in Washington read the newspaper story, he called Landsman and suggested it would be good for *Nightly News.* Landsman agreed. An NBC reporter was dispatched to Dallas to interview the birth mother.

And that was the trouble. The story on *Nightly News* showed only that interview; it included no pictures of the children and no word from the adoptive parents in Virginia. Their side of the story was completely missing. After we watched, Landsman asked me what I thought. I was clever; I told him it was a good half a story. I believe I waxed medium eloquent on the importance of getting the *whole* story, every time, no matter what. You want to impress your new boss the first day, let him know what a serious journalist you are.

Landsman explained to me that the assignment editor in Washington, whose idea it had been to do the story, and who, in one week, would be my more immediate boss, said he had called the Virginia family and those people had said they didn't want to talk to reporters or see anything that even looked like a television camera near their house or their children. (Good for them.) I said that was swell, but still it made for only half a story.

After the broadcast and our chat ended, I went to my hotel room. It shows my inexperience and lack of thought that it never occurred to me assignment editors talk to each other. Apparently the national assignment editor telephoned the Washington assignment editor and told him the new reporter they'd hired didn't think he was doing his job especially well. About eight o'clock in the evening, the phone in my hotel room rang and a desk assistant in Washington explained he was calling on behalf of the Washington assignment editor, who thought it would be right nice if I went to the airport immediately, caught the nine o'clock shuttle plane to Washington, where I would meet the NBC camera crew that would be waiting for me on board a small airplane NBC had chartered to take me to Blackstone, Virginia, where I would get the other half of the damn story by the next damn broadcast, thank you very much. I believe the "or else" was merely implied.

I got the story. Much as I would prefer to say I got it by dint of journalistic endeavor, that's not how it happened. When I got to the major's house in Blackstone and the major's wife came to the door, I began to babble about my own children, who would soon be on the street and hungry because their mother had shot off her mouth and, gee, I'd only been a network correspondent one day and it would be a big help if I could finish out the week before I got fired this time, which surely would happen if she slammed the door in my face and I had to go back to this evil assignment editor in Washington empty-handed. I may have cried a bit; I try not to remember, but I will always remember those nice people in Blackstone. They gave me the interview, two cups of tea, and a Kleenex.

The fight for custody of the children went on for months. Meanwhile, I was assigned to cover the House of Representatives. Another reporter followed the story of the children, and I have to confess here that I cannot tell you who got the children. Perhaps I did not want to know. I would not have wanted to be a reporter at King Solomon's court, either. It's just too bloody awful to watch babies reduced to "stories."

I learned something on this one, though. I learned that—contrary to popular opinion around newsrooms—assignment editors *do* have senses of humor. Bad ones.

I spent most of my time in Washington covering the House of Representatives. There were 435 congenial clowns there, and if you fired a shot into their midst, they rode off in 435 legislative directions, all talking at once. It was as unlike the White House as it could be; at the White House they put reporters into a room over what used to be the swimming pool and force-fed them information through a slot in the door. And they made up the rules as they went along. I know. I remember the first day I filled in for a White House correspondent who was sick. That was unusual; they almost never get sick, those people—they're too afraid someone will take their spot for good.

That day I covered a briefing by Jody Powell. My assignment editor wanted to know about plans for President Carter's trip to Poland. Powell began the briefing by giving us that very information. I took it down, then listened as he went on to tell us it was National Sweet Potato Week and later the president would be in the Rose Garden with Miss Sweet Potato and some farmers if anybody wanted to take advantage of the "photo op."

A "photo op" means there is no opportunity to do anything other than take a photograph. Questions are not allowed. That's why President Nixon thanked Ron Ziegler for inventing the "photo op." In 1983, in a story about President Reagan, NBC White House correspondent Andrea Mitchell described the beauty of the "photo op" by pointing out that being photographed driving a tractor beats trying to explain unemployment. "Do we," asked Andrea, "have a president or an actor playing commander in chief?" A fair question and one that should be asked as well about presidents who don't happen to have formal experience in front of the camera, because they have all become public-relations presidents, masters of the "photo op."

But a "photo op" on the sweet-potato issue? I didn't think we had all that much interest in sweet potatoes, so I left the briefing before Powell finished, called my assignment editor and told him the plans for the Poland trip.

"How long did Jody talk today?"

"Hard to say. He's still talking."

"What? You left before the briefing was over? That's completely against the rules. Go back immediately."

It seems all those news organizations that took out ads telling you how competitive they were had gotten together and agreed no one would ever leave the briefing before it was over. That way nobody would scoop anybody. Cozy.

In that case, I told him, we were in real luck. I'd already left. The damage was done. Now we could scoop everybody on the sweet-potato story.

Some people don't recognize a gift when they're handed it. I went back to the briefing, waited until Powell was done saying nothing at all, then returned to the NBC booth to type up my notes on the Poland trip. A voice over the public address system interrupted me.

"The lunch lid is on. I repeat. The lunch lid is on."

Now that was the sort of announcement guaranteed to send a reporter back for further instruction, especially one who'd already messed up as a White House correspondent. Another call to the assignment editor.

"Hi. It's me. At the White House. Thought you'd want to know the lunch lid is on. I don't know what that means but it sounds important. Maybe we ought to tell *Nightly News* right away, in case they want to change tonight's show. Meanwhile, what should *I* do?"

He said I should go to lunch. The announcement meant reporters could go to restaurants with their sources, or each other, and not have to worry about war being declared while they were away from the press room. No news would happen until after three o'clock. Well, fancy that. Not only did competing news organizations make sure no one would be competitive on the briefing, but the White House joined in the game when it came to the important stuff, like lunch. My next call was to ask the assignment editor to send a replacement. I wasn't cut out to cover the White House.

I truly feel sorry for the men and women who, on a daily basis, do cover the White House. They work without access to the man they're supposed to cover and, instead, must deal with people around him, people who want to see on the air and in print only those things they think the public *needs* to know. A reporter who reports something else may find himself frozen out for a while; no one will tell him anything, and when you can't talk to the president, you depend on people telling you things. Naturally, some of those people will lie to you, if they talk to you at all. What is in their interest probably is not in yours.

It is a wonder any first-rate reporting comes out of the place, but it does—and even the smallest crack in the armor of the presidency can reveal curious insights into the man in the office. For example, during Ronald Reagan's first term as president, he made a speech about the economy. He made many; this one was in October, 1983. In it, he quoted from a letter sent to him by a woman he identified as "Judith." Judith lived in Selma, Alabama, he said, and she had written:

> I have been unable to sleep. After years of training and experience, we can't find jobs.

> There may never be a house (home) of our own—that dream we have worked for for so many years. We worked hard. We conserved. We planned. We feel so out of control. We want a better life.

For Reagan, it was the perfect letter. It implied the rotten economic situation was not his fault so much as it was his problem to fix. When he finished reading the letter—all this on national television—he said, "Judith, I hear you." It was quite moving.

He may have heard her. He didn't know her. A nasty old White House reporter went to the telephone and began making calls. Judith was Judith McMurtrey. Reporters who went to her address were invited into her comfortable brick home, which Mrs. McMurtrey *owned* with her husband, an *employed* accountant. It was true that Mrs. McMurtrey had no job, but Mrs. McMurtrey had *never* worked, it seems, and so had no job to lose.

She said she wrote the letter symbolically, as an unelected representative of others, not people she knew, exactly, but people she heard about on, you know, the news. Besides, she said, she liked Ronald Reagan and didn't think the press treated him fairly. White House spokesman Robin Gray was asked if the president or anyone had checked on Mrs. McMurtrey before the president used her letter in his speech. Gray said no, and he didn't see what the noise was about. After all, there were plenty of real examples of hardship across the country, just like the kind described by Mrs. McMurtrey.

That was the truth. There were too many examples of hardship, but Judith McMurtrey was not one. The condition typified by the use of her letter was another kind of condition entirely. Remember that the nationally televised speech was made at the president's request—and he also requested the date: October 13, a scant few weeks before 54 Republican senators, 192 Republican representatives, 23 Republican governors and who knows how many Republican candidates for state legislatures would stand for election or reelection. The condition here was politics, and in politics, what you say doesn't have to be absolutely true as long as it sounds good.

That is a small, very small story. White House reporters might wince at the idea someone would use a little story like that as an example of what they can do. After all, haven't they uncovered and reported serious, important stories about presidents? Yes, they have, but in a morality play—and governing our country is, if nothing else, a morality play—it's the little things that count. Consider Richard Allen and the pizza.

In December, 1981, the news was filled with stories about poor Richard Allen, national security advisor to President Reagan. In that month, Allen had been put on "administrative leave" because he'd accepted one thousand dollars and a Seiko watch from a Japanese magazine writer for setting up an interview with Nancy Reagan. The president didn't like that. The president's men didn't like that. In the last quarter of the twentieth century, administrative leave is the bureaucratic equivalent of a day or two in the stocks.

The president and his men did like the pizza, however. The same week the story about Richard Allen broke, the president was in Cincinnati for a fund-raising dinner. Afterward, the president and his men went back to their hotel rooms and decided they were still hungry. White House aide Ed Rogers got on the phone, ordering forty extra-large pizzas, all with extra cheese. Mike La Rosa, the owner of the pizza parlor, was suspicious of such a big order; he went to the hotel to check. Sure enough, it was the White House calling, as much as the White House could be said to be in Cincinnati.

La Rosa told reporters that Ed Rogers wanted him to donate the forty pizzas, all with extra cheese, and offered him a pair of presidential cuff links in return. La Rosa agreed to give them the pizzas; it would be good publicity for him, even if it cost him four hundred dollars, with tax. He liked Reagan. He didn't object to giving him some pizza.

Richard Allen should have objected. If taking one thousand dollars was wrong, was taking four hundred dollars worth of pizza right? If Allen had taken one thousand dollars worth of pizza, would that have been okay? If, in return for the money he did take, Allen had given the Japanese writer a pair of presidential cuff links instead of an interview with the president's wife—would that have made it all right? Finally, remember that Richard Allen never spent the one thousand dollars, but the president and the White House staff *did* eat the pizzas. And what about the Seiko watch? Too much thinking about the relative values involved here, the ethics, makes my head hurt. If anyone ever asks you how the government is like a pizza pie, however, the answer is easy—the government is like a pizza because when it comes to morality, they can always slice it any way they want, and someone else will pay for the cheese.

Detail, detail. While it may be true that in a septic tank the really big chunks always rise to the top, it's also true that the smaller pieces clog the system, too. If little things tell a lot at the White House, they also tell a lot about the bureaucracy. Remember the giant windmill? The federal government built it on top of a mountain outside Boone, North Carolina. The blades were 97½ feet long, each of them. The windmill was supposed to generate two thousand kilowatts of electricity when it was finished in 1979. It cost thirty million dollars to build. But it didn't work. Either the blades were broken or there was no wind; it was always something, and there were the neighbors to think of. They said the windmill's "whooshing" sound interfered with television reception. The windmill repairman said he could fix the "whooshing" for another $500,000. In May, 1983, the government gave up and sold the world's most expensive windmill for $51,600—a loss of $29,948,400, but who's counting? Not the government. By that time, the federal government was already into eels, also in North Carolina.

It seems the government decided it would be terrific if migrant farmers in the state raised eels and froze them; then they could sell the frozen eels to Japan and China. In June, 1983, *one month* after it sold the windmill, the government began taking bids on its abandoned eel farm in Swan Quarter, North Carolina. I'm sorry I can't tell you how much the eel farm caper cost, but you might ask Senator Jesse Helms of North Carolina. Bureaucracy and boondoggle are so hard to tell apart sometimes. Maybe they can develop a taste for eel pizza over at the White House.

During the years I was in Washington, the Congress was troubled by no more than one or two attacks of morality, and with diligence these were overcome. Naturally you never saw anything about these attacks *on* television; at that time, cameras were not allowed on the floor of the House or the Senate. In 1979, for the first time, the House permitted cameras to record its proceedings, but the cameras were controlled by the House itself, so people would see only what the House wanted them to see. During the debate about who would operate the cameras—the House or the networks—congressmen said it *must* be the House. The networks, they said, would distort everything. What if a camera were allowed to show a congressman asleep during a vote or picking his nose? What if the camera showed a congressman (or congressmen) to be absent. No, they said, people would misunderstand if they saw all that on national television.

They would not. People would understand just fine. They would understand that their instincts about Washington were correct. It tells you something that during the debate about whether or not cameras would be allowed on the floor of the House and who would control them, no congressman suggested it would be dandy if, while conducting the business of the nation, congressmen showed up, stayed awake and left their noses alone.

As I write this, the Senate still does not allow its work to be photographed. That's too bad. When I covered the Congress I had wonderful fantasies about being able to show on television some of the more absurd acts performed in that circus. I recall a day when the Senate, still flush with a little post-Watergate virtue, suffered one of those brief morality attacks I mentioned earlier. It decided to consider the matter of how much money a senator should earn. At the time, the pay for a senator was $57,500 annually. Many senators added to it by practicing law on the side and making speeches for money.

It was suggested senators should limit what they could make from "outside sources." It was suggested that by doing so, more senators would stay in Washington and attend to business, since running off to Des Moines to make a speech would be less attractive if it were for free. It was suggested that a senator should be allowed to earn no more than $8,500 a year from outside sources.

The senators thought it over for a while, agreed it was a sound, moral idea, on principle, but why not ease the burden by first raising the salary of a senator by $10,500 a year? That would help senators to, well, accommodate. So they did that. They passed a bill giving themselves the raise in pay. Next they were supposed to pass the bill limiting their outside earnings to $8,500.

When the bill was brought up on the floor of the Senate, Senator Ted Stevens, Republican from Alaska, argued that senators were victims of inflation just like ordinary people: therefore, they really needed all the money they could get from the practice of law and the making of speeches. Why, if they couldn't avail themselves of that extra money, they might have to dip into their savings, or, shudder, borrow money. Some senators, said Stevens, might be forced to ask their wives to go to work.

It was a glorious speech and would have made great television, as would the speech of Senator Patrick Moynihan, Democrat from New York, who said, in effect, that United States senators had really important things to worry about and should not *need* to worry about financial matters.

The Senate agreed with these gentlemen. After voting to *raise* their salaries, senators voted to postpone for *five years* the notion of putting limits on outside income. (Five years later, the Senate seemed to forget completely that it ever had such a silly notion.) The vote itself would have made the best television of all. Although it was announced ahead of time, only twenty of one hundred senators showed up to vote on the limiting of outside income. Senator Moynihan, who had made such an eloquent speech defending their right to earn all the extra money they could, said he had a dental appointment. The Senate Majority Leader, Robert Byrd, Democrat from West Virginia, left the chamber one or two minutes before the vote—and disappeared for a while. Although it was an important vote, it was quickly passed without a roll call. They did it on a voice vote, which meant there was no record of who voted how. After it was done, a couple of senators rushed up to the Radio-TV Gallery to tell the cameras it *should* have been a roll-call vote, but none of them had demanded a roll-call vote at the time, which *any* of them could have done.

So, had television cameras been allowed in the Senate on that day, they would have shown twenty percent of a governing body acting swiftly and in relative secrecy to pad the pockets of all one hundred distinguished gentlemen.

Remember, this was the same Senate that had passed a resolution promoting, almost *demanding,* openness in its actions—sunshine in government. You heard a lot about sunshine in government in those days. Hadn't everybody learned a lesson from Nixon about the perils of government conducted in secrecy? It turned out the warm glow of sunshine was not meant to include the harsh glare of television lights.

Because television came late to the job of covering government, for years the Congress was able to enforce a handful of stupid rules it would never have tried with print journalists. For example, not only could I not take my camera crew—my equivalent of pen and notebook—into the chamber of the House or Senate, I could not take my camera crew to some places in and around the Capitol that were, at the same time, open to all tourists with their cameras. If I wanted to film or tape something on the steps of the Capitol, I needed permission from the office of the Capitol Architect. I don't know why. I wasn't going to hurt his building, just photograph one congressman or another standing on its steps. If I wanted to make pictures walking down the hall of one of the congressional office buildings around the Capitol, I needed to get permission from the occupant of every office whose door I would pass. Some halls have twenty or thirty offices along them. Try getting permission from each.

If I wanted to take my camera crew and wait outside some congressman's office to ask him a question he did not want to answer, I needed the permission of the congressman who didn't want to answer what I wanted to ask. Figure that one. Why, you ask, did the various television news organizations put up with such nonsense? A good question. I never got a good answer.

Why was the Congress so suspicious of television? Television could disrupt—that was true—but mostly it wasn't in the congressional interest to have information available to the public that the Congress could not control. Take the *Congressional Record*, a printed document that is supposed to reflect what happens in the House and the Senate. The words said in those chambers are purportedly there for all to see, that day or forty years from that day—except, and this is a big "except," congressmen are allowed to do something called "revise and extend." That means after they say something on the floor, they can think about it later, go back, and change the words to reflect what *they wished they had said.* Handy.

I believe there was still another reason some congressmen objected to television. Some congressmen really didn't understand television. It caused some confusion. I remember one wonderful day when a reporter covering a story for the *Today* show went to Congressman Dan Flood, Democrat from Pennsylvania, to ask him whether he thought a particular education bill would pass the next day. He went to Flood on a Tuesday evening, explained to him that the interview would run Wednesday morning on *Today.* Could the congressman please keep that in mind when answering the question? The congressman answered that it was a good bill and he had every hope it would pass tomorrow when the House voted, but he would know more after he went to the meeting of the House leadership about six o'clock that night.

One more time, the reporter explained he was working for the next day's program. Could the congressman please change his statement to reflect that? Sure, said Flood, who then answered the question as follows:

"I think it's a good bill, and I have every hope it will pass today, but I'll know more when I go to the meeting of the House leadership at six o'clock yesterday."

Either Dan Flood didn't understand television—or he understood it too damn well.

Some people think Washington reporters are too cozy with those they cover: that they both get up, put on their gray suits, go to work, one doing something, the other writing about it, then they both go home, change into their blue suits and go to the same dinner party in Georgetown.

One NBC News television reporter, the first time she was asked to be on *Meet the Press,* was so anxious about not making a fool of herself that she studied for days, talked to the best friends and worst enemies of the man she was to question, then showed up at the studio six hours early on the day of the broadcast, just to go over her notes and prepare her questions. The lady was ready. The week after the broadcast she was taken to lunch by one of her superiors and told that if she wanted to be on *Meet the Press* again, she must not ask such hard questions. They were too tough, and if everybody asked that kind of question, pretty soon no one in Washington would agree to be a guest on *Meet the Press.* That's what she was told.

Happily, although reporters and politicians do depend on each other, they do not, I believe, get in bed together as much as it might seem. (I mean that figuratively. I don't know about literally and if I did, I wouldn't tell. Call it cowardice.) Consider the matter of the Christmas list, however. In 1979, a story circulated that the Washington *Post* had gotten hold of a list which had belonged to Ardeshir Zahedi, the Iranian ambassador to the United States during the Shah's rule. The list supposedly contained the names of four thousand people who had accepted gifts from the generous Mr. Zahedi and his generous government. The list was not made public, which may have been because so many of the four thousand names reportedly belonged to journalists, including some very important ones. Of course, there are no unimportant journalists in Washington. Just ask any of them (or me, when I was one). Here you had a situation where journalists who had hoped like the devil they *were* on Nixon's list of enemies (it was good for the image), were all of a sudden praying just as hard they were not on Zahedi's list (not at all good for the image). And the Washington *Post,* which gave the nation Watergate, would not give anybody the list, which also was said to include the names of and gifts to several hotshot journalists and editors employed by the Washington *Post.*

That seemed pretty funny, so I decided to see what I could find out, probably because I love caviar, and no one had ever offered *me* any. I called some Washington journalists I thought might know a thing or two about the list. One told me that, yes, some people were said to have gotten caviar, but others were said to have received gifts worth up to $10,000—Persian rugs and other goodies like that. Another journalist told me there were degrees of gifts involved here. Not everybody got the rugs, obviously. And there were two sizes of caviar. Those who really didn't count much to the Shah got a translation of the *Rubáiyát* (with pictures, in case you were a television reporter and couldn't read). Still another reporter explained to me that the gifts really didn't count. The press didn't think it was being bribed, not at all. "After all," said one, "we went to those parties of Zahedi's to get news. That's how things operate in Washington." The parties were big, extravagant shindigs, and it meant something to be invited. And it meant something if you weren't. If Zahedi didn't like you, he might send a bottle of Dom Pérignon to your house, but he wouldn't invite you to his house, where he might have to talk to you.

That's how it was explained to me.

What I don't understand is how the man gave so many parties when nobody ever went to one. I know that nobody ever went to his parties because everybody *I* talked to about it said they knew about the parties but, no, certainly *they* hadn't gone to them. They had been very busy somewhere else, like down in the courthouse basement, reading transcripts. As for the gifts, the only people I spoke to who would admit ever having gotten any were people who had sent them back. Those people's memories were crystal clear. One reporter who allowed she had benefited from the Shah's generosity, said it was all right because she gave the Gucci scarf to someone whom she didn't like very much, and she didn't eat the caviar until it was stale—rather like not spending the money until it's wrinkled.

I felt sorry for all the high-powered Washington journalists, but it was fun to watch them squirm. Many of them decided paying two hundred dollars a pound for caviar was cheaper in the long run. Too many people in Washington were keeping lists about too many things.

I felt sorry for Zahedi and the Shah, too. All that money, all those parties, all those fish eggs—all that trouble—and still it wasn't enough. It didn't work. In the end, Zahedi found out he could not buy the Washington press corps with caviar. Maybe he should have tried bourbon.

It's fair to say that in Washington, the prevailing attitude of politicians toward the press is simple. They hate us. Take the matter of "good news." Politicians are always wanting to know why we don't report more good news. In 1983, President Reagan asked the three networks to devote a whole week to the reporting of good news. The networks refused, and hurrah for them. I have seen countries where there was plenty of good news on television, and in every one of those countries, television was owned and controlled by the state. When the anchorman is wearing a colonel's uniform, it tells you something. Besides, news is the exception. How would it be to go on the air and report the number of people not killed on a given day? When there is good news, and it is *news,* we do report it, but usually news is a record of human failure. Those wanting to celebrate human accomplishment are, as someone said, advised to go to the sports section.

I don't think we hate politicians. I don't think the only way to look at a politician is down—but sideways makes sense. It is the same way one should look at journalists. Just as the reporter should put a critical distance between himself and a politician, the viewer—reader, listener, whatever—should put the same kind of distance between himself and what he sees, hears or reads about politics and politicians. There *are* good, honest, hardworking politicians in Washington, but there are the other kind, too. The same is true of reporters.

In 1733, a man named John Peter Zenger published the first newspaper in New York. In it he said a recent local election had been fixed by some crooked politicians. Zenger was thrown in jail for what he'd written. When the jury refused to convict him, the judge ordered the jury thrown in jail. They still refused to convict him. He and the jury were turned loose. Zenger was right and the jury knew it. The election *had* been fixed. Nearly fifty years after the incident, the men who wrote our Constitution cited the story of John Peter Zenger as reason enough to include the First Amendment in the Bill of Rights. The press had to be free and the public had to know certain things. That was what reporters were supposed to do—tell people what the government would not.

Two hundred fifty years from the day Zenger published that newspaper, the United States invaded the island of Grenada and said the press couldn't go because the press wouldn't tell people the truth. The press would distort. On the day of the invasion, a man named Mike Carlson decided to exercise his rights as a citizen. He lived in Milwaukee, was in the advertising business and had not known about the invasion of Grenada until he heard the report on his car radio, going home after work. Mr. Carlson was concerned about the invasion, concerned about the press being barred from covering it, and, while driving home, he'd thought about it and decided to tell his government how he felt. He was a right-wing Republican who voted regularly, and regularly contributed money to the Republican party. But he didn't like this Grenada business.

First he'd called the Washington office of Senator Proxmire, who was, of course, from Wisconsin. It was six o'clock in the evening, Washington time. He got no answer in the Senator's office. Mr. Carlson had recently moved to Wisconsin from Illinois, so he'd called the Washington office of Senator Charles Percy—a Republican he admired. No answer. He'd tried Senator Dixon. No answer. Mr. Carlson had remembered he had once done some work for Congressman Jim Leach of Iowa. He'd called Leach's office in Washington. No answer. By this time, Mike Carlson was angry. He'd called the office of Tip O'Neill, Speaker of the House. No answer. That left the White House. He'd called. He'd gotten an answer; they told him to call back in the morning.

Thoroughly upset, citizen Mike Carlson, *Republican,* had dialed the number of the Washington office of Senator John Glenn, *Democrat.* This time he got an answering machine. Next he called NBC News. I took the call. He told me his story and said that the next morning he intended to stop payment on a check he'd written to the Republican party. Then he was going to call Senator Glenn again, because an answering machine was better than a nine-to-five government.

I told him he was wrong about the government. Having worked in Washington, I knew it wasn't a nine-to-five government. Usually they quit at four.

# THE LOST WEEKEND

Any education worthy of
the name is bound
to be dangerous.
PROFESSOR L. NEIL
Australian teacher

Spring. 1979. Neither Lloyd Dobyns nor I wanted to go to Palm Springs. That's why Reuven Frank sent both of us. Lloyd and I anchored *Weekend,* but Reuven was executive producer. As for Palm Springs: a few years earlier, NBC News had bought the rights to an interview with former President Gerald Ford, the interview to be conducted on the eve of the publication of his memoirs. At the time the arrangement was announced, some of us in the news division felt it was wrong to put a politician on the payroll, or even that contradiction in terms—a retired politician. The deal was made; Ford took the money, then we sort of forgot about it. Maybe we thought he would never finish the book, but he did, and in April, 1979, Gerald Ford, in Palm Springs, was ready to publish and, per agreement, ready to tell all on national television, on my network, on our show and, apparently, to Lloyd and me. Reuven explained it this way: "It's going to be dull, because Ford is not going to tell all: he's going to tell only the 'all' he chooses to tell, but no other program at NBC wants the interview, so we've been told we want it. I haven't the heart to send either of you; that's why I'm sending the both of you. Goodbye. Pack. Go. Have a nice day." Something like that.

The plane to Palm Springs was late. It was midnight when we got to our hotel and the restaurants were closed, so we went to the hotel bar. If the restaurants had been open, we still would have gone to the bar—that's how joyful we were about our assignment. We'd been in the bar about an hour when Lloyd was called to the telephone. It was Nigel Ryan, a vice president at NBC News, a British fellow with, as it turned out, a proper dose of good manners. Ryan told Lloyd that the president of NBC News had taken a plane to China. We knew that already. Ryan told Lloyd that what we didn't know was, just before leaving, the president of NBC News had announced the cancellation of *Weekend.* He'd told the press. He just hadn't told us. (This was the same president of NBC News who once said to someone on the telephone: "Yes, I know we're in the business of communicating, but not with each other.")

Ryan was on vacation in Los Angeles. He said he'd been driving on the freeway when it occurred to him that no one had told Lloyd and me our show had been axed; that we were likely to get up and read about it in the newspaper. Ryan thought that was one bloody poor way to find out, so he'd taken the first exit ramp off the freeway and gone in search of a telephone, any telephone, which was why, he explained, it was so noisy on his end of the line. He was calling from the toilet of a Beverly Hills restaurant. Seemed right to us.

If ever there is a Trivial Pursuit game about television news, it's likely one of the questions will be: Can you name all twelve television news magazines NBC has put on and taken off the air? It broadcast its first news magazine the same year CBS first broadcast *60 Minutes*. Should it have escaped your notice, *60 Minutes* is still on the air. There's a reason. News programs, like other programs, need ratings to survive, but no news program ever got good ratings when it first went on the air, with the possible exception of *ABC News Nightline,* which began as a nightly update on the story of American hostages in Iran—and had the added advantage of being anchored by Ted Koppel. Usually, news programs need time to build an audience. *60 Minutes* was on the air for nearly seven years before it became a hit and the most profitable program on television. (The most expensive news program is cheaper to produce than the least expensive sitcom.) For CBS patience paid off, and not in pennies. Staying with *60 Minutes* was good business. NBC, lacking that patience, but wanting the rewards it had brought CBS, put magazine shows on the air, sat back and waited for the profits to start rolling in immediately, and when they didn't, canceled the shows, all of which were pretty good and none of which ever got ratings better than the low end of "not bad." Some didn't do *that* well, but none ever was given time on the air to change that. *Weekend* was NBC's fourth try at a news magazine and my first.

I was in Washington, covering the House for NBC News, when it was announced that *Weekend* would stop being a monthly program and become weekly. That was in December, 1977. *Weekend* had aired once a month at 11:30 on Saturday night since 1974. During the rest of the month, *Saturday Night Live* occupied that time slot. Now *Weekend* was moving to prime time, moving to once a week, and seeking a second anchor. Lloyd Dobyns had anchored it alone, but he would need help with the new *Weekend.* I thought I ought to be that help. It was the first time I'd said to myself, "Now there's a job I really want." Could I write well enough for *Weekend,* with its reputation for using the right words, not too many of them, and in the right order, something Lillian Hellman said most people don't do—something almost no television program did?

I thought so and was certain my bosses would think so, too, once they got around to it. After all, hadn't I, in two years at NBC, made clear my reverence for Good Writing, my intention to be a Good Writer? Hadn't I established a reputation as someone who could write a simple declarative sentence, when pressed? Well then, I would just wait for Reuven Frank to come to his senses and come to Washington. That's how sure I was. It was January and two weeks after the announcement that NBC would add a second anchorperson to *Weekend;* it happened exactly as I had predicted, except that Reuven Frank came to Washington to see Jessica Savitch, not me.

When I found out, I called the president of NBC News, Les Crystal, and asked if this meant I wasn't going to be considered for the *Weekend* job? Les said that's what it meant, all right. I was cool. I went to my office and shut the door, but I didn't cry. The Big Boys didn't cry, but they expected girls to cry, and right then

I was in no mood to do anything The Big Boys expected of me. I was furious. What I did was grab the saw from the wall where it hung and add another notch to the bookcase, a big notch. Then I decided that while nowhere is it written that anything will be fair, it simply wasn't fair; Jessica Savitch had been at NBC for only a few months, and she was already Senate correspondent and anchor of the Saturday night edition of *Nightly News*. I begrudged her neither of those assignments, but *Weekend* was what *I* wanted, and I didn't give a damn whether I was being a good sport. Then I decided to hell with them. Who wanted to work for Reuven Frank, a man who had been president of NBC News and must have done something horrible because now he was only a producer and all he produced was *Weekend,* a dumb, dumb show. I added a second notch to the bookcase. *Then* I cried.

Three weeks later Reuven Frank came to Washington and asked me to dinner, a consolation dinner, I figured, and since I didn't want to be consoled or patted on my head or told what a great trooper I was, I opened the dinner table chitchat by asking him how he'd managed to keep a job at NBC News after he'd been fired from his job as president of NBC News? By the time Reuven Frank finished answering my question—and correcting my facts (he had not been fired)—the pasta was gone, along with my resolve to spend the entire evening being openly, genuinely and perfectly shitty. This white-haired fellow with a face like a Jewish sphinx, Dennis-the-Menace eyes, a shirt that didn't go with his suit, and a tie that went with neither was the smartest person I'd ever met, and the funniest. He still is.

I caved. I asked for the job, at least for a chance at

the job. I told him I wanted to work for him badly. Reuven said he hoped not; if I were to work for him he would rather I were good at it—and by the way, working for him was what he'd come to Washington to talk to me about. That was the first of Reuven's gentle attempts to alter my abuse of the language. Getting the message was easy, getting the job took longer.

What about Jessica Savitch? Oh, she was still the odds-on favorite, but Reuven had persuaded the president of NBC News to audition at least one more person. It would be fairer that way. (I figured he meant it would *look* fairer that way; I knew the competition was rigged. It was already in the newspapers that Jessica was going to get the job.) Reuven said the president of NBC News had agreed to the audition idea. Here was how it would work. Each of us would be given a copy of a twenty-minute story that had appeared on *Weekend* two years before, but on our copies, all the narration would be erased, all of Dobyns's words gone from the film, leaving only picture, natural sound and pieces of interviews, edited together with holes left for new words. Jessica and I each would write our scripts, record them and transfer them to the identically cut stories. When that was done, we would fly to New York, sit on the *Weekend* set, introduce our stories, roll our film, then go home and wait. Reuven apologized for the contest aspect of it, which he said he knew was shabby.

Shabby, my ass. Finally I had a chance. In 1963, while I was still at Vanderbilt University, the United Methodist Church decided to send five American college students to spend three months working in its missions in Bolivia. I was taking Latin American history; I wanted to go to Bolivia. There was only one tiny problem. I hadn't been to church since I was thirteen, which was why my mother sent me our church bulletin every week; it was in the church bulletin that I had read about five students getting to go to Bolivia. If church attendance counted, they weren't going to pick me. But then I read that the five students would be selected on the basis of a written essay, and although I'd skipped church, I had not skipped English class. In the essay I explained how, by sending me, they had a chance at saving an extra soul—mine. I learned a lot that summer in Bolivia, but when it was over I still wrote better than I prayed.

Maybe *Weekend* would be another Bolivia, another writing test that would allow me to tap-dance around certain inadequacies—such as the fact that unlike Jessica, I'd had what amounted to *no* experience anchoring. This time, however, the writing test wasn't a Sunday School essay.

When putting together a television news story, the usual practice is to write the words, record them, then go into the editing room and match pictures to them. The pictures are supposed to fit your words. Words first, pictures second. At *Weekend* the pictures came first. That is, the film was shot, the producer arranged the pieces he chose to use in the order he chose to use them, the film editor assembled the pieces, then the reporter wrote and recorded the narration that would complete the story. It is a better way. Changing the words to fit the pictures makes more sense, because once the film is in the house you cannot change the pictures. But it's tougher for reporters; it makes you work harder and think more. It makes you write *to* the pictures and *with* the pictures. I'd never tried this technique or heard of it. Worse, I wasn't going to try it for the first time on some two-minute story; no, I was going to begin with a twenty-minute story.

Jessica and I each had three days. On Friday, we were to bring our stories to New York. I spent hours at a Steenbeck machine, running the film back and forth, stopping and starting, trying to figure out what to say in this 15-½-second gap, that 6-second pause, how to arrange the information I had so that it wove smoothly in and out of interviews, music and background noise. Consider it, if you like, a sort of supercomplicated crossword puzzle. The subject of the story was a twelve-year-old Brooke Shields, and her mother, Teri Shields, but what it really was, was a story about stage moms, a prurient public and greed. It was inventively produced, shot and edited, and lacked only something to match in the way of words. The whole time, I felt like a cowboy heading for the shoot-out at high noon.

In order to be alert Friday morning in New York, I planned to take the shuttle from Washington Thursday night. On Thursday morning it began to snow in Washington and to snow even harder in New York. By midafternoon I decided not to risk the shuttle and caught a train to New York. Seven hours later the train completed its three-hour trip. I arrived at Penn Station to find a city shut down by the worst blizzard since 1947. Cab? I looked up Seventh Avenue and saw something I'd never seen before and may not again: nothing was moving. Seventh Avenue, New York City, was solid with snow as far as the eye could see. No cabs. No trucks. *No tracks*. Nothing. And nothing to do but pick up my film and suitcase and start walking the twenty-eight blocks to the hotel. It took two hours, and the hotel was so sorry, but when I hadn't shown up earlier, they'd given my room to somebody else: they'd given all their rooms to somebody else, in fact, and perhaps I had a friend nearby? Not one, I assured them, who had a sleigh. Couldn't they call another hotel for me? They could, but I should know it wouldn't do any good. There were no rooms in town. There was a blizzard. Didn't I know?

Kindness is measured by need. The hotel let me sleep in a chair in the lobby. It was two in the morning, and they were so helpful; when the cleaning people woke me at five in the morning, they let me use the hotel employee's toilet to change clothes and wash my face so I could be the well-rested, alert would-be-anchor-woman-gunslinger, primed for the shoot-out, if only my eyes would open.

At nine o'clock, I was at Reuven Frank's door, clutching my film, ready to sit on the *Weekend* set, play it fast and loose and take my best shot. I went through the door the way Shane did when he came in the saloon, looking for Jack Palance.

"Reuven, I'm ready."

"Good. You've got the job."

"I beg your pardon?"

Reuven said Jessica had called the day before and said she wasn't going to bring *her* version of the twenty-minute story to New York because she'd thought it over and she didn't want to work on *Weekend.* She said she already had the Saturday *Nightly News* anchor spot and the assignment of Senate correspondent; therefore, she thought it only fair that some other reporter have a chance to anchor *Weekend.* Reuven said they'd tried to call me and tell me, but nobody knew where I was. Somebody said they thought I was on a train to someplace.

I had the job. I had the job. I had the job by *default.*

It bears witness to the competitiveness or outright insanity of journalists that my first reaction to getting what I wanted was a terrible, fierce anger. Nobody left Gary Cooper standing in the middle of the street with his gun hanging out, waiting for the other guy to show up. I mean, I was *ready*. Where the devil was Jessica?

As good fortune would have it, reason returned, pique subsided, and I managed to tell Reuven I would be pleased to join *Weekend*, but did he want to see the film I'd brought, just in case? He did, I still got the job, and although I don't like Western movies very much anymore, to this day I'm right fond of Brooke Shields.

For me, *Weekend* was a classroom. The program, never to be confused with *60 Minutes*, had a reputation for "lighter" or "softer" stories, yet, said Reuven, when done right, those stories were "heavier" or "harder" because they spoke to human behavior but made their points by implication rather than direct statement. They let the viewer think, decide. What an unusual idea, I remember thinking. Reuven believed television was a narrative medium and that understanding, if any, came out of the story, not from describing the story—or explaining the story. We were to tell the story, that's all. He said that on *Weekend* almost all our stories would be about people. The others would be told through people.

The first people I was going to tell a story through were all in Alabama, selling or about to sell Bibles. They were students who had been recruited by a certain religious publishing company, hired to spend the summer going door to door, giving their all and collecting their commissions. In training them, the company liked to get the students so hyped up, so zealous with the desire to sell and, therefore, *win*, that they might not notice the thirty-dollar down payment they took in cash and the signature on the contract both came from a woman who had three kids, tar paper on her walls and no milk in her refrigerator. Students who did notice and were bothered by that sort of thing rarely lasted the summer, or if they did, they were changed by it, and not for the good. Some students thrived on the competition of the "game." Some complained the company sucked them into ordering more than they could sell, then forced the student to pay the difference. It was a story with layers and it deserved the fifteen minutes needed to tell it on the air. Also, it was a story that left something for the audience to do; it would be seen differently by different people.

What it didn't leave was much for me to do. The story was produced by Craig Leake, who has the kind of cherubic face and manner that causes people to tell him anything he wants to know. They just open up and talk, seeming to forget about the camera. In Alabama they opened up and talked so much and so well that almost all the story was told through their words, combined with pictures that told the rest. There really wasn't anything left for me to say, but Craig was graceful about it; in editing the story, he managed to create a few gaps where my voice would be needed. I'm sure he did it just to be kind; it was my first magazine story and, well, it would be nice if I said something in it. So I did. In a fifteen-minute story, I spoke for thirty-four seconds. Welcome to the television news magazine. Well, at least *I* wrote the thirty-four seconds.

If the story really didn't need me, it did need Craig Leake. On *Weekend* (as on *60 Minutes*) the real reporter is the producer. Most of the time TV magazine reporters don't like to dwell on that, but it's the truth;

*Weekend* had two reporters—Lloyd Dobyns and myself—but it had thirty producers, each of whom was a journalist and in some stage of preproduction, production or postproduction at all times. Long stories take longer to do because, usually, they are more complicated in subject matter. The producer goes out with the crew, shoots the story, or most of it, then calls in the reporter for a few days. The reporter does the major interviews, films his stand-uppers, then catches a plane to the next story. He won't hook up again with the first story until after the producer has brought back his film, screened it and made a rough cut of the piece. By then, the reporter may have been out on five other stories.

So, when you see a piece like "Always in Fashion," a story I reported about modern sweatshops in the garment industry, know that it was the *producer,* Stephanie Meagher, who took the camera crew into places where old women cut thread for almost nothing and children worked fourteen hours a day in rooms with no ventilation, making clothes that would be sold in major department stores. It was Stephanie who, when told by one boss that he did indeed pay his workers by the hour, pointed out that there was no clock in the factory, which was itself tucked away, hidden from the labor inspectors, the union and—most of all—the Immigration people. Southeast Asia had given America a new crop of slave labor. It was a good story, a good piece of journalism, but it wasn't mine—it was Stephanie's.

In April, 1979, *Weekend* reported the advances made by a group of parents of children with Down's syndrome (we used to say "mongolism"), parents who disregarded the general body of medical thought on the subject, kept their children at home instead, and worked with them, patiently teaching them, pushing, encouraging and leading them past their "limits." The results were breathtaking, but it pointed to the sad, sad fact that by acting on the advice of doctors, and institutionalizing Down's syndrome babies, sometimes within hours of their birth, many parents had allowed their children's lives to be wasted. Again, the story wasn't simple and wasn't made out to be. Victims were more easily identified than villains. The parents who put their kids away did so because "experts" told them to, but no doctor acted out of malice when he told the parents of a Down's syndrome child it was hopeless. He spoke from experience and education, two things we can usually depend on and probably should not.

It was a special story, and when it won an Emmy, the Emmy went to Christine Huneke, the producer. I may have been the one to write the script—and by this time I could be trusted with more than thirty-four seconds—I may have been the one to sit, on camera, and listen to a five-year-old boy, the kind we once called a mongolian idiot, read to me from a first-grade reader, but Christine Huneke was the one who found the child, the story and the way to tell it.

Well, if that's all I did on *Weekend,* why wasn't I a Twinkie? *Was* I a Twinkie? I looked like one. My hair was slicked back and pinned on top of my head, my blouses were silk and frilly, my hems were even and were attached to skirts, not pants—and my shoes often matched my eye shadow or lip gloss. I did not wear glasses. I wore pearls. How was this happening? Easy. It's how Reuven Frank wanted it, it's how his bosses wanted it. They must have wanted it a lot; for years anchorpeople at NBC had tried, unsuccessfully, to get the company to buy their clothes, but NBC bought our clothes, mine and Lloyd's—and we didn't ask for that or want it, particularly. We were perfectly willing to wear what we wore all the time, which was the trouble, according to NBC. Figuring, correctly, that Lloyd would wear safari jackets and tacky leisure suits while I would show up in jeans, tacky tee shirts and sneakers, NBC insisted on buying our clothes and paid somebody else to pick them out. As further evidence of trust in our sartorial sensibilities, NBC kept the clothes at NBC, thus avoiding a more than slight chance that we would show up to tape the program wearing parts of two or three of our new outfits all at once. Lloyd and I agreed; they were fine clothes, all right. You could do almost anything in them, except work.

Which brings me to the subject of Lloyd Dobyns. He was my partner on *Weekend,* later my partner on *Overnight,* and in between we shared offices, opinions and reputations for having no team spirit. After so many years, I can say with absolute certainty that the reputation is deserved; *Lloyd* has no team spirit, none at all. It's one of his best qualities. He is Welsh, American Indian and God knows what. He has a feel for words—or a taste for lying. He neither suffers fools gladly nor sees anything worthwhile in abstension—from anything. He loves and appreciates all women, all ages, indiscriminately, and although he is from Virginia, he is no gentleman. That, too, is part of his act.

We know too much about each other for me to write comfortably about him, and we keep each other's secrets. Things get fogged: I've watched Lloyd's hair go from mostly brown to mostly gray, and helped the process along when I could. I remember when he didn't have to wear glasses to read a TelePrompTer or to keep from falling into things. I've watched him go from leisure suits to custom-made vests, from up to down, from sad to almost happy, which is as close as he can come to happy. I've watched Lloyd cry and watched Lloyd work. He liked it when a critic described him as "ham on wry." I forgave him for telling the same critic that I was a "walking disaster." When the critic called me "brass" and him "steel," we fought about which was worse. Lloyd and I liked to fight with each other and we were good at it; sometimes it was the way we talked to each other best. I suppose Lloyd is the least sexist man I know since he shows no mercy to anyone, female or male. When it comes to polite conversation, Lloyd believes in shooting the wounded. However, he does know how to spell Buffalo, how to get bail in Tel Aviv, the capital of Abu Dhabi, the proper way to eat an ortolan—and he can call by first name at least three bartenders, two police detectives and one newspaper editor in each of the ten biggest cities in America. Best of all, in my presence he always tells stories about me in such a way as to make me look good. How he tells them when I'm not around is not something I need to worry about—or want to know, not that I really want to know how to eat an ortolan, either.

It was not love at first sight. The first time I met Lloyd Dobyns was on the set of the *Today* show in July, 1976. Jim Hartz and Barbara Walters had left the show. Tom Brokaw was scheduled to begin hosting *Today* after the presidential election in November; until then he would continue his assignment as White House correspondent. It was not known who would replace Barbara Walters, and NBC, unable to make up its mind, chose to hold auditions during the summer. Those asked to audition were Cassie Mackin, Betty Furness, Kelly Lange, Linda Ellerbee and Jane Pauley.

During the audition period, Lloyd Dobyns would

host the *Today* show, but would have no say about which woman got the job. He was in a peculiar position; one of the women would be a permanent part of that program but he would not. Therefore, being friendly to all of them made sense. And he tried, he did try. During a commercial break on my first day doing the *Today* show, he suggested that when it came time in the program to indulge in what television refers to as "cross-talk"—and the real world calls conversation—that we talk about me. I'd been at the network less than a year; Lloyd thought it reasonable for the audience to get to know me a little bit on the air. For example, was I married? I said I was and told him my husband's name.

"That sonofabitch?" said Lloyd. "I fired him once and I'd do it again."

We went back on the air right after that. For "cross-talk" we chatted about the federal budget.

The next time we met was when Reuven, knowing nothing of the *Today* episode, suggested to Lloyd that it would be smart if the two of us went out to dinner and got to know each other, since we were going to work together on *Weekend*.

We did what he told us to do and suspect we had a grand time, but we can't be sure because the only record is a handful of receipts, the total number of which suggests we got along just fine. The most either of us can remember is a rambling conversation having to do with why we *should* get along, a conversation that rambled, apparently, over a large part of Manhattan and through a sizable number of its saloons.

Later, some people said we were alike. Other people said we were too much alike, and that was a damn shame, they thought. We assumed it was a joke until the letter about the pigeons. It arrived a few days after I had reported a story about people who lived in Brooklyn and raised racing pigeons on their roofs. As I said, I reported the story, I wrote the story, I narrated and I appeared in it on several occasions. The letter began, "Dear *Lloyd* . . ." It went on to tell Lloyd that *his* piece on racing pigeons was wonderful, possibly "the single best feature I've ever seen on television." The letter was from Charles Kuralt. I wrote him back. "Dear Leslie . . ." The truth is, Lloyd and I are more different than we are alike, except for the fact that at different times and for different reasons we both fired the same man.

One reason Lloyd and I stay friends is that each of us believes she (he) is the better writer, and neither of us has ever put it to the test. Sure, he would correct my grammar and I would correct his spelling, which he claimed didn't matter—it was television. Occasionally we would engage in friendly competition, trying to outdo each other with obscure "good night" items on *Weekend.* If Lloyd said, as he did one night, "Good night for the Edward Powell selection committee of Philadelphia. Appointed by the mayor to pick a Philadelphia citizen to receive a twenty-thousand-dollar cash award, the committee picked—the mayor of Philadelphia," then I would come back the following week with, "Good night for *The New York Times,* which, in reporting the wedding of Patty Hearst, was able to say with a straight face, 'The maid of honor was Miss Hearst's friend, Trish Tobin. Miss Tobin's father owns the Hibernia Bank, which Miss Hearst was convicted of robbing in 1974.'"

Lloyd knew more than I did about writing words to pictures when I first joined *Weekend,* but I was learning, and I choose to believe that was what saved me from Twinkiedom. A radically new concept—writing *with* television. Letting picture tell story. To explain, let me suggest an experiment. Turn on the newscast and go into the next room. Now, listen to any story on the newscast—from beginning to end. If the story is perfectly clear to you at all times, it is a normal newscast. There is a name for this manner of telling a story. It's called radio. If it's television, you will be unable to stay in the other room and still get it all. If it's television, it will compel you to watch. At least it should; if it doesn't, throw out your television set and get a better radio. Be sure your neighbors are watching; show them once and for all you don't *need* television. Why not? It may be true. We keep trying to make it true.

The idea that television had to be more than radio with pictures was unfamiliar to me until I met Reuven Frank, but that's understandable. At the time, I'd been a television reporter for only *six years.*

Pictures, I was coming to learn, were different from words; as different, Reuven pointed out, as smells are from sounds. Words, he said, go mostly to the intelligence; pictures go more to the feelings and responses. Reuven once used the example of a plane crash to explain. What are the best pictures from a plane crash? (I know. There's nothing "best" about a plane crash, but mine is a business that is supposed to inform you of the crash, anyway.) According to Reuven: a stocking hanging from a tree, a doll with a broken face—these, in their way, tell you more than words do, more even than pictures of body bags being carried down the hill. Beyond that, good writing meant good thinking, and no combination of words and pictures could save the reporter who rushed to the scene, found the mother of the doll's owner, told the cameraman to shoot her face close up, then stuck his microphone into her face and asked her anything, anything at all. It's the act of a moral dwarf, *and an example of a complete bankruptcy of ideas.*

"Another thing," said Reuven, "almost nobody writes silence anymore." Well, I tried to write silence; with a score of thirty-four seconds out of fifteen minutes on my first story, I figured I had a chance of learning how to write nothing—nothing with words, that is. With practice, I found I liked the idea and wanted very much to learn how to write with pictures, the words of the people in the story, sounds—and the lack of sounds.

A year later, when I put together the first story for *Nightly News* in which I used no narration at all, *Nightly News* refused to credit me in the introduction. How could I claim to have written it? There was no narration. I continued to try the technique whenever possible; they continued to deny me a byline. A compromise was reached. The anchorman would not say, "Linda Ellerbee reports"; however, he would say that what people were about to watch was "assembled by" Linda Ellerbee, which, to me, sounded as if I were about to show the class my collection of dead toads—but it was better than nothing. It still is.

Don't misunderstand. The technique works only when the pictures do tell the story. One of the most pointless pieces ever seen on television was a little something on *Weekend* in which the reporter strolled around the Taj Mahal and the city of Agra while Bing Crosby sang "Far Away Places" in the background. The reporter looked unhappy about being there—and it is proof there *is* such a thing as fairness in this world that the reporter was Lloyd, and not me. He still leaves the room if I say "Taj Mahal" a certain way.

Because *Weekend was* television, it addressed the subject of television, but again, indirectly. One time the subject, ostensibly, was employee theft, but mostly the story was about cameras and the number of companies using them against workers. Unions hated it; they said it was spying. They said it was not Big Brother but Big Business who was watching, with cameras hidden in overhead lights, air conditioning ducts and dress mannequins. In other words, private industry was doing many things police couldn't by law. According to big business, people's morals had changed; the days of the mom-and-pop operation were gone, nobody felt close to the people they worked for, and so they felt that when stealing from large corporations, they were stealing nobody's money. Insurance companies would pay.

Private industry, instead, was choosing to do many strange things in the name of protection, and along with hidden cameras, one company had resorted to brainwashing. For $2,700 it had piped into its plant a subliminal message blended into music. The message said, "I am honest. I won't steal. If I do, I will be caught and go to jail." The story was produced by Merle Rubine, a feisty woman some people called pushy just because she was willing to take her cameras where they weren't necessarily wanted, to ask questions people generally didn't want to answer, then ask them why they didn't want to answer, and finish off by telling them she didn't care what they had to say, anyway.

Sometimes it worked. I remember a night in San Francisco, six years later, when Merle and I, working for a program called *Summer Sunday, USA,* spent hours waiting for a keyed up and thoroughly obnoxious Hunter S. Thompson to stop his prancing performance and sit down for the interview he'd agreed to do. Thompson was enjoying his coyness, perhaps believing it was the first time we'd ever encountered an asshole, and, therefore, we would be impressed. Merle, looking up from the floor, bored and, like me, wondering why we were there, told the cameraman to turn on his camera, then go sit down. She told Hunter that the camera was rolling, it was over there, he could walk over, pick up that microphone, face that camera and talk if he wanted to, or he could take the microphone and stuff it, for all she cared, but in ten minutes she was going to tell the cameraman to turn off his machine and we were going back across town to the Democratic convention, which was looking, right then, like an oasis of sanity. And—she wanted to know—was there any word in what she'd said that gave him trouble? That was one of those times it worked. Hunter Thompson, like other people in other stories who thought they didn't want to talk about something, ended up wanting to be on television more than he wanted to play his game.

Television can—and does—change people at both ends of the camera. Consider what happened with the parents of Karen Ann Quinlan and the media.

Peter Poor produced the story for *Weekend*. It was called "Karen Ann Turns 25." Ms. Quinlan, you will recall, had been in an irreversible coma since April, 1975. Karen's parents went to court to obtain the right to take her off her life-supporting respirator after doctors had determined her brain was damaged beyond recovery and might, in fact, be "dead." In a milestone court decision, the parents won that right. The respirator was turned off. But Karen lived. (In a rest home in

New Jersey, in a coma, until summer, 1985, when she died.) At the time of *Weekend*'s story, Karen Ann Quinlan had just turned twenty-five. Peter Poor filmed the birthday party at the Quinlans' house: Karen Ann's birthday, shared by her family, close friends—and the media. What had happened was curious. From the beginning of the Karen Ann Quinlan story, the Quinlans had been swamped with coverage, especially from local television stations in New York City. The Quinlans had made a decision to cooperate with the media, in hopes they could make people understand the choice they'd made about their daughter, make people face the problem and think about it. There was one restriction. *No one* in the media would be allowed inside the room to see or photograph their daughter, and except for one brainless reporter who tried a nun's habit as a disguise, the media cooperated. As time passed, the parents adjusted to the magnifying glass that wouldn't seem to go away. In Peter's story about them, you saw a family who knew by first name all the local television reporters who, for four years, had covered the story; in many cases they knew the reporter's wife's or husband's name—and would ask about them. Watching Arnie Diaz report on WCBS-TV, one of the Quinlans remarked that he looked better since he'd gotten back from his vacation and wouldn't it be nice to see Arnie again soon. Of course they did see him soon. The Karen Ann Quinlan story, like Karen Ann Quinlan, was slow to die.

It was an example of one of those times when people in a story came to see reporters as humans—*and the other way around.* In fact, when *Weekend* did its story, the only slightly detached person, as best I could determine, was me.

That was because I had never covered the story and never met the Quinlans before *Weekend.* Besides, reporters aren't supposed to have emotions, remember? We're supposed to be objective and to choose cynicism over involvement. Of course, there is no such thing as objectivity, which is where the trouble starts. Some reporters merely reject the notion of objectivity as old-fashioned and leap into the fray choosing sides, but a reporter who sets himself up as an avenging angel—a righter of wrongs—is just one step short of running for office. We're not supposed to change things, we're supposed to report them. On the other hand, any reporter who tells you he's objective is lying to you. "Objective" *is* impossible; there is no such thing as a random number and there is no such thing as a reporter who comes to a story able to forget everything he's ever heard, seen or had happen to him.

Or *her.* That was the problem with the abortion documentary. Technically, it wasn't a documentary; it was a special edition of *Weekend* in which the entire hour was given over to one subject—the antiabortion movement and its growing political power. It was *a news story.* The movement had been underestimated; it had become a force of sorts in American politics—a single-issue force. This was in January, 1979. Two months before, in Senate elections, Thomas McIntyre had not been reelected in New Hampshire, Floyd Haskell lost the race in Colorado and Dick Clark, a popular incumbent, lost in Iowa—all of them defeated *because of or partly because of their proabortion stands.* In all three states there had been a concentrated and professional lobbying effort, one that extended to lobbying people in churches and passing out pamphlets that said, "Change your party to save a baby's life."

In New York State, the antiabortion groups had mounted an all-out effort to get votes for their candidate for governor, Mary Jane Tobin. Nobody thought she would get elected, but by New York State law, if she got 50,000 votes, the "Pro-Life" party would then be assured a line on the ballot in *all* state elections for the next four years. The Communist party had tried the same tactic. So had the Socialist party and the Free Libertarian party. None of them had succeeded. The "Pro-Life" people did. She got more than 50,000 votes.

It was a story about single-issue politics, and not a story about abortion or about whether abortion ought to be federally funded, legal or performed under any circumstance. But there was one big obstacle. Reuven had assigned me and not Lloyd to report and write the one-hour special, and I knew it was a bad choice, because Lloyd Dobyns had never had an abortion. I had.

Years earlier, before the 1973 Supreme Court decision made abortion legal, I'd been one of those women, young, unmarried, who'd gotten pregnant, then gotten the name of someone through a friend of a friend, paid six hundred dollars cash, and waited, terrified, at my apartment until midnight when a pimply-faced man showed up, exchanged code words with me and came in, bringing cutting tools, bandages and sodium Pentothol—but no medical license I could see. I was lucky. I did not bleed uncontrollably. I did not die. I recovered. I was no longer pregnant. But I wasn't the same, either. No woman is. I'd felt it was my decision. I believed then and believe now that a woman has a right to choose. I'd been prepared for the consequences to my heart and to my opinion of myself, but not for the abject shame I apparently was supposed to feel. Not having six hundred dollars cash, I'd gone to the man who owned the radio station and asked to borrow it. Unable to come up with a plausible lie, feeling, somehow, that the truth was called for, I'd told him why I needed the money. He'd given it to me, but not until he'd had an hour of mocking me, ridiculing me for "being a dumb broad to believe some man when he said he was 'protected'; didn't you know any better?" He'd said it proved I was a slut, like all women who worked when they ought to be married and having babies, not killing babies and taking men's jobs. He said I was lucky he was such a generous boss, that he would loan me the money but he ought to fire me. He charged me thirty percent interest, instead.

I didn't quit. I needed the job—and I needed the six hundred dollars in order to carry out my decision. But I never forgot any part of it, and so all those years later, when asked to write an hour on anything at all having to do with abortion, I balked. I didn't want to churn up my own feelings—and I didn't want to come right out and say I wasn't objective, or to tell anyone why I was the wrong person to do the story. Even in 1979, women didn't admit openly that they'd had an abortion. Many still don't. I don't know of any other woman in my business who has, and in doing so now, I may run some risk, but if you can't be objective, hell, at least you can be honest, which is what I'm trying to be now, and what I tried to be then on *Weekend.* I told no one but Lloyd what the problem was. He advised me to do the story anyway. He said if I couldn't be *fair,* I wasn't worth what they paid me, never mind that I probably wasn't worth that, anyway. Lloyd was always a comfort to me.

I reported the story and worked like a demon to keep my opinions out of it. Frankly, I think I succeeded, because after the show aired I got an equal amount of hate mail from both sides of the issue, each claiming I had favored the other side. Objectivity. Pure objectivity. Everywhere but inside.

Something about writing this has reminded me of Frank Reynolds. In 1970, when Reynolds was removed as the anchor of the evening news at ABC, he said, on his last night on the air, that he guessed he should hope his words had offended no one, but (as a matter of fact) he didn't hope that at all because there were, in this world, people who ought to be bothered. In choosing to do the abortion special, I had bothered people; and I was one of the people I'd bothered.

Frank Reynolds, you may remember, was the most on-again, off-again anchor in the history of television news. He would anchor ABC's evening news, then be taken off it, to be replaced by someone else until the next time they needed him. This went on for years, and it is interesting to note that in the spring of 1983, when Frank Reynolds was sick and could not appear on ABC's *World News Tonight,* the program dropped in the ratings and stayed there past his death in July of that year. The most fired anchor in TV news finally had his ratings revenge.

By spring of 1979, ratings were on all our minds at *Weekend,* despite Reuven's warning that when the likes of us started trying to understand and explain ratings, it was usually tooth fairy time. *Weekend* had been airing weekly since September, 1978. You will recall that until then, *Weekend* had aired on Saturday nights, replacing *Saturday Night Live* once a month. Probably it has not escaped your notice that by 1978, *Saturday Night Live* was a hit television show; certainly it did not escape Fred Silverman's notice. Silverman was president of NBC, brought over from ABC where he'd been known as the wonder boy, the man with the "golden gut." It does not take metal intestines to figure out that a hit show that airs three times a month will make even more money if it airs four times a month. Of course, it wouldn't look good for Fred to join NBC and, right out of the box, cancel a prestigious, critically praised, award-winning *news* program simply because it had such a small audience—and was in the way. Better to promote the show to prime time, take credit for rewarding the news division, give *Saturday Night Live* its fourth Saturday every month—and give *Weekend* the chance it deserved. The Chance It Deserved. Right. Silverman said he had every faith in our success as a weekly, prime-time program. He said he was firmly behind us, a statement to be taken the same way one must take George McGovern saying in 1972 that he was behind Tom Eagleton "one thousand percent," or Liza Minnelli saying in 1979, "I get high on life."

"But what," said Silverman, "could go wrong?" I believe something was mentioned about *60 Minutes* being a commercial failure for its first seven years, and it was pointed out that *60 Minutes* got to go on the air opposite *Walt Disney*. Silverman said it didn't matter, we shouldn't worry about things like that, and proved he wasn't worried by scheduling our first prime-time program opposite the final installment of *Roots*. Later, he made it possible for the truly committed viewer to find *Weekend* by making sure newspapers were notified of changes in the *day* and *time Weekend* would air each week—and notified in time to make the paper no later than the day of air, or at least the day after.

One night, I found myself going on the air to say, "Good evening. The name of this program is *Weekend*. Yes, we know it's Wednesday, but try to think of *Week-*

*end* as a state of mind rather than a time of the week, which is how we've come to think of it around here."

In March, Reuven threw up a slide just before the commercial. The slide read: "First in War, First in Peace, 65th in the Nielsen's." I thought it was funny, which is part of my problem. It's also part of Reuven's. This was a "verbal," which was what Reuven called them, and why not? He could call them what he liked; he wrote them. They were little sayings that were printed on the screen going into and sometimes coming out of commercial breaks. Some were philosophical: "When things can't get worse, they get worse." "Most men lead lives of quiet desperation; film at eleven." Some were political: "Name any three Republicans not running for president." "Jerry Brown has hurt Linda Ronstadt's image." Some were, well, the result of a particular sense of humor: "Deng Xiaoping once pretended to be Teng Hsaio Ping." Once in a while Lloyd and I would try to stop Reuven, to keep something off the air for his own good: "If someone socked Mike, would *60 Minutes* use the film?" Finally, there was: "If you like *Weekend,* share the secret with a friend."

We never succeeded in stopping him or even slowing him down, and, meanwhile, Fred Silverman was not laughing. Television news is not about humor—or journalism—it's about money. It always was, but as long as the news made no money, it remained a throwaway, basically something done to keep a station's or a network's license. And it might have stayed that way if John Kennedy had not been shot. During the measured, fragile days that followed, the country gathered round its TV sets, grieving as a family, joining to share the formal feeling of participating in a national catharsis. When we got up from our sets and went back to our separate tables, the habit was established. It can be argued that this is pure speculation on my part, and that may be so, but it suits my purpose here; therefore, it's true. One thing is verifiable; no television newscast made money before John Kennedy was shot, but the first time one did, everything was changed. Television news programs came to be considered the same way other television programs were considered, at least by management. The television news program became one more tool used to manufacture the product.

Please remember that in television the product is not the program; the product is the audience and the consumer of that product is the advertiser. The advertiser does not "buy" a news program. He buys an audience. The manufacturer (network) that gets the highest price for its product is the one that produces the most product (audience). It might be said that the value of any news program is measured by whether it increases productivity; the best news program, therefore, is the one watched by the greatest number of people. Argue the point if you like, and when you get tired, argue with the weather. Altruists do not own television stations or networks, nor do they run them. Businessmen own and run them. Journalists work for businessmen. Journalists get fired and canceled by businessmen. That is how it is.

We were a big disappointment to Fred Silverman, and real quick. A two-year commitment to *Weekend*'s prime-time position expired after eight months. *Weekend* let Fred down. It had terrible ratings; it did not matter that people wrote nice things about the program, when they thought to write about it. *Weekend* had to go—and it couldn't go back to its old spot on Saturday night; that spot was taken now. *Weekend* would simply have to disappear. There is this to say for Fred Silverman. He let *Weekend* stay on the air longer than *Super Train*. And so *Weekend* chugged feebly along, until April, 1979, which was when Lloyd and I went to Palm Springs to listen to Gerald Ford and find out our show was canceled—but not in that order.

Being canceled made you feel just terrible. I took it personally. It wasn't as bad as being fired, but that was all you could say for it. The worst part was, we couldn't keep doing *Weekend*. That was what canceled meant, all right. I was going to miss that show, miss the classroom. It felt as if someone had closed the school door in my face. The interview with Gerald Ford in Palm Springs was uneventful, as Reuven had said it would be. I wished he had been wrong. It would have been sweet to go out with some flash, but the only thing that moved, the only thing that woke anybody up was not seen on television. It came after the interview was finished and Lloyd, President Ford and I were standing in President Ford's yard, which probably is not what they call it, but it was outside his back door and covered with grass, even if it was also a golf course.

The three of us were standing there so the official Gerald Ford photographer could take pictures. While we waited, President Ford said he'd noticed something strange when he'd read my biography, the one NBC had sent him. He said he'd been surprised that it contained the date and *year* of my birth; he didn't recall seeing that on any other network reporter's "bio." I told him that was right; I didn't lie about my age. I lied about my height. On my tallest day I can do no better than five feet six inches. I told him I'd always wanted to be tall, so I lied.

"You really lie about your height?" said President Ford. "Just how tall are you?"

"Mr. President, I am five feet eleven inches tall."

That was when I got a little worried for us all, because that was when Gerald Ford, the man who had been leader of the free world and in control of the little red button that could kill us all by his touching it—this man, who stood well over six feet, stared down onto the *top* of my head from nearly a foot above it, and said, "I can't see why you'd want to lie. Five feet eleven inches is a very nice height for a woman."

Everything seemed a little funnier after that, funny enough to get us through the day. I bought a pair of sneaker roller skates, which were available in Palm Springs but had yet to make their way to the East coast. A sometimes mild-mannered NBC News cameraman named Houston Hall joined Lloyd in helping me to make my way, on skates, back to our hotel, where the desk clerk insisted I take off the skates until Houston and Lloyd offered to kill him, just for the sport of it. Maybe we weren't taking cancellation so well, after all.

On the way back to New York, I thought about Reuven Frank. This had to be tougher on him than on me. He had invented *Weekend;* I'd only helped put it off the air. Reuven once explained television by saying that what it did uniquely was to transmit experience, to let people know "What was it like?" And that it was a rare—and usually accidental—accomplishment. To me, the time on *Weekend* had been like that, the transmission of an experience, a glimpse of a different way to see television and to make it. A lucky accident for me.

Monday morning, I wore my roller skates to work. What was the use of working in a building with shiny marble floors if you couldn't skate on them? I made it through the lobby of the RCA building with only two guards chasing me, and only one serious about it—the old one, happily. When the elevator doors shut behind me, I started wondering what Reuven Frank would say to me about *Weekend* being canceled. I was sure it would be something wise, something I could remember and carry with me to whatever came next. I was right. What he said was something I can remember clearly. I got off the elevator and started down the hall to his office. He came out his door, saw me, and from thirty feet away gave me lasting advice.

"Linda, how many times must I tell you? Never roller-skate on the rug."

I try to keep it in mind.

# LEAVE IT TO BEAVER

God bless the squire and his relations
And keep us in our proper stations.
OLD PRAYER

There was a beef shortage in 1973, also a shortage of butter, eggs and toilet paper. We reported all this, but it didn't end there. Marya McLaughlin, a political reporter for CBS News, was called into the office of the producer of the *CBS Evening News* and told she had a new assignment. CBS wanted her to cover cooking stories. Not fluff, explained the producer, not girl stuff, but "hard news" cooking stories—food was news. Marya, whelmed by the assignment, thought for a minute.

"Oh. Now I understand. If a 707 crashes this afternoon, you want me to take my camera crew to the pilot's house, and when his wife comes to the door, you want me to ask her what she *would have cooked* for dinner if he *were* coming home. Is that right?"

Marya told me this story in 1977, when the two of us were covering the House of Representatives, McLaughlin for CBS, Ellerbee for NBC. She told it to me in the House Radio-TV Gallery. At the time, I was wearing a sweater, blue jeans and sneakers. It was what I wore most days—still do—and it never failed to anger some of the men reporters who covered the House. They had to wear coats and ties, serious clothes. The reason was simple. The dress code said that they did. The reason I could wear jeans and sneakers was simple, too. There was no dress code for women. It had never occurred to the men who had made the rules that women might one day be covering the United States Congress.

In 1978, I left Washington and covering the Congress to work for *Weekend,* which, as I've said, involved considerable travel. One night I had dinner with a friend who traveled more than I did. She was a "still" photographer and in great demand because she took wonderful pictures. While we sat at the bar, waiting for our table to be made ready, we discussed the possibility of meeting at her house in Switzerland for a long weekend of skiing. It was January. Our schedules made such a weekend difficult to arrange, but we thought we'd try. The next weekend was out; she would be shooting publicity stills on a movie set in Utah. It didn't matter; I would be shooting a story in Phoenix that weekend and the week after that I would be in Mexico. What about three weeks from then? No luck. She would be in Hawaii. The week after that? Sorry, I would be in China—if the visa came through. How about the middle of next month? That was out; she would be in Pakistan, but maybe the end of February? Forget it; I would be in Pakistan.

While the two of us got out our calendars to see if we had any blank space before spring thaw, the bartender, who, during this conversation, had been standing there, wiping one glass, listening and looking faintly puzzled, suddenly smiled.

"I got it. Stewardesses, right?"

Those three stories illustrate some of the relative disadvantages, advantages and all-out silliness that go along with being a woman in this business, a business in which most men believed we didn't belong and couldn't last.

We did and we have, at least so far. What happens as we age, as our hair grays, our eyesight fails, our faces fall and our breasts sag? Will we be retired, as once was the custom with stewardesses? Will we be shifted from in front of the camera, in front of the White House, the Capitol, the explosion, the courthouse, the war zone—to more seemly assignments like covering cooking stories and one hundredth birthday celebrations of senior citizens?

On the subject of birthdays, consider this. In 1983, there were 32,000 Americans one hundred years old or older according to the U.S. Census Bureau. Of that, 24,000 were women. It seems clear we're outliving men. The question is, how shall we pass the time until then? In 1982, Barbara Walters pointed out that she was generally considered to be the "Grande Dame" or the old broad—depending on your bias—of television news. She was fifty. Dan Rather was considered the brash young kid who had replaced Walter Cronkite. He was also fifty. It raises a question.

In order to answer questions about where we're going in this business, it's necessary to look at how we got here. It wasn't enlightenment. It was the Federal government, and it wasn't enlightenment on the government's part either—it was the civil rights movement. In the late sixties, there developed a growing mandate in this country to extend employment opportunities to those who did not happen to be blue-eyed white men. The Federal Communications Commission, under pressure, finally suggested to the white men who ran the news operations at the networks that it might be a generous gesture on their part if they hired a few women, also a few blacks, Hispanics, Orientals and other minorities (blacks, Hispanics and Orientals are minority groups—women, being fifty-one percent of the population, are *not* minor). The message was clear: hire *some* of these people so we can get the rest of them off our backs here in Washington.

The suggestion was met with less than raging enthusiasm at the networks. Women had no place on the front line. Certainly, they were too frail to carry those big cameras. They would faint at the sight of a little blood. They would blush at the language of your average camera crew (so would a longshoreman). They would complain about spending hours standing outside the courthouse, waiting. They would trip over their high heels chasing some fellow who didn't want his picture taken. They would giggle, shriek, simper, fall, bitch, flirt, screw up (and around), blow the story, blow the boss and take jobs from men.

In short, putting the broads in broadcasting would flat out ruin the party.

Or so it was thought, if not said. It was said that the only kind of women who would want to work in this business would be aggressive and combative—compliments when applied to men. Well, they were dead right. Most of us "ladies" who work for television news are aggressive and most of us like it that way. It helps, you see. Some of the qualities that go into making a good reporter—aggressiveness, a certain sneakiness, a secretive nature, nosiness, the ability to find out that which someone wants hidden, the inability to take "no" with any sort of grace, a taste for gossip, rudeness, a fair disdain for what people will think of you and an occasional and calculated disregard for rules—are also qualities that go into making a very antisocial human being. Somehow, as a society, we are less able to abide those things in women than we are in men. It's one of our fantasies that women are softer or better than that—or ought to be.

It's true, I suppose, in all professions and trades. Certainly it explains why Kenneth Ulane no longer flies for Eastern Airlines. Ulane flew—and won medals for his flying—in Vietnam, then flew twelve years for Eastern, but in 1980, Kenneth Ulane had his sex changed, surgically, and became Karen Ulane. Eastern fired them both. Ulane sued, charging sex discrimination. Since Eastern had no female pilots, Ulane figured she had a case. During the trial, Eastern argued that it was a safety problem. Ms. Ulane might distract the other pilots, or at least confuse them. One pilot testified that Ulane had a serious problem: otherwise, *why would he want to be a she*? The court agreed. There was no question about it; Karen Ulane no longer had the "right stuff" for the *cock*pit.

As for television, it's not surprising that the first women hired for TV news operations were almost all hired to be reporters. It was easy to point to women on the television screen and say, "See, we *do so hire women*." You could *see* them, for heaven's sake, and that distracted attention from what you could not see, which was this: behind the camera, operating the camera, editing the pictures, producing the programs and running the networks, there were damn few, if any, women—and that situation continued for many years after the first rush to hire women in television news. That situation still exists in the executive suites at the three networks. You can count the number of women executives on both hands and have two thumbs left over with which to twiddle, and wait.

Because there are so few women in management, it is men who do most of the hiring, which may account for the disproportionate number of pretty, pearl-wearing vacant-headed paper dolls—the kind of women you swear blow-dry their teeth—that you see reporting the news on television. If too many women in my business seem to concentrate more on their looks than on their brains, perhaps it's because men do the hiring and, as someone pointed out, men see better than they think. (I mean that in jest. Maybe.)

The first women hired for television news were not all gorgeous, although none was ugly—there are no ugly women on television news—but they were all, or almost all, women who previously had worked in print. Because television had employed few women who were not secretaries and had no intention of promoting secretaries to journalists, there was no pool of women from which they could pick, so they went to newspapers, magazines and wire services to find women to work as television reporters. Sometimes they went to radio, but radio hadn't been employing bunches of women, either, so that pool was more of a puddle.

It wasn't a bad idea, raiding print for women reporters. At least that way they hired reporters who had actually reported, then taught them—or allowed them to learn—television. Later, networks and local stations would, in some instances, hire models, actresses, Miss Americas, Miss Artichokes and Miss Alliances, then try to teach them television *and* journalism. In 1985, the British Broadcasting Corporation announced it would no longer televise beauty pageants because they were demeaning to women. If that were to happen here, some future anchorwomen would have to find other ways to audition. It's interesting to note that in recent years about half the contestants and several winners of the Miss America pageant, when asked what they wanted to be when they grew up, answered "a television anchorwoman." It's also interesting to note the great number who have gotten their wish.

This is not to imply that anyone who is beautiful is dumb. I know one fresh-faced, honey-blonde, dimpled darling who can write a story faster and finer than most men and who once, while covering a story on military preparedness, stopped to show a confused private how to fieldstrip a Thompson submachine gun, just to help the kid out.

The women coming into television news today, pretty or not, bright or not, are at least secure there is a place for women; if they can do the job, they won't be laughed out of the job. They owe it to some of the women who went before. There weren't many. One of them was Cassie Mackin.

Catherine Mackin was just a few years older than I and had worked in television only a few years longer, but those few years were rough ones. A number of men really didn't want Cassie around, although she was a hardworking, talented reporter who thought the viewer deserved her honest best, and if the viewer didn't deserve it, well, she gave it anyway. She also gave her opinion to everyone with whom and for whom she worked, like it or not. Some did not. They said she was abrasive. Usually, that meant they didn't like whatever it was she was telling them. Once she promised an officious campaign worker, who was using what little authority he had to keep Cassie from getting her story, that she was going to kick his balls through his brains, if he had either. Now I ask you, is that abrasive?

Cassie and I took part in a little known and not very important moment of history in television news. We did the very first network news program ever anchored by two women. It happened this way. Every two years NBC News broadcasts a program about the new Congress. Traditionally it is anchored by the Senate correspondent and the House correspondent. In 1976, that happened to be Cassie Mackin and Linda Ellerbee. At first, management was uncertain what to do. A program anchored by two women? There was talk of putting a man on the show as a sort of "umbrella" host. He would introduce us; we would report. In the end, NBC News did the courageous, right thing. They allowed the two women to anchor the program by themselves. Then they put the program on at dawn one Sunday morning, so nobody but my mom and Cassie's ever saw it. History, indeed.

I didn't like that, but I smiled and took it. I needed the job. Cassie, who also needed the job, told them all to go to hell. She was right, but she was seldom popular and she didn't care, or if she did, she didn't tell. Cassie made her own way, took nothing from anyone, be he senator or boss. She was a plain, old-fashioned reporter, and if she never made the cover of *People* magazine or was never made the regular anchor of *Nightly News,* well, that was how it was. She demanded respect, however, and got it, and she made life at the networks easier for those who followed her. She fought some fights first.

In November, 1982, in her late thirties or early forties—she never would tell—Cassie Mackin died of a particularly ugly form of cancer, at home, in private, with her family and without any yelling. She asked for no sympathy and she told few people about her disease. She wasn't the first tough, strong woman reporter in television—there were other even older women who had been there first—but whenever I am confronted with some monumental piece of political lying, whenever I feel like kicking some especially stupid executive—it's always Cassie I remember.

Compare Cassie with another woman television reporter I used to know. This one was hired, she said, by a news director who saw her legs in a stocking advertisement. She also had been a researcher at a weekly news magazine. When I knew her she covered feature stories in New York City for a local television station: celebrity auctions, old men who built ships inside bottles, fashion shows and Christmas parties at orphanages. Once, filling in for a "hard" news reporter who was ill, she found herself looking into a fifty-five-gallon drum to see the very dead and decomposed body of a victim of foul play. She did, she said, what she felt was the right thing. She fainted.

The lady is happier now, married and living in Beverly Hills, forever separated from journalism, and when last I spoke with her, the biggest crisis in her life was when her French instructor asked her how many bathrooms she had. It wasn't that she didn't know how to say it in French—she did. What she didn't know was how many bathrooms she had. Nine, as it turned out. And not a fifty-five-gallon drum in any of them.

You see, there are as many different flavors of women who work, or have worked in television news as there are women. The same is true of men.

Do we use our sex in our work? No. And yes.

If there's but one woman at a news conference, that woman will get a chance to ask her question. She won't need to giggle or wiggle anything. The fact that she is the only woman in the room—less likely these days—will be enough. Is she using her sex? No. Men are.

If a woman has been raped by six linebackers while five of their friends cheered them on, does a female reporter stand the better chance of getting the story? Yes. And for cause.

If a woman is sent to the Middle East, where some men still believe men are men, women are cattle and goats are fun, will she be able to cover stories there as well as a man? Yes. They may think she's a whore, but often they will talk to her more openly than to a male reporter. In fact, it's hard to think of a situation today in which, all other things being equal, a woman cannot do as well as or better than a man. That was probably always the case, but too few men, and women, realized it.

Having said that, I must also say that I do remember one story in which being a woman interfered. In 1976, Carl Albert, Speaker of the House, announced his retirement. There was no question about who the next Speaker would be. They were practically going to anoint Thomas P. ("Tip") O'Neill. NBC asked me to put together a long piece about O'Neill for *Nightly News*. In the course of preparing the story, I went with O'Neill to Boston one weekend. O'Neill is not actually from Boston; he's from North Cambridge, pronounced "Narth" Cambridge. It's not the part of Cambridge where Harvard is located; it's the part where workingmen and women live. On the plane to Boston, I asked O'Neill what he had planned for the weekend. He told me that on Friday night there would be the annual meeting of "Barry's Corner." It seems that when he was growing up, there was a group of boys who hung out together around what they called "Barry's Corner." This wasn't an actual street name or specific place anymore, if ever it was (O'Neill was a little vague about that), but the notion and the group had endured. In fact, the group had grown over the years, but everyone in it—maybe one hundred men or so—was part of the old neighborhood and part of O'Neill's past, even if he seldom saw them anymore, and hadn't been to a "Barry's Corner" gathering in years—usually he was in Washington.

I told O'Neill that we wanted to tape the get-together; it would show viewers a side of O'Neill they hadn't seen, a side I believed was important to the story. O'Neill sat there for a few minutes looking out the window, then told me there was a problem—a woman had never, ever been allowed to attend a meeting of "Barry's Corner." Did I really need to tape that? Yes, I did, and didn't he remember he'd given his word I could follow him around during the weekend? He did, and agreed, hesitantly, that my crew and I could go to the meeting.

That night, when we got to the hall where the gathering was to take place, I stopped O'Neill before he went in the door.

"Are you sure I can go in?"

"Yes, I promised."

"And you're not going back on that promise, right?"

A clearly reluctant Tip O'Neill assured me that he might not like it; in truth, it made him damned uncomfortable, taking a woman into that room—but a promise was a promise. I could go. I told him that was all I wanted to know. I wouldn't go. I would send my crew and I would go back to the hotel.

I didn't want to interfere with my own story, and I sensed we would get pictures of a more relaxed O'Neill among his old pals if I weren't there. Also, I knew that by voluntarily taking him off the hook, I would do myself some good as far as the future went. He was going to be the Speaker of the House. I was going to be the House correspondent at NBC News. He would remember that I'd let him out of an uncomfortable box. It would come in handy, back in Washington, where information was currency. (It did.)

The footage we got at "Barry's Corner" was worth it. You see a very relaxed, un-Washington-like O'Neill, back among his own. A man in the room yells out, "Hey, Tip, can you still call 'em down?"

This white-haired, diesel truck of a man stands at the front of the room, then smiles and says, "You betcha I can." He starts at the back of the room. "Timothy O'Brien, James Patrick Shaughnessy, Al Casey and his younger brother, Tommy Casey—and how's yer mom?—Sean Callahan, Red O'Leary." He went on, naming every man in the room, some of whom he hadn't seen in thirty years, "calling down" the boys of "Narth" Cambridge who'd come, many of them, thinking that O'Neill, a powerful congressman about to have even more power, wouldn't remember them. It showed, among other things, why Tip O'Neill was the politician he was—and it was a scene that would have been altered by my presence.

Dick Clark—not the one from *American Bandstand* but a producer at CBS News and later at ABC News—had a theory about when and how to use women on stories. During the early seventies, most women reporters in television were covering feature stories, but whenever a story involved a crowd—say a medium riot—Clark said he would send a woman. He knew she would get through the crowd because most men, by habit, would make way for her. By the same reasoning, he said, if the story were really a tough one, he would send a woman because she was so grateful to have the job she would work twice as hard and long as a man—usually for half the pay. Indentured gratitude, it's called, and to some extent it still works. Was Clark using women? Yes. Was it wrong? You decide.

Clark also told me a story about Michelle Clark, a young black reporter hired by CBS News and quickly given more and more important assignments because she proved she knew what she was doing. I suspect her name would be very well-known had she not died in a plane crash in 1972. Back then, everybody in our business knew she had a no-limit-in-sight future in television. Clark told me the story about Michelle Clark and the time she interviewed Hubert Humphrey.

Hubert Humphrey liked to talk. Oh, did he like to talk. At the inauguration of President Carter, I tried to shorten a live interview with Humphrey by pointing out that the ceremonies were about to begin, and I was sure he didn't want to miss a moment of them. "Oh, no," replied the cheery Humphrey. "I've got all the time in the world, I do."

Michelle Clark found a faster way to shut him up. The two of them were sitting on the set of *CBS Morning News*. The time allotted for the interview had expired, but Humphrey kept talking, missing or ignoring all hints Michelle gave him to stop. In the control room, Dick Clark signaled the stage manager to signal Michelle to *make* him stop, somehow. He didn't want to go to a commercial while the man was in mid-sentence. It didn't look polite.

Michelle got the message. What people watching the program saw was this: Humphrey was talking. Then suddenly Humphrey wasn't talking. Humphrey, in a close-up, was smiling, weakly, vaguely. Cut to commercial.

What Clark, in the control room, saw was Michelle Clark reach out and, without changing her expression of rapt attention, close her hand around the gentleman's upper thigh—the *upper*est part of the thigh. Humphrey shut up.

Was she using her sex? Yes, but I've often thought other senators, caught at their desks during one of Humphrey's interminable speeches in that chamber, might have taken a cue from Michelle Clark, had they but known.

Once or twice I've wondered if Reuven Frank knew about Michelle Clark and Hubert Humphrey when he insisted Lloyd and I sit on separate benches while we anchored *Weekend,* which brings me to the topic of men for whom I've worked, and mostly I've worked for men. Some were fair, some were not; some were stupid, some were not; and while only *some* of them had things to say about my work, my writing or my attitude, *all* of them had things to say about my appearance. I guess I can't blame them. They tell me it's a cosmetic medium, whatever that means, and it's true I regard anything beyond the aforementioned jeans and sneakers as costume. However, having bought into their costume party, I must—when necessary—dress the part. The dispute has been: when is it necessary? I don't happen to think it's necessary as often as they do, but we have come to terms about this over the years—although not so long ago I was told to lose weight if I wished ever to anchor again at NBC News. I wonder if anyone's ever said that to Charles Kuralt.

Still, the way I look and dress appears to be acceptable to most of my employers most of the time, and I have, over those same years, given in to their suggestions and worn my share of pearls, pastel suits, silk shirts and high heels. A discreet silk bow at my neck is out, however—I don't care what it says in *Dress for Success*. Regarding my hair—I have lots of hair—I've paid attention to commands to tie it back, bring it forward, put it up, take it down, cut it, let it grow, curl it, straighten it, tame it—and I stopped doing so before someone asked me to shave it off. In fact, when Reuven Frank asked me to anchor *Overnight*, a late-night news program which aired for seventeen months, beginning in July, 1982, I said I would—on three conditions. One, if the late hours caused too much strain on my family, I could quit the show with no penalty. Two, I must be allowed to leave the studio from time to time to go out and report stories before I forgot how. Three, I would kneecap the first sonofabitch who wanted to tell me what to do with my hair.

Maybe I'd just gotten older, not mellower, or maybe I'd had it up to here with men telling me to *do something* about my hair. In any case, Reuven agreed to all three conditions. He was and is a very nice man and besides, as Lloyd said, "She means it, Reuven. She really does." She really did.

Reuven gracefully allowed me to use the part of the budget allocated for a hairdresser to buy a videocassette recorder for my office, instead. After all, I *needed* a videocassette recorder.

Frankly, the attention given to how women look when reporting the news is just so much garbage, and it focuses on the wrong issue. Witness the case of Christine Craft, an anchorwoman who sued because she was fired, she said, for not meeting her station's standard of dress and appearance. You may remember the case caused a stir. She won, then lost on appeal, but the real trial was in the newspapers and on the talk shows. "How pretty must a woman be to be on television?" people debated, and debated. It was boring and it missed the point, which is: How smart must a woman be to be on television? Too often, the answer is—not very. That's true of men, also. There's no shortage of bubble-headed, bleached blonds who happen to have penises, and happen to be anchormen.

To be fair to the men, it must be said that they, too, have been told to part the hair on the other side, shave the mustache, grow the mustache, throw out that suit and get a new one—and smile.

Once upon a time there was a newly hired correspondent for NBC News based in Washington who was not liked by our employers. The truth is, they didn't think he was very good at his job, but no one, it seems, wanted to come right out and tell him that. Instead, they told him to stop squinting. The fellow was born with eyelids that would rest forever at half-mast. It wasn't his fault, but they told him it ruined his appearance on camera, and they told him often. Then this fellow took his vacation, and no one seemed to know where he'd gone. The day before he was due back at work he telephoned and asked if I could come to his house; he had something to show me. He met me at the door and asked what I thought of it. I stared at him for a long time. "It" was his operation. The man had had his eyes "fixed." The man paid good money to have his eyelids surgically altered—for *television*. What did I think? I thought it was obscene, but I guess I wasn't thinking anything too clearly, because I said the first thing that passed through my mind. I told him if it didn't work he could always marry a G.I.

It didn't work. They fired him anyway. The eyes were just an excuse all along. There is a moral here: Do what you can, don't do what you can't (or won't), and if they don't like the way you look, well, screw 'em, because that is precisely what they will do to you—man or woman, if you let them.

Somewhere back there I was speaking about women in television, and I have more to say on that. It's time to talk about the impression—held by some, even if they don't say it right out loud—that most of us bedded our way to where we are. I know how the rumor got started; it began because in some cases it's true, and that is something that bothers the rest of us tremendously. It's hard to defend against such a charge when you know of at least two or three women who got where they are by sleeping with the boss.

Although they are not representative of women in television news, we are all damaged by their behavior. For example, when Connie Chung, one of the hardest working journalists I know, did an investigative report on abortion clinics, she made one doctor so angry that he hired private detectives to get the dirt on Connie; he was sure the bitch was another round-heeled woman reporter, and sure he could prove it. Later, when the Los Angeles police raided the doctor's office, they found the reports on Connie, reports which were summed up with the line: "Goes home after work." And I add: When she's at work, *she works,* like most of us.

It seems clear to me that women have proved themselves on the job, time and time again. We're still here, and resentment of us has receded *somewhat.* The pay seems to have evened out, at least for those of us on the air. The work of women such as Lesley Stahl at CBS, Mary Alice Williams, not only an anchor but a vice president at CNN, Lynn Sherr at ABC, Sylvia Chase at ABC, Diane Sawyer at CBS and Jane Pauley at NBC, to name but a few—all of whom happen to be good-looking blondes—has shown anyone who cared to notice that women know a thing or two, and if they don't, the smart ones learn. Jane Pauley, who, at twenty-six, took the *Today* show anchor job from Cassie Mackin and several other older, more experienced women, has proved to be one of the cleverest, most able people ever to occupy that spot, and one of the most underrated. Not only that, Jane has never lost her manners, her temper or her good nature. When I grow up, I want to be Jane Pauley.

Good for us, then—except for two things. Sometimes you get the feeling we haven't come a long way, and we already know we're not babies. For instance, in 1983 I was asked by NBC to take part in a speaking tour sponsored by the network. Several correspondents would travel around the country, making speeches about television for NBC's affiliated stations. Concerning the tour, one NBC vice president wrote a memorandum to another NBC vice president. In it, he said, "I have made sure that in each city you will have a high-identity correspondent, a Washington correspondent and a woman." Notice he didn't even say "woman correspondent," nor did he see anything wrong with what he'd written, since he sent me a copy of the memorandum.

It's an attitude that's hard to defend or explain, or would be if some of the criticism of women in television were not warranted. What follows bears that out. Tom Pettit was an NBC correspondent for many years, until he went into management. This story took place when he was national political correspondent and a woman, recently arrived at NBC—not Cassie Mackin—was Senate correspondent. The night the Senate was to vote on the adoption of the treaty giving the Panama Canal back to Panama Pettit was stationed outside the Capitol in order to interview certain senators for the NBC News special that would air after the vote was complete. The woman was inside the Capitol, in the rotunda, at a desk, waiting to report the vote.

It was raining.

The hour got later and the rain harder. Tom and Senator Mathias stood there, Tom with a microphone in one hand and an umbrella sheltering the two of them in the other. Both men could hear in their earpieces everything that was being said in the rotunda. What they heard was a woman complaining that her hair didn't look right and this was network television and if the network couldn't hire a hairdresser who knew what he was doing, well, they should hire another one right after they fired this one.

The rain didn't let up and neither did the noise from the rotunda. After a while, Tom felt his nose begin to run, but with both hands occupied, there was precious little he could do about it, except stand there in the rain and listen to beauty-parlor talk coming into his ear from inside the warm, dry rotunda. Tom's nose ran on.

Finally, the senator, saying nothing, reached into his pocket, took out his handkerchief and, with it, gently wiped the nose of a twenty-five-year veteran political reporter. Neither man mentioned the scene inside. They were professionals.

Now for what an ABC executive producer once called the "recent future." If women aren't going to leave television news, where are we going in it?

In one sense, we're going up. *60 Minutes*, for example, finally has a woman reporter on its team. That's good. On the other hand, in August of 1985, walking by a newsstand, I noticed Diane Sawyer's picture on the cover of a magazine. The caption read: WHAT DO MIKE WALLACE, ANDY ROONEY AND THE OTHER MEN ON *60 MINUTES* REALLY THINK ABOUT DIANE SAWYER? Now there's a sexist headline. Sadly, the magazine was *Good Housekeeping*, a "women's" magazine, supposedly.

As for anchoring, most women who anchor on television do it in "fringe" time: very early in the morning, very late at night or on weekends. They do not anchor the big shows, but someday some woman will, and who that woman will be may depend on what a friend of mine calls "the rules change." She defines it this way: when we began, we were told that in order to sit in the big boys' chairs, first we had to go out and pay our dues. We had to cover fires, courthouses, politics, crimes, wars, riots—beef shortages—any of it, and all of it. Then we could come back and talk to them about the big boys' chairs, and not before. And so, she says, she did those things, and when her dues were paid in full and her card was duly stamped, she came back to find Phyllis George sitting in the chair. Somewhere along the line, there had been a rules change, only no one had said so until it was too late. Sorry.

Now my friend talks about going to work for a university, teaching; but what, she wonders, should she tell young women who want to succeed in this field? Should she tell them to go out and pay their dues? Might not they be wasting their time, time they might spend to better advantage at, say, Bloomingdale's? Should she mention the rules change? Would they believe her, or shrug it off as one more excuse from someone who just couldn't cut it in the big time, you know? She knows.

Don't get me wrong. Phyllis George is a sweet, talented woman, but she's not a journalist, and it's not her fault that she had trouble playing a journalist on the *CBS Morning News*. She didn't pick Phyllis George for the job; CBS management did. CBS management apparently decided being beautiful and pleasant was all that was necessary to be a journalist, and that no one watching would know the difference, or care. Unfortunately for Phyllis, they knew the difference. Phyllis lasted eight months.

Me, I wonder if the rules have changed, *ever.* In the spring of 1985, I attended the annual convention of the National Association of Broadcasters, an intimate gathering of forty thousand, comporting themselves in Las Vegas with the quiet, understated good taste that is the hallmark of our trade and that city. I went because I was invited to be one of a panel of five women. This was somewhat surprising, because by 1985 the N.A.B. had not taken what you might call sharp notice of the fact that many women work in broadcasting. The other women on the panel were a correspondent from ABC News, a correspondent from CBS News, an anchorwoman from a television station in Washington, D.C., and a woman who hosts a program that is syndicated, nationally, on radio and television.

There was this teeny, tiny misunderstanding. Silly us. We were not, it turned out, invited to speak to the broadcasters. We were invited to speak to the wives of the broadcasters. Make that spouses. If they use the word "spouse," you are supposed to know right away it is an enlightened group, never mind that the spouses are almost all wives. Our panel, as I recall, was wedged between a class in flower arranging and a makeup clinic. Unless I'm mistaken, our panel also was an alternative to a trip to the Hoover Dam, and our topic, chosen by the N.A.B.: "Women in Broadcasting—The Rise to the Top." Catchy title.

By 1985 I had learned, if I'd learned nothing else, how to count. Therefore, I did not write a letter to the N.A.B. At best, the letter would be read by no more than forty or fifty thousand people, assuming all members of the organization read it, which wasn't going to happen. Instead, I told the story on the *Today* show, which has much better numbers, and numbers, as everyone in television keeps telling me, count. Three days later, a viewer sent me a letter that contained a copy of another letter, one written to New York University, which said:

> I received from Mr. Chase, your Chancellor, in a letter dated April 26th, the information that New York University wishes to confer on me the honourary degree of Doctor of Humane Letters. In the same letter Mr. Chase informed me that Mrs. Chase would be pleased to receive me as guest of honour at a dinner given for a small group of ladies at the Chancellor's house on the evening before Commencement.

Her happiness did not last. The next letter she received informed her that while she would be dining with the Chancellor's wife, the other recipients of honorary degrees, all men, would be attending a separate dinner at the Waldorf-Astoria. Although she would be there for reasons of scholarship, she was, as she put it, "solely for reasons of sex, to be excluded from the company and conversation of my fellow doctors."

She writes that had she known this, she would have refused, but it would be impolite to do so at such a late date. She closes:

> I beg of you and the eminent Council whose representative you are, that I may be the last woman so honoured to be required to swallow from the very cup of this honour, the gall of this humiliation.

The letter was written in 1937. By Edna St. Vincent Millay. Rules change? So maybe the rules have never changed. Maybe they just got a little fuzzy here and there. The real changes will come when management changes; when women begin to get some real power in this business. To explain what I mean, let me explain first about the monkeys.

In 1983, scientists at the University of California at Berkeley completed a six-month study of male power. For their purpose, they used a colony of African monkeys, the way doctors studying cancer use rats. Their basic conclusion was that the biggest and strongest male monkey does not always get the girl. Blue monkeys live in the forests of western Kenya. It was believed the dominant male of the group had first choice when it came to mating privileges—but no. The researchers reported they regularly saw females sneak off into the woods with a variety of males they seemed to like better than the dominant one. Even the other male monkeys didn't seem to like this fellow. The dominant monkey, called "Ta" by the researchers, was indeed able to fight off other males to protect his mating rights. That, in fact, was his trouble. According to the researchers, "Ta" spent so much time proving he *was* the dominant monkey that he seldom got to enjoy the rewards of his battles—and when he wasn't fighting, he was too *tired* to get the job done. Poor old dominant "Ta." He didn't understand how easy it is to make a monkey of yourself when you're behaving like a jackass.

Neither, sometimes, does management. I have worked for "Ta" enough to see how very often the fight to remain the boss leaves too little time and energy left to do the job. They weren't all "Ta," but they were all men. It's not my fault, maybe not theirs, either. We are raised how we're raised, conditioned how we're conditioned, but the "Ta" syndrome is as good a reason as any to explain why I have come to appreciate the value of letting women run things: not all things and not all the time, but some things, sometimes. Two experiences persuaded me of this, and I don't care whether two experiences constitute a proper statistical sampling.

The first was *Overnight.* When Herb Dudnick, an extraordinary producer himself, and never a "Ta," left *Overnight,* he was replaced by Deborah Johnson. He recommended Deborah for the job.

For the first time, we had a woman executive producer at NBC News. Not only that, Cheryl Gould was senior producer, I was general editor and a good three-quarters of the *Overnight* staff were women.

None of those women were there because they were women. They were good at what they did. Also, I guess, none of those women would have been in those jobs if *Overnight* had not been a low-budget, late-hour, rather unimportant—to management—news program.

Before *Overnight,* I had never worked around or for so many women, and neither had any of the men on the program. We learned, for the most part, that everything and everyone worked easier. Fewer power games were played. Perhaps it was because women, having had little real power in our business, didn't know the games. Some learned. I remember one woman who got a chance to be an executive and after a while she became "Ta," snapping at people under her, complaining, taking credit and passing blame. The only bosses she'd ever seen were men, and I suppose she thought that was how you were supposed to manage.

On *Overnight,* there was something human—I don't know how else to describe it—about how things worked. If a telephone rang and the senior producer happened to be closer to it than a secretary, the senior producer answered it. Of course, most people, hearing a female voice, assumed it *was* a secretary. Lloyd and I shared an office for years and answered each other's telephones. During that time, everyone assumed I was his secretary. No one assumed he was mine.

On *Overnight,* women made coffee *and* policy. If there was a production meeting, and someone walked in with tears in her eyes and told us her husband or boyfriend had left her, someone got that woman a cup of tea, someone gave her a squeeze, someone said a kind word—*and then the meeting continued.*

You might wish to say that this is the frothiest of female thinking, but let me tell you something. For years I have worked for big corporations, and at every one of them there were problems—and they're getting bigger and more widespread—with employee drinking, ulcers, illness, heart attacks, broken marriages—all the nasty little by-products of stress. Are you a social drinker, sir? No, all my drinking is work-related.

It is more than probable that too much of this stress is caused by a system of management that chooses not to recognize that an employee is more than the carcass he or she hauls to work, and it is certifiable that management is prey to the same stress. Usually, the boss is the first to get the ulcers. Remember, nobody suffered from the "Ta" syndrome more than "Ta." A husband or wife leaving *is* a big deal, and you don't check it at the door when you come to work. If a child is sick, that's on your mind while you're on the job—but that is not how the game is supposed to be played. We are supposed to be so committed to our work that we leave all our other parts back at the house and we never, ever let on that they count as much as the part we bring to the office.

Would John Wayne admit to pain? The first man to walk into your average male-dominated production meeting with a tear in his eye might not be fired on the spot, but I suggest he could probably kiss his future goodbye. How could you trust anybody weak enough to show a little human emotion at work? How could you respect a boss mushy enough to squeeze the shoulders of an employee with troubles? Is he queer or what?

I'll get nailed for this, but I feel sorry for men. Our society, current popular psychology to the contrary, seldom wants boys to cry and almost never wants boys to admit to weakness, let alone tenderness. It's not, well, male.

Consider this, however. Just before *Overnight* went off the air, the engineering department at NBC initiated a study to find out why the people working the *Overnight* shift, just about the worst shift in NBC in terms of lousy hours, had the lowest absentee rate of *any* shift in the company. We can't know what they would have found out. The program went off the air right about then. For most of them, the shift ceased to exist. Certainly, the program did. However, I contend the absentee rate was low because on *Overnight* workers were treated as human beings. I do not contend this is all because of women. It began with Herb Dudnick, a man so smart he could be a woman.

I do think most women are more able than most men to recognize that a person is the sum of any number of parts, each of them important, and that he works best when all parts are taken into consideration. Women are allowed to think that way. Women are even expected to think that way. They're just not expected to be in charge.

I have been lucky. I have worked with and for some remarkable women, women like Christie Basham, who ran the Washington bureau of NBC News for much of the time I worked there, and who left only when NBC refused to give her the title of bureau chief, which she deserved, but at that time there were no women bureau chiefs at NBC News and no thought of having any. Lucky for us, she came back later.

Then there is Cheryl Gould. She is younger, smarter, skinnier, prettier, nicer and probably a better writer than I am. I like her anyway. She is a teacher in the best sense, a woman so sure of her skills and talents she never minds sharing them with those of us less skilled, less talented.

I met Cheryl in the summer of 1981 in London. I was

there to cover the wedding of Prince Charles and the Lady Diana. Cheryl lived there, working as a field producer in our London bureau. I thought I dressed funny, but here was this small person in yellow pedal pushers and red gladiator sandals laced up her calves. And there was all this hair. Cheryl has the original Jewish Afro; it adds two inches to her height, then curls every which way down to her shoulders. When she wears an angora sweater, she gets Velcrolock. She was talking about food. I was to learn Cheryl talks about food often, and likes eating food even better. On tasting her first escargot, at age seven, she decided she was French—she is from Exit 7 on the Jersey turnpike—and began to study the language. When she graduated from Princeton, she moved to France. She says it was to write. I say it was to be near the snails.

We became friends when Cheryl was senior producer of *Overnight.* Later, as senior producer of *Summer Sunday,* a weekly news magazine that appeared and disappeared in the summer of 1984, Cheryl kept me sane and was responsible for much of the good stuff that appeared on that show.

She worked seventy-two days straight on *Summer Sunday,* with no time off and no escape from the telephone, even at home. Yet she made us laugh and she kept us calm. With Andrea Mitchell that is not always an easy assignment, as Andrea would be the first to tell you. Andrea, a White House correspondent, is intense, coiled—on full alert at all times. She is rapid-fire funny, industrial-strength smart and as courageous a White House reporter as there is, and she is a kind person. She has a bit of trouble, however, with the word "relax." Andrea Mitchell is the only person I know who I think should drink *more.*

We made a fine pair. She made me look as if I were standing still, which often I was. Once, when the two of us were being interviewed by a newspaper reporter, Andrea was asked what she did for stress.

"I drink coffee," she snapped.

But Cheryl could calm down Andrea, or me, or a bear. Sometimes she did it with her sense of humor. On *Overnight,* one of her responsibilities was to write the headlines that appeared on the screen at the beginning of each of the stories in the "newsreel" segment of the show. They were all good. The one I liked best concerned the ruling by a California judge that Sheik Al Fassi did indeed owe his ex-wife a great deal of his fortune, though not, as she had contended, all of it. The headline: "Sheik, your booty!"

It would be wrong to paint Cheryl as another fast kid with a fast line. She is wiser than most people twice her age and her news judgment is solid. Because she lived overseas for so many years, she has a firm grasp of the politics, economics and people there. I asked her once why she didn't return to Europe after *Overnight* went off the air. She could have. The network would have been delighted to have so experienced and valuable a producer return to Europe. She told me she thought it was a bad idea; she was already spending too much time trying to figure out why she felt more at home in places where she didn't speak the language. NBC finally had a better idea. In the spring of 1985, it named Cheryl Gould senior producer of *Nightly News.* Now that's progress, and more important than asking a woman to anchor *Nightly News.* Besides, it is the first time, to my knowledge, they've had a senior producer who keeps on her desk a vase of plastic, yellow roses which light up if you plug them in.

The lessons I learned working for and with women on *Overnight* and *Summer Sunday* make me ashamed I used to feel complimented when someone told me I thought like a man. Women may or may not be the best managers, but they should be given—must be given—more opportunities to find out. A woman executive must stop being a contradiction in terms when it comes to network news. Am I a feminist? Yep. Do I like men? Same answer.

On *Overnight* we sometimes read viewer mail on the air. One fellow wrote:

> Dear Ms. Ellerbee:
> I like your program. I even like you. But I was wondering where you got such a wimpy last name?

There was a letter that surely deserved an answer, so I gave him one.

> Dear Sir:
> From a man, where else?

The man wrote back. This time he did not address the letter to me, but to the program, in general. He said I was "promoting negativism" between the sexes. He said men and women needed to learn from each other, instead of fighting each other. That letter also deserved an answer, so on the air I told him that I agreed; certainly I didn't want to "promote negativism" but, I added, the next time he wrote a letter to a program that had a woman as executive producer, a woman as senior producer and a woman as general editor, it might be better if he did not begin his letter "Dear Sirs."

Why did I call this chapter "Leave It to Beaver"? Because that's what some of the men at NBC News called *Overnight,* the first network news program run by women.

# HAPPY TRAILS TO YOU

I couldn't hit a wall with
a six-gun, but I can twirl one. It *looks* good.
JOHN WAYNE

It wasn't George Bush's fault. As he told me on the plane from Iowa to New Hampshire: "I'm not really as dull as you think I am."

Still, if it hadn't been for George Bush, I wouldn't have been spending a dull afternoon walking around a plant that manufactured movable widgets, wondering why anybody would want to go to New Hampshire in February every four years. Most people, most sane people, wouldn't, but that's where they hold the first presidental primary, every four years, so there I was, following Bush, who was following the governor of New Hampshire, who was shaking hands with and smiling at anything that moved and wasn't a widget. George Bush did not like to shake hands with strangers, or dance with strangers, or kiss babies. He told me that, too, but it was before he was vice president.

Bush wanted to be president, which was why he ran for the office in 1980. Actually, he ran for the Republican nomination. The month before the New Hampshire primary, he had come in first in the Iowa caucus. The week he toured the widget plant his picture was on the cover of *Newsweek* magazine. His campaign was riding as high as it ever would that season. Ronald Reagan, who had stayed away from Iowa and lost, went to New Hampshire and won. After that, for George Bush, if it wasn't one thing, it was another.

This was before that New Hampshire primary, before he knew he wasn't going to be president, not in 1980, maybe not ever, so George Bush was smiling. He was even smiling at the governor, a man with whom he didn't seem very comfortable. I was not smiling. I was trying to ask the governor a question about voter registration in New Hampshire, and I wasn't getting an answer; I was getting ignored. I followed Bush and the governor outside and across fifty yards of slush and snow so they could shake hands with people waiting at a bus stop.

My sneakers were soaked. My jeans were soaked. My parka was inadequate. My hair was a sad sight; I believe it was frozen. Any makeup I'd put on that morning was behind me by at least four towns; I had no mittens; my hand was frozen to the extra light I was carrying for my cameraman. I had a knitted cap that belonged to my son pulled down over my ears and almost to my nose, which was running. There had been no more than five hours' sleep a night for any of us in the past five weeks or so and, dammit, I wanted an answer from the governor. It was hardly a tough question, but the governor kept brushing me off. He would smile right at my crew, smile right into the camera, then walk away. It didn't make sense.

Bush slogged his way to the governor and, shivering, asked him when he thought the two of them might go back inside and get warm. The governor leaned over and, in what he must have thought was a whisper, said, "Let's go inside right now. It's the only way that NBC *electrician* is going to stop asking me questions. Jesus, is *she* pushy! Why is an electrician asking me questions, anyway?"

That pretty much explains the glamorous world of the campaign trail, at least for me. As has been noted, I am not the proper person to send to cover someone's run for destiny. I don't look the part, obviously. Some say I don't think the part, either. It's not that I'm unwilling; it's that very often I don't understand what's going on when it comes to elections. For example, during the general campaign in 1980, polls indicated most people didn't like either Jimmy Carter *or* Ronald Reagan, and didn't much want to have to choose between them. How do you explain the fact that the two major American political parties picked as their candidates men more than half the people didn't like?

I understood just fine why those men wanted the job and why each of them thought they might get it. Carter, running for reelection, was betting on tradition. Sitting presidents usually got to keep their seats. Ronald Reagan, meanwhile, was offering daily prayers that voters would follow the Mae West rule. Ms. West once said that every time she had to choose between two evils, she picked the one she hadn't tried yet. John Anderson was harder to understand. He seemed to believe there was enough voter dissatisfaction to make him the first independent candidate ever elected president, even though he'd won not a single primary and showed up first in absolutely no poll at all.

The polls: they may have been the real trouble. I didn't then and do not now understand polling. Used to be, if you wanted to run for president, you had to know how politics worked around the country, who ran what at the precinct level, what trick had to be turned to get out the vote in East Des Moines *and* South Chicago, when to push and when to plead. If you didn't know all that, and a lot more, you had to have people around you who did: all the bright young men—who didn't really have to be young, and later, didn't really have to be men. But they had to have plenty of political savvy. That's how it worked.

We still have bright young men and women, but by 1980, the bond was not a working knowledge of American politics, but a working knowledge of polling. In any campaign, the most important person somehow seemed to be the pollster. The candidate, if he was lucky, came in third—right behind the media consultant. Consequently, although it may have looked like a Ronald Reagan–Jimmy Carter race, it was equally a Richard Wirthlin–Pat Caddell race. They polled for the candidates so the candidates could know what the people wanted. Then they could want the same things.

It didn't stop there. The news organizations, not content with the candidates' polling, did their own. There was the NBC–Associated Press poll. There was the CBS–*New York Times* poll. And there was the ABC–Harris poll. Once, a meeting about political coverage was a thing where reporters and editors sat around and exchanged thoughts, if they had any, about what was going on. I remember a meeting in 1980 to discuss the Republican convention. NBC pollsters gave me a packet of research. In it were thirty-two words and 1,687 numbers (yes, I counted—I *can* count). Now, if I could read numbers—if I understood numbers—I'd have more sense than to be a writer. Only pollsters and my son understand numbers. Pollsters, by trade, are computer experts, programmers. As has been noted, I don't understand computers, either. As for the argument that polling and the extrapolation of polling information through the use of computers will give a more precise picture of what is going on than will your average ward heeler, ask yourself this: If polling is so accurate, why are there so many different companies doing it?

For anyone who ever, for one moment, savored the outrageous circus of American politics, the dominance of the pollster and his computer is bound to trigger a certain brick-throwing instinct. What have they done to our politics? Like liquid diet products, the calories are still there, but where's the fun?

Still, politicians like polling—and I could be wrong about it. A relationship exists between politicians and journalists that almost insures that more often than not, we will be wrong about each other. Remember when Richard Nixon told a news conference, after he had lost the race for governor of California, "Well, you won't have Richard Nixon to kick around anymore"? We dutifully reported Richard Nixon was finished as a politician. We were wrong about his career. He was wrong about us kicking him around some more.

The peculiar part is that even though we do not understand each other at all, we need each other desperately. This is especially true of campaigning politicians and television reporters. Until television came along, I strongly suspect the majority of the people in the United States had no true appreciation of how unalterably silly the major-party political conventions can be—and how silly we can be while reporting them.

I'm getting ahead of myself, though. Conventions come after primaries and we're talking about primaries here. I have never, ever distinguished myself covering primaries. I remember pissing off a couple of my more reputable colleagues in 1980 with a small story about the press in New Hampshire. For lack of other news, reporters were covering each other, then partying together, and in general putting on more of a show than the candidates. (In our defense, there were more of us than there were of them.) Closing the story, I quoted the old line: "You'll meet a lot of interesting people in journalism, my son—most of them other journalists."

Over the line, I used a close-up of the profiles of two journalists having drinks in the bar of the Sheraton Wayfarer, home-away-from-home for reporters in New Hampshire every four years. It was a wonderful shot. The two men were John Chancellor and Walter Cronkite. It looked like Mt. Rushmore, if Mt. Rushmore drank. Bill Small, the president of NBC News, said he thought it would be a good idea if I sat out the next few rounds of primaries.

Four years later, in 1984, I reported only one story from New Hampshire, a state *obsessed* with its perception of itself as a culling ground for presidents. I drove around the state with a camera crew, asking people if there had ever been a president who was *from* New Hampshire. Almost no one was sure. Finally one fellow said, "Yes, there was Franklin Pierce. He was from

New Hampshire, but really he was out of his league as president."

The man was right. Franklin Pierce was a proslavery president from an abolitionist state, an alcoholic, a man who carried bad luck with him like a backpack. He was his party's choice on the forty-ninth ballot, his vice president died after one month in office, his son was killed on his way to his father's inauguration, his wife shut herself up in the White House and refused to act as his hostess, and he was the only president denied renomination by his own party. All I did was report this. No wonder people in New Hampshire seemed to want to forget about Franklin Pierce. For the end of the story, I went a few blocks from his grave in Concord and asked people where he was buried. Nobody knew. The conclusion of the story was a shot of his grave, ignored except for a plastic wreath. I may never have to go back to New Hampshire again.

The same is true of Ohio. In 1984 I went there to write about its primary, and in the story, I pointed out that when Ohio joined the Union in 1803, the Congress, busy with other matters, *forgot* to pass the resolution making Ohio a state. It was a situation that went unnoticed until 1953, when the Congress, on being told of its oversight, quickly passed the necessary legislation and President Eisenhower signed the bill making Ohio a state. In *1953.* In my story, I suggested that all six presidents to come from Ohio between 1803 and 1953 were never really presidents at all, since they were ineligible. I suggested the primary we were there to cover in 1984 was so legally fogged, it might have no more validity than your average straw poll. You see, there are reasons I don't go to all the primaries. Good ones, my bosses tell me.

Covering campaigns is rough on reporters, but some of them love it, and all who do it get caught up in some small measure in the silliness that attends a campaign. That is how plane surfing got started. Members of the press who regularly cover someone's campaign spend too much time on airplanes—airplanes that land and take off maybe four or five times each day. The people get bored. One day, in 1980, someone discovered you could take the plastic cards the airline puts in the back of the seat in front of you—the ones that tell you where the emergency exits are and how to open them—and if you put one card under each foot and stood in the aisle near the front of the plane while it was climbing after takeoff—you could surf the aisle for the length of the plane. It's a wonder no one ever surfed his way through the back of the plane and into the nice, thin air. I saw a tape of Gary Hart surfing on his campaign plane during the 1984 primaries. All Reagan ever did on his plane was to bowl with oranges. Maybe that's why he won.

The pace gets hectic. That was especially true on the Kennedy plane during the first few months of 1980. It was more crowded than the other planes because each of the networks had not one but two crews assigned to cover Ted Kennedy. There was a reason, a sad one. Ted Kennedy was running for president, and no network could forget what happened to his brothers. No one at any network wanted it to happen again—but if it did, no one at any network wanted to miss getting the picture. Thus, the deathwatch, as it came to be known. With so many people following Kennedy, organization got slack. They say the food on the plane dwindled to cold, dry ham sandwiches for several days running. They say the press, after a while, chose one day to use gaffers' tape to affix the sandwiches to the ceiling of the cabin of the plane. I didn't see that, but I did see the Kennedy press corps leave a banquet and, following Kennedy, pass a salad bar on the way out. It was the only time I ever saw people eat lettuce with their hands.

Of course, primaries are rough on candidates, too. Try to imagine giving the same speech day after day. That's tedious. *Now,* try to imagine listening to the same speech day after day. That's worse. The only candidate who ever correctly grasped that feeling of boredom was George Wallace. He always gave the same speech, the one about pointy-headed liberals. If you've taped or filmed it once, there's not much sense in doing it again, but the rules require that every time a candidate speaks, we set up and roll, no matter what. Wallace knew this. He tried to make life easier for the cameraman. I'm told that Wallace would use the phrase, "And you better believe this . . ." to alert camera crews that he was about to deviate from the text of the speech. "And you better believe this" was the signal to roll. Something new was about to be said. It was the cameraman's wake-up call, so to speak.

The fact is, politicians aren't supposed to make it easy for us—and we're not supposed to make it easy for them, but sometimes we do. Sometimes we slip carelessly into the politicians' way of looking at things. Take the matter of titles. For a country of just plain folks, we've gotten awfully partial to titles. It's almost impossible to run for office without one. Mind you, it doesn't have to be a current title. In 1980, we called John Connally "Governor Connally" even though he hadn't been a governor since the days a dozen years before, when Lyndon Johnson was president. Connally liked being called "Governor," however, and we went along with it. During the same campaign we called Ronald

Reagan "Governor Reagan," and he hadn't been governor of California for a while, and we called George Bush "Ambassador Bush." "Mr. Ambassador"—I'll bet he thought it had a fine ring to it.

But those men weren't those things anymore. What they were, were politicians running for office, and a reporter who continued to add honorifics to their names gave those men an edge over men without titles, or men whose titles were lesser ones—even if it was tradition to do it. Titles always give an edge. Anyone who disagrees should try calling the most popular and crowded restaurant in town late one evening, requesting a table for Mr. Smith and eight of his friends ten minutes from that time. When it doesn't work, wait ten minutes, call back and tell them Senator Smith and his friends are hungry. You'll eat.

Who decides what a politician will be called? It's not reporters. Consider this. We called George Bush "Mr. Ambassador," but he'd had other jobs and other titles—in fact, Bush never met a job he didn't like. Why didn't we call him "Congressman"? He was one, once. Granted, to call him "Mr. C.I.A. Chief" would be awkward, but how about "Lieutenant, J.G."? He was one of those, once, too, and although many ambassadors are stuffy, dull people, I've known a couple of swell Navy lieutenants.

If we insist (or they do) on basing the title on past performance, we might just as easily have called "Governor" Connally "Mr. Secretary—slash—Navy," or "Mr. Secretary—slash—Treasury." How about a simple "The Defendant"?

As for Reagan, he once starred in a movie called *Bedtime for Bonzo* and no one calls him "Bonzo"—likely because that was the monkey's title and no doubt he retained the honorific. Reagan also was a sports reporter at one time, but you never heard anyone call him "Hey, you," or even "Governor Hey You."

No, we call them—not as we see them—but as they wish to be seen, and because all titles are not created equal, they choose the *best* title, no matter how far back it is necessary to go to find it. In 1980, I suggested we call them all "Your Grace" and have done with it; then we could have gone on to judge their other merits, if they had any. Until somebody—everybody—figures out I'm right, we will continue to muddy campaigns by calling people what they're not, anymore, bumping up their images in the public eye, awarding an unfair advantage to one candidate over another and, in general, insuring that *Mr.* Smith will never, ever go to Washington again.

There's something else. What *we* call them is almost always nicer than what *they* call us. After Bush lost in New Hampshire in 1980, the number of reporters covering him dwindled. Those who stayed were assigned to cover Bush's campaign, period, win or lose. Bush didn't actually blame the media for what he called "the loss of momentum" in his campaign after New Hampshire, but he did think what we wrote contributed to it. What he said was that the reporters were a bunch of "mournful pundits." That was a particularly George Bush type of thing to say. Mournful pundits. Gerald Ford would never call a reporter a mournful pundit. He would have thought it was a football term, maybe. (The mournful pundited it for a twenty-yard gain.) Would Lyndon Johnson call a reporter who wrote he was losing a "mournful pundit"? No, he would have the reporter's balls for lunch, instead. Would Richard Nixon call reporters "mournful pundits"? Probably not, but he might have made a list of those he suspected were. Jimmy Carter would have prayed for the pundits he thought most mournful. Ronald Reagan would have asked one of his advisors what to say about the mournful pundits, if asked on camera.

Here, though, was George Bush, "Poppy" Bush when he prepped at Andover, a man who campaigned in suits specially bought for that purpose at Filene's Basement in Boston, so he could look like a man of the people (keeping his hand-tailored suits for later, in case he won), a man whose basic nice-guy instincts couldn't allow him to say, "Listen, you bastards, you're ruining me with your stupid stories saying I'm losing." No, George Bush just said we were all a bunch of "mournful pundits." It had a nice ring.

A group of reporters who were there when he said it got together to throw a small party at the Republican convention in Detroit that summer. It was a kind of going-away party for Bush. The next day, the Republicans were going to nominate Ronald Reagan for president—everybody knew that—so what was going away was Bush's last chance to be president, at least that year. Bush was a man who always believed the glass was half-full; throughout the primaries he kept insisting the opera wasn't over until the fat lady sang. It wasn't his line, originally, but he liked it and to him, it fit. Well, in Detroit, the glass wasn't half-full. The glass in front of George Bush was empty. Someone thought it made a lot of sense, therefore, to end the party with the entrance of a large, large woman from the Detroit opera, carrying a spear and singing, "You got to know when to hold 'em and know when to fold 'em."

That, of course, is always good advice, and it is advice that also must apply to the television networks when they decide how to cover political conventions from now on. For years, we covered them as if, at the time, there were no other news on the face of the earth. Cynics among you will say it's because networks make money covering conventions. Wrong. Network financial people burst into tears every four years. No network will give exact figures, even to its own people, but I recall one NBC executive telling me that in 1984, NBC News spent somewhere around twenty-five million dollars covering two conventions that summer. He said it was a conservative estimate. It's a good way to become a non-profit corporation.

So why do we do it? One reason is the belief that it is our civic responsibility to do so. We are bound to let people see democracy in action. That's nice, but is it really what we see at conventions today? No. Not since television and the primary system combined to alter political conventions forever. It wasn't a conspiracy, merely a bit of accidental timing that the growth of the number of states holding presidential primaries and the expansion of (and fascination with) television coverage of conventions came along and changed conventions into overmanaged, overproduced and overrated gatherings of the faithful. By the time conventions took place, there was seldom anything left to decide except who the vice presidential nominee should be and how that lingering little question could be made exciting for television.

Republicans haven't gone beyond the first ballot to choose a presidential nominee since 1940. Democrats have not done so since 1932. As a civics lesson, the conventions of the past few years have been poor teachers.

So what about the theory that we cover conventions

because it is our Olympics and the winner takes all? Once upon a time, in 1956, Chet Huntley and David Brinkley, a couple of new boys then, anchored the conventions for NBC and knocked poor Walter Cronkite at CBS for a ratings loop. Huntley-Brinkley went on to become the top-rated team in television news and their broadcast the top-rated news program in television. Networks think it's wonderful when that happens, and so the myth began. The network to get the best ratings for its convention coverage would also get the best ratings for its regularly scheduled evening newscast. Never mind that in all the years since Huntley-Brinkley, lightning did not strike twice, at least in so clear a way. Sometimes the network that went into the conventions with the highest ratings came out with the highest ratings. That's not the same.

So—again—why do we do it?

Easy. We like to cover conventions. Those of us who make our livings reporting doom and gloom, and in an election year, despair, look forward to those tribal gatherings. Political specialists among us know our license to pontificate will be renewed. Eager first-timers feel certain their efforts at a convention will elevate them so that they can pontificate, too.

In case you might be an eager first-timer, or want to be one, let me remind you right now that these days you can only pontificate if you're fast. Used to be a network correspondent needed to be a thoughtful, deliberate journalist, someone who could shed light, put a little historical spin on what was happening on the floor of a political convention. Now you need to be a linebacker with a first-class pair of running shoes, although there is something to be said for the uses in a crowd of a pair of pointy-toed, spiked heels.

You see, there are all these other network, cable and local television reporters and their crews on the floor trying to make the same big story out of the same small happenings. Speed counts. Speed counts almost more than anything else. Pat Trese, a droll, experienced, professional newsman who has worked for NBC since before the Huntley-Brinkley days, wrote the convention handbook for NBC in 1984. The handbook went to all NBC correspondents covering the conventions and it went to all the local reporters NBC uses to cover the different state delegations. I quote from the preface.

> If, by chance or by glitch, some bit of data is not in the computer or on a spindle at the news desk, one of our delegation reporters will go get it: walking to the scene, asking someone who knows, writing it down so it won't be forgotten, then coming back to tell the person who wants to know.
>
> For those of us just starting in this business, that is the way it is done. The process is the same at a convention or at a two-alarm fire in the Bronx: stay cool and write it down. Some rewrite man or editor *will tell you what it all means* later.

Speed: that's what it comes down to. Not understanding—speed. In 1980, Chris Wallace was generally recognized as having scored *the* scoop at the Republican convention in Detroit by reporting a few seconds before everybody else that George Bush was Reagan's choice for vice president. At the Republican convention four years later, I reminded Chris of that and asked him how important, in the history of journalism, was an eight-second scoop?

"Actually, Linda," said Chris, "it was forty seconds." Forty seconds. Which network vice president, I wonder, is in charge of the stopwatch? When there's no real news, we do strange things. For example, I covered the Democratic convention in New York in 1980, and there wasn't much news there, either. President Carter was going to be renominated. I was not a floor reporter. I was there to cover the spillover news, if there was any. There wasn't. I spent time staring at my credentials. You stare at anything long enough, you get a little weird. I began to think the credentials issued to me by the Democratic National Committee looked like money.

In a way, they were supposed to look like money. The Democrats had done that because American money is hard to counterfeit and they wanted the credentials to be hard to counterfeit, so bad people wouldn't come to their party.

Trouble was, it seemed to me they had done too good a job. There is a law against making copies of our money. The government is extremely serious about that law. Having little better with which to occupy my time, I called a Secret Service agent (Treasury Department, remember?) who I knew was at the convention. Could we talk? We met and I told him it was kind of silly, what I was going to ask, but idle minds do strange things and mine had decided the credentials at the Democratic convention looked funny. Had he, as an agent of the United States Treasury Department, noticed anything wrong with them?

There was a bit of silence, then he laughed the way most of them do, which is not real loud or real sincere.

He said if he answered me, I had to promise not to use the information until he said I could.

We argued awhile. I didn't like his terms, but I was curious about the credentials and, what the hell, this wasn't a declaration of war we were discussing. I agreed to wait before reporting anything—if there was anything to report, which I doubted.

He said the Secret Service was in a tough place. The Democrats, in their zeal to maintain a secure convention, had broken the counterfeiting laws of the United States. Oh, yes, they knew the Democratic National Committee wasn't trying to pass phony paper; it didn't look *that* much like money, but they were going to have to prosecute, nevertheless. If the case weren't prosecuted, several characters awaiting trial for attempting to substitute their artwork for the government engraver's might argue they hadn't done as good a job as the Democratic party, so why were *they* going to jail and not the Democrats? He said a judge might see it their way; you could never tell about judges. And so, he said, a reluctant Treasury Department had that day filed charges against the Democratic National Committee. Felony charges. In Federal court. The reluctance was understandable. It was, after all, a Democratic administration. Obviously, something had to be worked out. Nobody, he said, wanted to put handcuffs on Bob Strauss, Chairman of the Democratic National Committee and organizer of the convention. I told him that was too bad; it sure would be something to see. He reminded me of my promise not to use the story—yet. I asked him when I could. He said I could when he said I could. Some reporter I was. Finally, I had something to report about the convention and I couldn't report it. I told him I'd see him around. He wanted to know why I was the only reporter who had noticed the credentials looked like money? I told him it was dedication.

The next day, while my crew and I were rehearsing camera positions for stories that would never happen, our stage manager came running up, all excited. He was about twenty years old and the son of a Broadway producer. He knew production and had worked in television before—but never in news. He thought news was swell. He wanted me to know he'd been walking around outside Madison Square Garden, where the convention was being held, and he'd found an open door: a small door, black, like the wall, flush with it, and without *any* guards near it. Remember, this was a convention that took its security seriously. There were guards, police, Secret Service agents and others we lump into the category of "authorities" crawling all over and around the place. Nobody just walked into the Garden. It took reporters with credentials an average of fifteen to twenty minutes to pass through all the electronic and human checkpoints each night.

However, the kid said he'd walked in that open door, pretty as you please, then just as prettily walked up a back stairway near the door until he got to where we were standing—with our good, clear view of the podium, where the President of the United States would stand that night. I didn't have to see *The Manchurian Candidate* more than once. I told him to show me the door. We took a walk. He showed me the door. And he was right. We got the camera crew and went outside, then, with tape rolling, we walked in that door and up to where we had been standing. No one stopped us. There was a great big hole in the security at Madison Square Garden.

Being a good citizen, I knew I must tell the Secret

Service at once. I called my friend. Of course, he wanted to know where the door was. This time the moment of silence was mine.

"Look, about that little credential story you said I couldn't use . . ."

There is a moral to this story. I guess it has to do with mistaking what is piddling for what is something, just because it's the only piddle going. Yes, I got on the air with the story about the credentials; that is, I got on the air with about ten seconds of the story. Then my voice went. It just dried up and went south—the first time that ever happened to me. I never got to finish telling the story. John Chancellor, in the anchor booth, explained we were all a little tired from the hard work of covering a convention, of being dedicated journalists and all.

As fortune would have it, most of my convention "scoops" have ended less than well. In 1976, I covered my first political convention. That one, too, was a Democratic convention and that one, too, was at Madison Square Garden in New York City. (Yes, I have covered Republican conventions, and if I could think of a good story about one, I would tell it.)

Again, I was bored. Again, I was not a floor reporter and when you're not, there's seldom a lot to write about; however, at least there was a story at the 1976 Democratic convention. An outsider, "Hi, I'm Jimmy Carter and I'm running for president," was going to get the nomination. That was news. It always is. But after you'd said that, what did you say next? The only question left: Who would be his running mate? (Are you sure it wasn't eight seconds in Detroit, Chris?)

Since I hadn't covered the primaries and didn't have sources in anybody's campaign, I didn't see how I could find out the answer to that question before anyone else.

But there was this button maker. I had met him at the convention. He didn't make the kind of buttons you undo. He made the kind of buttons that said "VOTE FOR JIMMY CARTER." He made almost all the buttons that said that—and he was going to make the buttons that said, "VOTE FOR JIMMY CARTER AND———————." He said he was going to print those buttons *that night,* so they would be ready the next morning when Carter held a news conference to announce his choice for running mate. It meant he knew who the vice presidential nominee would be.

I knew two things about the printer, because he told me. I knew where his print shop was, and I knew the printing press was on the fourth floor. A quick cab ride told me one other thing. The building across the street from his was five stories tall.

I did not know what time the presses would start to roll, and I did not know how to present my idea to my many superiors, so I went to Stanhope Gould.

You have to know Stanhope. He is a first-rate producer of journalism as it is practiced in television. And he is bizarre—a lot bizarre. Some people say he's a genius. Some people say he is not too tightly wrapped. Some people say that's an act. It's possible all of them are right. Stanhope has worked for, succeeded at and then been divorced from two networks. When he went to work for ABC News, his third network, I asked him what he would do, where he would go, if he got canned by that one—there was no CNN then. Stanhope said he would go back to CBS, where he had started, because the people who had fired him were either fired themselves by now and working at another network, or promoted beyond the place where they would care much about him so that it was safe to go back. He believed he could continue moving around as long as he stayed one step *behind* the posse. Any conversation with Stanhope always leaves me thinking I will get out of television soon.

Anyway, in 1976, Stanhope worked for NBC. I did not think Stanhope was strange—I *knew* Stanhope was strange, but I also knew he was smart and had street sense. I told him about the button maker and the buttons he intended to make later that night. The two of us went to Les Crystal, executive producer of NBC's convention coverage that year. (As of this writing, Les is at PBS; Stanhope will have to wait awhile.) We told Les what we knew and said we would like to be relieved of our regular convention assignments that night. I was assigned to cover the "perimeter," which generally is a description of the kind of news one finds there. Stanhope was assigned to cover the riots outside Madison Square Garden. Unfortunately, nobody outside the Garden was even angry, except for the reporters waiting to get through another fail-safe security check.

We told Les we wanted to go to the roof of the building across the street from the print shop. We would wait until the presses began their run. The presses were in front of big windows. We would have binoculars. The buttons would come off the presses and they would say "VOTE FOR JIMMY CARTER AND—SOMEBODY." We would telephone. NBC News would beat everybody else with the story by at least twelve hours. NBC News would credit Stanhope and me. We would be scoopers.

Les Crystal said he would approve it as long as we understood he had never heard of either of us.

We went to the apartment building across the street from the print shop and got into it the way every kid, thief and reporter has since someone first invented those buzzer releases for the outside door. I'm not saying how—in case you don't know—but it's not illegal. At least I don't think it is. On the roof we settled down to wait. An hour passed. The presses were silent. We got bored. Another hour passed. We got more bored. We'd told each other all our best lies; finally, Stanhope decided to show me some steps to a dance he'd learned in Afghanistan or Marrakech or maybe it was Singapore—I forget. The dance was short on delicacy and long on stomping.

The next thing that happened was everything at once. The presses began to roll. The door to the roof banged open. Several large men charged onto the roof. One had a gun. Two had knives. None spoke English. All I could understand was something about bands of robbers and mother-rapists thundering across their roof. Across the street, the buttons, with the name of the vice presidential candidate on them, began to roll off the presses. Our binoculars, wouldn't you know, were about two feet the other side of the gentlemen who were yelling and brandishing things at us. Stanhope and I raised our hands, slowly, and just as slowly we began to back toward the door to the stairs.

"Don't shoot," said Stanhope. "We're not dangerous. We're in television."

If I have given the impression that I believe covering politics and political campaigns is a trivial pursuit, I do not mean to. My part in it may have been trivial, but there is nothing a news-gathering organization does that is more important than monitoring the government. The First Amendment was not included in the Constitution to protect stories about how to raise avocado trees in your closet or get through a divorce gracefully.

However, we do get sidetracked in the covering of things political. The year 1980 was rife with opportunities to make a fool of yourself as a reporter. I think we took advantage of damn nearly every one of those opportunities. We knew so much. We were political observers, political hotshots, political *prophets*. We knew, for example, that Ronald Reagan was too old to be elected president—but we knew he would win the Iowa caucus. The NBC poll predicted he would beat Bush in Iowa by eighteen percentage points. That was the night before Bush beat Reagan in Iowa by fourteen percentage points. The next week, in New Hampshire, we knew it was all over for Ronald Reagan. One national magazine had a picture of Reagan on its cover with the words "REAGAN'S LAST HURRAH." I remember thinking it was gospel. We knew about the Democrats, too. Early in the campaign, we knew Teddy Kennedy would stir the hearts of Democrats as his brothers had done. Why, he would probably be appointed president. Jimmy who? Later, we knew that since Reagan had been nominated, Carter would be elected president, but we knew it would be close. The week before election day, all three networks ran stories about the race being too close to call. I spent five minutes and several thousand of my network's dollars explaining and illustrating this on *Nightly News*. A handful of undecided voters, I said—and I was not alone—would swing the election. That was the story. The night before the election, NBC said on the air it could not speculate on the outcome. The polls were that close. The day of the election, our producers told us to go to our assigned positions and be prepared to wait until two, maybe three in the morning before we knew who had won. That's how close it was, they said.

By 8:15 P.M. (Eastern time) it was all over. Ronald Reagan had won with 50.7% of the votes.

Surprise.

So much for us veteran political observers. So much for the polls. So much for what we knew. The entire national press corps missed it. To my mind, it happened because we let ourselves get in the business of handicapping races instead of reporting them. We're not supposed to be prophets; we are supposed to be reporters. As prophets we are unreliable.

In December of 1980, I said on NBC radio that given what happened, I hoped when election day came around in 1984 I would be working on a story about schools in Rugby, North Dakota. I figured it was all I deserved, all most of us deserved. Sadly, when 1984 came, we didn't get what we deserved.

I've written about national politics for almost eleven years now, off and on and between other, less tricky assignments. After six conventions, three general campaigns and a clutch of primaries, there are damn few instances I can point to with any pride, probably with just cause. Your estimation of my character will not be enhanced if I tell about the golf cart, but it does say something about the honor of reporters.

I first saw the golf cart in the small hours of an October morning in 1980, in Springfield, Missouri. It was sitting there in the parking lot of the Howard Johnson's, harming no one. The golf cart had fringe on the top and was, I recall, painted blue and white. The cameraman and I must have drunk some spoiled beer because it seemed to us the golf cart wanted to take us for a ride right then, so the golf cart, the cameraman and I toodled around the HoJo parking lot for a while, then we decided to see how the cart would like the field next to the motel. The golf cart didn't like the field one little bit and proved it by rolling over. We got it upright but could not then get it back into the parking lot. Spoiled beer saps your strength. We did the right thing; we left the cart in the field, and returned to the motel, which was home for the night for the Reagan campaign: staff, Secret Service agents, candidate and press.

There was to be a rally at noon. I had business to take care of with the Carter campaign and so I didn't stay for the rally. On an early plane out of town, I read in the local paper that the woman who ran the HoJo's wasn't concerned about handling all those people at her motel because she had "a brand-new golf cart to help her get around." Oh, dear. It speaks for the honor of reporters that when the plane next stopped, I went to a pay phone, called the woman and told her where she could find her new golf cart. It speaks for the cowardice of reporters that I did not, naturally, identify myself. And it speaks for the compulsion of criminals to confess that I just did. Madam, I'm truly sorry about the golf cart. It was the cameraman's fault. But if ever I return to Springfield, Missouri, I promise to stay at the Holiday Inn.

As for being proud of my political reporting over the years, well, I do favor one story I wrote in 1980 that had to do with politics and the media. It was my second favorite story of that campaign, maybe of any campaign. During that year, I wrote what seemed to be a lot of stories about politics and television, about the airtime politicians paid for and the airtime they pimped for. These were not major stories, they never led the broadcast, but it's not a bad idea to help people understand some of what they see on television, especially political commercials.

For instance, the Carter campaign ran a series of television commercials in California just before that state's primary. They were made up of what are known as "man-on-the-street" interviews. The interviews were taped in several cities in California. In each one, people were asked what they feared about Ronald Reagan. Scare stuff. Each commercial included interviews with four or five people and each commercial was shown only in the city where it was shot. Thus, people in Sacramento saw the Sacramento "man-on-the-street" commercial. San Francisco saw what was said in San Francisco. What was said in Los Angeles was seen in Los Angeles. Obviously, Sacramento never saw what San Francisco saw. That was all to the good, as far as the Carter people were concerned. You had to see the commercials from *all* the cities to see that the "people-on-the-street" in Sacramento used the same words as some of the "people-on-the-street" in Los Angeles and San Francisco, or any of the other cities where a commercial had been shot. Almost the exact same words, again and again. "I think Ronald Reagan shoots from the hip." "Reagan—he shoots from the hip." "Reagan seems to like shooting from the hip." "Governor Reagan? He shoots from the hip." By this time, I was hip to what was going on. If you work in television, you know that the only way you get two people in two cities, much less four people in four cities, to say the exact same words about anything is when you tell them the words to say.

You're not supposed to do that.

*They* are not supposed to do that. If they do and you find out, it is called an okay story, maybe even a good story. What they've done is not against the law, but it *is* cheating and it's useful to know when a candidate will allow cheating on his behalf. Reporting it likely will not change anything—but it is something worth knowing about before you vote. So that was an okay story, to my way of thinking, but it wasn't my favorite. My favorite political story was even smaller, on a journalism scale of one to ten. It took place in a grocery store in Lima, Ohio.

In October of 1980, the Reagan campaign decided to take advantage of high-tech television techniques. It would create "instant ads." They would work like this: something would happen in the world, something about which the Reagan people felt Reagan should comment. Wherever he was that day, Reagan would say the right thing about what had happened, whatever it was. His campaign staff would tape it and that night it would be played as a commercial on television. The idea had two advantages. One, Reagan would appear to be up on everything that was going on. Two, his message would not be on the news, where it would be edited by us. It would go straight to the viewers instead. The Reagan campaign informed the networks it wished to buy time for this purpose.

It wasn't an earthshaking plan, but I was curious to see how it worked. The problem was that no campaign ever allowed reporters around when they were filming or taping their commercials. I guess they thought we'd make a candidate look silly or something. Still, this wasn't your usual commercial, and I wasn't out to make anybody look foolish. It just seemed it would be interesting to watch one of these "instant ads" being made.

I told that to James Baker, Reagan's campaign manager, and I meant it. Because the Reagan campaign thought it might be good publicity to show how current Ronald Reagan was on everything, Baker agreed to let me tape the making of the commercial. He said they were going to shoot the first "instant ad" the next day, in Lima, Ohio, but I was not to spread it around because they didn't want a lot of television people in that grocery store and he wasn't going to tell the other reporters, who would be outside, that an NBC crew and reporter would be inside. That was fine with me. I asked him what news event Reagan was planning to talk about in his commercial. Baker said Reagan would talk about the economy. Since the economy had been in the news for some time and Reagan had been saying all along that it was Jimmy Carter's fault things were so bad, I failed to see how this was going to show everybody how on top of the news Reagan was; however, it was going to be his first "instant ad," and if you're a reporter, well, you have to write about something.

I flew to Ohio, met my crew and got to the store before Reagan did. There were two other crews already inside the store, freelance crews hired to shoot the commercial for the Reagan campaign. The candidate arrived. The shooting began. Reagan stood in the aisle of the store, holding on to a grocery cart filled with food, as if he'd been shopping the way normal people do.

"Hello. I'm here in a grocery store in Lima, Ohio—a town of fifty thousand people," said Governor Reagan to the camera.

"Cut!" yelled the director. "It's not fifty thousand, Governor. It's sixty thousand. Do it over."

"Oh," said Reagan. "I thought it was fifty thousand."

"Just read what's on the TelePrompTer," said the director.

The shooting continued. Reagan read his part again. And again. The director was not satisfied.

"Wait a minute," said Reagan. "When do we get to the part where I ad-lib? They told me I could ad-lib."

He looked uncomfortable. I didn't blame him. Nancy Reagan, sitting on a stool in the aisle, under the Cocoa Puffs and Shredded Wheat, looked angry. She was not pleased with someone, but I couldn't tell whether it was the director or the candidate.

"You forgot to say how sorry you feel for people," said Nancy Reagan.

The cameras rolled again.

"I feel sorry for people who have to shop on a limited budget these days," said Reagan.

"Cut!" said the director.

"They *told* me I could ad-lib," said the candidate.

"Take six," said the director.

Well, it went on like that. I felt sorry for Ronald Reagan. It was tough enough running for president without a bunch of jerky television people telling you what to say and how to say it. When finally he was finished and the director was as satisfied as he was ever going to be, the people who worked in the store, and who for the duration of the commercial had been crowded together behind the butcher's counter where the director told them they had to stand, gave Reagan a round of applause. He seemed genuinely grateful.

"Well, thank you. Thank you very much," he said. "I like that sound."

I raced like hell. We edited our story and got it on the air before the instant ad played that night. After the story appeared, some people said it was clear I was out to get Reagan, to make a fool of him on television. There were a lot of phone calls to NBC. Some people said the tape of what went on in the grocery store made Reagan look human and vulnerable. They said it showed a part of him not seen in the controlled, slick world of campaign commercials and television shows.

A couple of newspapers wrote about the grocery store story. One called it an influential story. It wasn't. I don't write influential stories. If I did, I would not be writing stories in grocery stores in Lima, Ohio. It was nothing more than a simple little story without much narration, a little slice of campaign life. I don't know what the fuss was about. People kept asking me how I had gotten Ronald Reagan to make an ass of himself on national television. I disagreed. I was one of the people who thought it made him look like a real person instead of a cardboard candidate. But why, they wanted to know, had Ronald Reagan behaved as if he were among his own? Why hadn't he known that one of the three cameras in that store belonged to a television network news operation? Why hadn't Nancy Reagan known a reporter was watching her?

I don't know.

I guess his people didn't tell him. I didn't tell him because I didn't cover Ronald Reagan on a regular basis and I had never met the man. Or his wife. Perhaps they thought I was the electrician.

# JUST ONE OF THOSE THINGS

Your trouble is, you've never
understood that
seeing through the game is
not the same as winning it.
*NORTH DALLAS FORTY*

The camera opens on a wide shot of what may or may not be a newsroom. You hear something that may be music or may be the sound Donald Duck would make if you held his head underwater awhile. A man and a woman sit at wooden desks that are pushed back to back and littered with papers and what appear to be toys. Books are stacked along the backs of the desks. A rubber hand sits in front of them, and in front of the hand, a small, yellow, stuffed duck, wearing a red bow tie. Hazy figures can be seen in the background. Some of the hazy figures seem to be wearing flowers in their *hair*.

Cut back to the man and woman. She leans on a typewriter. He speaks:

> . . . all that and more, on this—the three hundred sixty-seventh edition of *Overnight*—the final edition.

Fade in. Fade out. It didn't go on forever, after all, and it didn't change the world or the networks. Oh, well. All it ever was to begin with was a low-budget, late-night television news program for humans. But it was ours. They said *Overnight* had an attitude. I never was certain what that meant, but many things about that program remain a mystery to me, and I am clearer about why it went on the air than about why it went off.

Begin at the beginning, sometime in May, 1982. Reuven Frank was once again president of NBC News. Maybe they meant him to keep coming back to that job until he got it right. Some of us thought he had got it right already, but never mind that. In the spring of 1982, Ted Turner was aggravating the networks, something he does often and well. This time it had to do with late-night television, those hours during which the networks showed reruns or nothing at all. Turner had begun offering his cable news service to network-affiliated stations. Some of the affiliates thought it was a great idea. None of the networks did, since nothing Ted Turner did ever meant anything good for them, but if the affiliates wanted news in the middle of the night, the networks were determined they would get it—from the networks.

Starting that summer, Americans likely to be the best informed would be those who could not sleep. ABC's entry: an hour-long program called *The Last Word*. CBS called its four-hour show *Nightwatch*, but the first to go on the air with an hour of late-night news, Monday through Friday, would be NBC, and the name of the program would be *NBC News Overnight,* generally shortened to *Overnight.*

To create *Overnight,* Reuven called in Herb Dudnick, a man who saw finishing a sentence as a waste of time, which was okay since Reuven rarely got that far, either. They understood each other perfectly. I've watched the two of them talk for fifteen minutes, say four words each during that time, then leave knowing what had to be done. What had to be done in this case was to figure out what *Overnight* would be, how it would work, who would do it and how fast it could be accomplished. It was scheduled to go on the air July 5.

Herb Dudnick had never been like the other up-and-coming producers at NBC, even when he'd seemed to be. For one thing, he'd come into the business late. At twenty-eight, he'd quit what he'd been doing up until then, and gone to work for the NBC Station in Philadelphia—as a desk-assistant. He was the only slightly balding, thirty-pushing, father of two, nearsighted desk-assistant there. Herb wanted in, and if it meant starting at the bottom, that's what it meant. He was competitive and ambitious like the others, but he didn't look or sound like them. A tall, tanned man who spoke through and around a pipe he seldom lit, he was given to coming to work in jeans, college sweatshirts and tennis shoes, or boots—but not the expensive ones. He wore a baseball cap to hide the fact that he was losing his hair, or because he knew he looked good in baseball caps, and he hid his emotions behind a pair of poker-player eyes, then hid those behind a pair of wire-rimmed glasses. Behind a hearty manner and a gee-whiz enthusiasm, he hid a lot of impatience. Behind a faked cynicism, he hid a good heart. He was a complicated man, hard to know, and not loose enough for this experimental show, I thought. But the decision had already been made.

Herbie would produce it. He would not be hindered by money, Reuven explained, because there would be no money. Well, damn little. It would be a no-frills newscast and it would depend upon the kindness of strangers. Reuven asked Lloyd Dobyns and me to write and anchor it. I told Reuven I wasn't a "night" person. Reuven said I would learn. I told Reuven that Herb Dudnick was the wrong man for the job—Herb was weird, but not that weird. Reuven said I would learn.

Herbie hired Don Bowers and Cheryl Gould as show producers, responsible directly to him and for everybody else, except Lloyd and me. After that, the hiring got tricky because few—try none—of the "grown-ups" at NBC News wanted to work on this jerkwater adventure. "One-thirty to two-thirty in the *morning*? Five nights a week? You must be kidding—nobody but insomniacs, cocaine addicts and those seeking an alternative to bed spins will watch the thing!" Reuven reminded them not to leave out East Coast bookies looking for the West Coast scores. Nobody was impressed. Since enlistment was, how you say, slow, Herb went after the young-and-untried, the old-and-overlooked, the screwups and the space cadets—in other words, the fringe element. Why not? It was a fringe program.

We had a lease on the hour and conditions to the lease: we could not afford to send NBC crews out to shoot stories, we could not afford to send NBC correspondents out to cover stories, we could not afford to buy satellite time to send stories back to us, and we could not afford fancy graphics, fancy sets or fancy trimmings of any kind. We were supposed to think our way out of this—with fancy ideas. There was one other condition. Come July 5, *Overnight* was going on the air, and it better find something with which to fill the hour. Reuven said he chose the date of July 5 because the NBC research department told him that statistically it was the night of the year when the fewest number of people watched television. It figured. If you don't have any money to put on a show, what do you need with an audience? I recall somebody saying it was going to be mighty interesting to see what happened that night when somebody in the control room said, "Roll tape," and there wasn't any to roll.

"Don't worry," said Herbie. "It's a piece of cake." Then he said—and I'm trying to reproduce this exactly—we'd open with "a something and a something, tell some news, a little of this, a little of that, watch a commercial, then a thing and a thing, a reel, some not-ready-for-prime-time stuff, more more news, sports-talk, some sports scores—Reuven said we gotta do scores because of bookies or something—then a roll, a reel a roll and a long five—they talk long at the BBC—a recap, some items, once overnightly, another something and a something, goodbyes—and we'll be off. A piece of cake."

It seemed I was wrong about Herb—he was that weird.

Was he on drugs? He didn't look the type, but the man was speaking *in tongues*. Reel? Roll? More more news? A something and a something? We were in big trouble. Lloyd and I took immediately to Hurley's saloon to talk things over. What was this fellow in a sweatshirt, baseball cap and felony sneakers talking about? Did Reuven know about this? Did Reuven do drugs, too? How could we get out of this project? That was our main concern. In the end we decided to stay, swayed by our affection for regular paychecks, Reuven Frank and the impossible. Besides, we hadn't anything better to do and by now we were curious to see what would happen, in the same way someone about to be hanged might be curious to see how they would tie the knots.

Somewhere along the way, Herb Dudnick began to make sense. Either he began to speak English or Lloyd and I began to understand whatever it was he usually spoke, which is the part that still worries me. But even if encoded, Herbie's message was worth the trouble. He believed that a good news program must connect emotionally as well as intellectually, that the only way to erase the barrier between the news program and the viewer was to make people *think*—and then make people *feel*. He said that everybody's life and everybody's day had peaks and valleys, and a good news program had to have the same, it had to *be* reality as well as present it—it must have peaks and valleys; it must be honest. When you're doing something you want to do, said Herbie, then and only then does your work become believable. "On *Overnight,* we were going to be believable," said Herbie, "or we weren't going to be anything at all. And we were going to give people some new views of the world." I definitely was wrong about Herb Dudnick. It seemed we were going to break some rules. We were going to dump most of the guidelines other news programs used, and dump absolutely everything we'd ever hated about other news programs. We were, for once, going to do it our way. We were going to be a "people's newscast." We were just going to talk to people, not shout at them or preach to them, and we *would* have pictures; he'd tell us how, later. First the talking part. He wanted Lloyd and me to make use of everything we'd ever learned about writing and anchoring, and then some.

Okay. First of all, we told him, Lloyd and I wouldn't talk to each other—not *on* the air. We are friends and talk off the air, but it's always burned both of us to watch anchorpeople chatting with each other during a newscast. They were on television—they should talk to the audience instead. Besides, neither of us generally had anything to say to each other that wasn't guaranteed to put the program off the air before it had any chance to fail on its own, if the FCC rules on good taste counted. Did Herbie understand that?

There was more, we said. We weren't going to call each other by name every time the camera moved from one to the other of us, as if we were there to tell *each other* the news. "Well, Lloyd, today the president said it seemed like a fine day to declare war on somebody." By the time we were on the air, Lloyd had already read the script, or should have—or, if it were his script, he'd already written the script, or should have. For the same reason, we weren't going to "act" the news, either. No sad faces for sad stories, switching to happy faces for happy stories. No cute reactions to cute stories, implying that—just like the folks at home—it was the first time *we'd* seen the story.

Since that wasn't so, any reaction of that sort would be manufactured. It always is, and any five-year-old can spot it, unless he's an anchorman. Nor were we going to open the newscast by saying, "Hello, I'm Lloyd Dobyns." "Hi there, I'm Linda Ellerbee." (On *Weekend,* we'd opened with me saying, "His name is Lloyd Dobyns," and Lloyd saying, "Her name is Linda Ellerbee," which wasn't ordinary but wasn't as good as opening by saying what the news was, instead.) In fact, we told Herbie, we wouldn't say our names on the air at all unless there were good reason, which there seldom was. Our names would be printed on the screen at the beginning, middle and end of the newscast. Wasn't that enough? Nobody was going to go blind trying to decide which one was Linda Ellerbee and which one was Lloyd Dobyns, except maybe Charles Kuralt. As for who got top billing—we would alternate.

And if Herbie didn't mind, we would prefer that when we were talking on the air, there be no pinball, pop, bam, boom graphics going off in little boxes next to our heads. If the words were good enough, they were good enough to stand alone, and if the words weren't good enough, he should fire us and hire two people who could make them good enough.

We were also going to ignore one of the central precepts of television news. We who work in television believe we are smarter than the people who watch television. Television news producers often turn down certain stories because, they say, the stories are too complicated or too dull to mean anything to the plumber in Albuquerque.

In 1984, NBC News was the first American network to air videotape of starving people in Ethiopia. Despite the fact that millions of people were dying of starvation, the story for the most part had been ignored by the American networks. The very next day, every network showed those pictures, every newspaper wrote about Ethiopia and the American people reacted swiftly and generously. NBC News was praised for bringing the story to the attention of a nation. Only those of us who work there know how very close we came to not airing the story. It took a fight to get the videotape from Ethiopia on the air, videotape that had been shot, by the way, not by NBC News, but by the BBC. Some people at NBC News argued against airing the story because, they said, nobody in Iowa gave a damn about Africa. It wouldn't mean anything to the plumber in Albuquerque. Research told them foreign news, especially news from the Third World, just wasn't popular. Thank God, news judgment won out over research.

One executive producer of a network newscast said he began each night with the assumption the viewer had never heard of Lebanon. If he wasn't bothered by the arrogance of that statement, he ought to have been bothered by what it said about his newscast. After all, Lebanon did not burst into the news this week, and if the viewer has never heard of it, the people responsible for the newscast should find other work.

In 1983, NBC News printed a booklet called *The NBC News Guide to Central America.* All NBC anchorpeople were required to promote the booklet on air. It was not a travel guide; it was a handbook to tell viewers everything they needed to know about that boring old civil war in El Salvador, which side to root for in Nicaragua and what the latest news was in places like plucky little old Belize, plus lots more. All anyone had to do was to write NBC News and the booklet would be sent to them, absolutely free.

Someone with courage or a long contract suggested to management that offering program notes might be an admission we were being less than clear on the subject of Central America in our newscasts. Were you supposed to need a scorecard to make sense out of a half-hour newscast? Would the next step be to offer the NBC News Classics Comic version of the Middle East?

Wasn't the *NBC Guide to Central America* a very clear sign we were doing something *wrong*? I read the booklet, and when I had finished I didn't feel terribly enlightened, but I did send off immediately for season tickets to all of Belize's wars. The country had pluck. Thank God NBC spotted it.

Never think my network is the only one to underestimate the viewer's intelligence. It is a condition of the trade, local and national, and it is this disregard for the mind of the viewer that has turned so many network newscasts into the Sermon on the Mount and so many local television newscasts into the Gospel According to the Cute. No wonder people laugh at television news and those of us who make it.

Imagine, if you will, the arrogance of some producer who is too scared to ride the subway after dark, too lazy to start a fire in his fireplace without a fake, self-starting log, too ignorant to change a tire and too confused to do his own tax return making fun of the plumber in Albuquerque just because he's a plumber, he lives in Albuquerque and he watches television news. How can they ignore the fact that the plumber in Albuquerque, unlike most television news producers, at least has steady work?

In the movie *Network*, a satire on television news, Paddy Chayefsky, the screenwriter, has a character say that television is "democracy at its ugliest." Chayefsky got a laugh but missed the point. It's not democracy at its ugliest; it's paternalism at its slickest.

Well, we weren't going to do that. We would begin every night with the assumption that our audience *had* heard of Lebanon—even the plumber in Albuquerque. Especially the plumber in Albuquerque. Lloyd and I had never been able to figure out why anchorpeople didn't write what they said, why they wouldn't want to, why any network would pay an anchorwoman or anchorman a zillion dollars a year—other anchormen and anchorwomen, that is—then let the words they spoke be written by some twenty-four-year-old in an entry-level position. It happens, and the funny thing is, most people who write the news you hear on television, the words the anchorpeople say, couldn't get jobs writing for those very entertainment shows many of them love to ridicule. In order to write for *The A-Team,* you'd have to be a much better writer than most of those who write the evening news at networks and local stations—forget about shows like *Hill Street Blues* or *The Muppet Show,* where writing *really* counts.

Herbie said that was fine with him; he didn't have any money to hire writers for us, anyway—as it was, we should feel honored *we* were going to get paid. He said it was also fine with him if we didn't talk to each other on the air. We would, however, be asked to talk to other people from time to time, to ask *them* questions. He said it was called "interviewing." I told him I didn't like to talk to strangers. Herbie said I would learn. Herbie had been talking to Reuven.

Between May and July 5, Herbie, Don, Cheryl and the rest of us talked about what we liked, what we didn't like and how *Overnight* should work. Herbie, Don and Cheryl did most of the work. Lloyd and I did most of the worrying. One of the conversations was about a logo. Since it was a late-night show, I suggested to Herbie that we use a moon as a logo.

"No moons," said Herbie. "Moons are bad. Stars are good. Think stars." It wasn't going to pay to ask him why, it just wasn't.

One week before we went on the air, Herbie called me at home.

"Forget stars. Moons are in. Stars are out. Think moons." This time I had to ask. Herbie told me he'd just found out that during our first broadcast there would be a lunar eclipse. He said it was a good omen. Moons were in, he said.

Moons were in, for good.

The night before the first broadcast, we were scheduled to tape two rehearsal programs. The first one was terrible; we needed to get better to die. There were technical problems, yes, but Lloyd and I were worse problems, and the most horrible part of the program was the sports segment. Neither of us had ever tried to read words live and make them match action in a sporting event. I was a baseball fan, but basketball bored me, football had lost its charm, I could never find the damn puck in hockey, and Lloyd hated all sports. About as pissed as I'd ever seen Lloyd was a few years before, when *Nightly News* assigned him to cover a baseball story because it was also a news story. He walked into the closet we shared at 30 Rockefeller Plaza, slammed the door and began yelling how they couldn't do this to him—and how he was going to ask me a simple question and he wanted a straightforward, simple answer, and if I told anybody about this or so much as looked like I was going to smirk like I usually did, he would hurt me *bad.* Did I understand and if I did, would I please tell him who the hell Billy Martin was? I told him, then I told everybody else so we could all smirk. Silly sonofabitch.

On that night, however, nobody smirked. We had enough trouble. A tape of that first rehearsal reveals a highly refined moment when Lloyd, trying to read baseball play-by-play copy yells, "Aw shit," to everyone in particular and throws all the pages at the camera. A real professional. The planned second rehearsal was called off, due to talk of blood on the floor. Herbie said maybe it was a good idea if we all went home and got a good night's sleep, instead. Right, Herbie.

I prayed to be taken to my reward before morning, but it wasn't going to happen; I was going to be allowed to live, I knew, so I could show up for work and die on the air, slowly, in front of everyone. *Weekend* had been *taped. Overnight* would be *live.* Live television wasn't what I did well, and because of that, it scared the hell out of me. It was why I didn't anchor regular news programs: I wasn't good at it, I'd figured that out. Years back, substituting for another anchor at WCBS—I'd been terrible and was not invited back. The week auditioning on the *Today* show—I'd been worse, and again, no return engagement. Failure was painful. Anchoring was painful. They were the same. I was not comfortable in front of the camera, sitting at an anchor desk. I could not "look natural"; everything about the whole thing was *unnatural.* Hadn't anybody noticed? I could not get my palms to stop sweating. When I'd stumbled on a word, I'd had to fight a strong desire to bolt from the set, to get out of town, if need be. My hands shook so bad I had to grip something so the audience couldn't see what was going on.

(For the first few months I anchored *Overnight,* I was always seen with my arm casually draped over my typewriter. People said it was an affectation, and I let them; better to think that than to realize the typewriter was not a prop but a crutch. It kept my hand from shaking and kept me in my chair.)

Naturally, I didn't talk about this. Making fun of what scares you is so much more comfortable. I was good at it, always had been. I can remember being afraid no one would invite me to the homecoming dance my freshman year in high school, ridiculing the idea of the dance, the idea of homecoming and the idea of dating; and finally, being hurt because, of course, nobody asked me to the dance. It's a tough pattern to break. Humor can be used to hide emotions as easily as it can be used to reveal them. I had mocked anchorpeople for years, shot my mouth off about how poor most of them were and how I could do it better, then said I wanted no part of it, wasn't interested—because they were fools. Only one who's been one, publicly, can know.

The night before the first *Overnight* show, I stared at my ceiling and watched the little movie in my head: the *Today* show. *Now* (a mistake I will confess to in another chapter) WCBS. The Associated Press. Homecoming. Failure. It was clear to me that once again I was about to humiliate myself in front of a large group of people, instead of one at a time, which is normal. The only person I'd told about this was Reuven. When he first talked to me about *Overnight,* I explained to him why I wasn't the person he wanted for this. Reuven said to forget about the network and my career; it was important for me as a person that I do this show, otherwise I'd never get past my fear, and that, he said, would bother me more than another failure. At the time, it sounded sensible. Twenty-one hours before air, I couldn't remember why. Herbie knew about me, too, but we never spoke about it until much later. He just knew, somehow. However, neither Reuven nor Herbie were going to be sitting at that desk, clutching at a typewriter when the red light went on and the stage manager signaled that it was time for me to do something. It hadn't happened yet, and already I was ashamed of my performance, and already I was working on a funny line I could use to dismiss it afterward.

Besides, there were other, equally real reasons to be afraid. Pictures. Tape. A reel. A roll. Herbie had promised there would be pictures. Herbie had promised tape would roll. *Herbie* had promised? Herbie? By seven o'clock, on the night of July 5, Lloyd and I were at our desks, near panic, but hiding it because, as Lloyd pointed out, many young people worked on this program, young people who had *their* careers still in front of them and it would be bad for their morale if they saw the two of us sobbing. Lloyd said we should think about life's rich pageant and not about how we were going to need to find new ways to earn our living, starting tomorrow.

A florist arrived. Someone had sent us flowers. How sweet. We opened the card. "Best of luck to *Overnight.*" It was signed, "Your friends at CNN." Great. NBC hadn't sent us flowers, but Ted Turner's Cable News Network had. What kind of omen was this, Herbie?

I thought about the duck. The year before, I'd picked up the duck at a hospital gift shop in California. Whenever I had to anchor one of those forty-two second news burps the networks air twice each night in prime time, I'd brought the duck along and it had stayed on the set, out of sight. It's not that I'm superstitious; it's just that your body never outgrows its need for small, yellow, stuffed ducks. Gerry Polikoff, who directed *Weekend,* also directed many of those short-take newscasts and knew about the duck. That night Gerry would be directing *Overnight.* Gerry's not superstitious, either. I don't think coming out of the control room four times to make certain I'd brought the duck *counts,* do you?

At ten minutes before the show was to begin, Lloyd and I were still writing the back half of the show. At five minutes to air, Gerry ran out of the control room one last time. He said rubbing the duck's head could do no harm. I showed him where the duck was stashed near the back of my desk, out of sight of the camera, and joined him in the rubbing part. At two minutes to air, Herbie came over to us, smiled and, for once, began to speak like a normal person.

"Okay, guys. All we're going to do is respect our audience, and if we do that, our audience will do us proud. And we're going to get on—and get off—on time. What else is there?"

The stage manager said it was thirty seconds to air. Herbie started to walk away, turned back, picked up the duck—and moved it to the very front of our desk, where the camera could not miss it and where it stayed for 367 nights.

We were on the air. I could tell because I could hear the sound of Donald Duck drowning. Maybe somebody out there would mistake it for music. Maybe somebody out there would mistake this for a news program. We began, and in spite of a moderately ragged first hour, Herbie was right—that night and for all the rest of the nights. Our audience did us proud and our audience became a full partner in the best news program most of us had ever seen or worked on. It *was* a piece of cake. Herbie was right about something else, too. We got on—and got off—on time. What else is there?

In time, I began to figure out what "a something and a something" was. It was Herbie's way of saying "something good and then something better." That's what we were to give the audience, and that's what we got back. When I write about *Overnight,* I run the risk of sounding corny, which is not my usual key. Without a doubt, this was the toughest chapter to write, and it took me a while to understand why. When things go wrong, as they often do in covering politics, Washington, crime or other pleasantries; when things are dumb, as they often are in television, local and network; when nothing works right and stupidity rules—well, it makes for fine storytelling. However, when things go right, there's a shortage of funny stories. Wrong is funny. Right isn't. The trouble with writing about *Overnight* is that too much went right with that program. I'm short material here.

It was a quick shakedown cruise; by the end of the first month, the reviews were in. They were better than good. Adjustments were made in the program: a little bit here, a little bit there, and we settled down to a life of news, nature, law, music, animals, parades, tacky sports, news, optimism, idiocy, sentiment, subtitles, news, hope, skepticism and more news, or as Herbie says, more more news. The news, we treated seriously—always—but the alternative to garbage is not self-important solemnity and, as Reuven says, there *is* no alternative to accuracy.

We had two advantages. The first was having no money. For one thing, it was partly responsible for the decision to air news reports from foreign news services. NBC and the BBC had an agreement that allowed us to use anything the BBC aired on its news programs. There were other foreign news services from which we could get tape for free or for precious little, and so *Overnight* covered the confirmation hearings of the new secretary of state by showing how four NATO allies covered them, which gave the viewer the extra benefit of seeing what Great Britain, France, Holland and

West Germany were looking for in an American secretary of state. Seeing how Poland covered the Solidarity movement told you why there was one. Consider covering the Falklands war by showing the British television report for that night, followed by the one from Argentine television. When was the last time you saw how Sandinista television covered El Salvador and Nicaragua? When the Soviet Union shot down a civilian commercial airliner over Sakhalin Island, we showed Soviet television every night, just to show what it was *not* saying about that tragedy. Australian television sent us moving stories about the drought there, a drought most of us didn't know existed; and until *NBC Nightly News* aired the heart-stopping pictures of starving Ethiopians in 1984, *Overnight* was the only American news program that regularly covered the famine in Africa. Actually, the BBC and Canadian television covered it. We aired it.

The accepted wisdom was that subtitles would not work in television news. They would confuse the viewer, poor baby. I suppose the assumption was that the viewer, if he could read at all, surely couldn't read and watch pictures at the same time. We used subtitles. The viewer was not confused. No matter what the language, there was somebody on the program who knew it, or knew somebody in the building who did, and would translate—for free, of course. The extra dimension added by showing how the rest of the world saw the rest of the world was such a splendid notion we were amazed no one had thought of it before.

The same applied to the notion of using stories from NBC's local affiliates in this country. Local news? How bush. That's the network attitude about it. We quickly learned how many people work at local stations—and not networks—because they want to, and how often their coverage is every bit as professional and regularly more lively than ours.

Reporters in Denver, not knowing any better, may be less burdened with the obligation to be as dull as we are. Cameramen in Salt Lake City tend to keep their jobs because they are good shooters and not because the union insists they cannot be fired. Editors in Shreveport or Houston or Toledo are less likely to take a lunch break in the middle of cutting a story.

We thrived on their work. Lou Pierce, a young man in South Bend, Indiana, sent us wonderful, imaginative stories he put together after work in his spare time. Neal Rosenau, a reporter in Portland, a fellow with a spare way with words and a heady sense of picture, once took us on an eerily beautiful tour inside the crater at Mount Saint Helens. Barry Bernson, in Chicago, understood the only way you cover a story about what happens to pink, plaster flamingos in the wintertime is with a straight face. Bruce Huss, in Wisconsin, gave us Wilbur, the jogging turkey, the only *genuine* turkey on television ever to get fan mail. Mary Wallace, in Los Angeles, a world-class smart-ass, gave us her cracked view of just about everything. Craig Wirth, in Salt Lake City, sent us his stories, each as human as it was funny, and—best of all—he became a friend, as did Mary and Barry. The Tucson station sent us a story about light pollution and how the city's growth was about to destroy the usefulness of the city's planetarium. The light made it hard to see the stars. It was a local story, but a local story that played just as well in Tacoma as in Tucson. A story about a woman whose telephone number was but one digit different from the president's was funny anywhere, but it took a local station to cover it—and *Overnight* to air it, nationally. Local news *was* national news if you picked the right stories—and Herbie did.

When a Pan Am plane crashed in a New Orleans suburb, NBC News sent its own correspondent—from Chicago. *Overnight* used the coverage of WDSU, the NBC affiliate in New Orleans. After all, the story was in their backyard, and their reporters wouldn't have to introduce themselves to the police chief. In fact, we aired the first ten minutes of WDSU's ten o'clock news, anchorpeople and all. It was less "slick" than a network news program, but it was better television because it was *their* story—and they had it *on* the air while the NBC correspondent was still *in* the air.

Still there was the problem of how to get NBC News people to work for *Overnight*. It would mean extra work for them. We couldn't pay them. Why should they do it? We gave them a reason. Most correspondents complained that *Nightly News* "committeed" their scripts and gave them a minute and a half when they needed two or three minutes. We suggested that the next time it happened, they recut the story the way *they* thought it should have aired, and send it to us. We wouldn't change it, if the facts were correct, and *we* would give them the airtime they told us it needed. We reminded them it might be unclear who was watching *Overnight* outside the building, but we knew for sure *Nightly News* watched it inside the building. Maybe *Nightly* would begin to see what it was missing. Well, it *could* work that way.

Some correspondents caught on fast and began to take chances, to swing a little wider with their stories. On the first broadcast, Andrea Mitchell sent us a report from California, where the president was on vacation and the White House press corps, stuck there, spent its time attending one briefing a day, then swimming, riding, sunning, eating and drinking the rest of the day. She let the pictures tell that story; her words talked about how difficult an assignment it was and how hard White House reporters were working. She finished her report about the rigors of covering the White House, lying on a massage table, wearing a towel and a microphone. It certainly eliminated the Sermon-on-the-Mount–style of White House reporting.

Jon Olson, an NBC cameraman in Burbank, shot a story for *Nightly News* about a train. I forget the point of the story, but I remember that Jon took the outtakes from it and put together a different story, one not encumbered by narration. That story he sent to *Overnight.* The train story won first place in the Los Angeles press photographers' competition, the state press photographers' competition and then took a first place in the national competition. Not the train story that aired on *Nightly News*—the train story that aired on *Overnight,* the one Jon put together from the shots *Nightly* discarded.

Rich Clark, a videotape editor for NBC based in Washington, D.C., noticed, while screening footage shot at the White House, that the president saluted almost everybody. Rich began collecting shots of this and, when he had enough, intercut them with shots of Reagan saluting, taken from his movies. The conclusion: President Reagan saluted everybody because he knew how. He'd had practice. Another Washington videotape editor, Vic Vassery, assembled (on his own time) the single most moving photo essay anybody ever saw about the dedication of the Vietnam Memorial in Washington. It was impossible to watch it without crying. He did it because his brother had died in Vietnam, and he called it "A Tribute to Brother Bob." What *Overnight* did was give him airtime. What he gave back was something from the heart.

These people are seldom mentioned on the air. We changed that. We said who shot a story and who edited it when what was shot and edited deserved it, and you'd be surprised how often it did—and does. But custom has it that people who do not appear on the air are not to be mentioned on the air, except in the printed credit roll at the end of a program. Rubbish.

In addition, people who work *off* the air are not supposed to anchor, which brings up the subject of Pat Trese. Pat Trese wrote the sports segment on *Overnight,* thank God, edited stories, made our copy better and told bad jokes, but, as was once pointed out, his real job on the program was to be wise. Pat had written for Chet Huntley, and had written and produced television news when some people working on *Overnight* were not yet born. Pat Trese is the only person other than Lloyd that I would let write words I say. He writes funny, and looks like Jimmy Stewart. Once, when my partner was on vacation, we asked Pat to coanchor the program. An off-air person appearing on air—anchoring? Such things were simply not done, didn't we know? Pat, too, was hesitant, until we told him to make believe it was Jimmy Stewart and not him. That way he couldn't fail, only Jimmy could. Pat did a first-class job anchoring and I would work alongside him any day, anywhere. If he'd stop telling such terrible jokes, I'd marry him.

Anchoring *Overnight* was never routine because whoever anchored it, wrote it. That is, they wrote the introductions to the taped pieces, the items, the weather and the essay. The trick was to write it all so that one story flowed into the other. The anchorperson's copy was used to set a rhythm, and to frame the stories so that finally, the whole show was one story, the story of that day, the way we saw it. That's what our writing was supposed to accomplish, and the attempt to do that each night—each day's stories being different—became my primary focus and my primary pleasure. Later, it occurred to me that it may have been what made the difference—for me—between anchoring, say, the *Today* show and anchoring *Overnight.* I had not written my own words when I'd anchored other programs, except on *Weekend,* which didn't count because it wasn't live. Maybe live anchoring was easier now because, having controlled the words, I could control myself. No, that was part of it, but there was more. I *liked* anchoring a live television show every night—now. I was comfortable in that chair, on that show—and the main reason for the change was simple as could be. Herbie was right again. You do your best work when you're doing what you want to do, and *Overnight* was the show *we,* those of us who worked on it, wanted to do.

Each night, the show began with the big story of the day and the entire first segment of the show generally was devoted to that story. If the lead story was, say, the Israeli invasion of Lebanon, the first piece might be a story from the BBC correspondent traveling with Israeli troops. The second story might be footage of the president of Lebanon, talking about what was going on there, with subtitles in English. There might be a piece from French television addressing the question of whether France would join a United Nations force going in to keep the peace while Israel got out. The segment might end by combining the best parts of two or three NBC correspondents' stories about the situation in Beirut and how people there were or were not surviving it.

Segment Two was, literally, page two—with more news, stories from affiliates that might have a common thread—the economy—or might be about separate subjects, depending on what had happened that day; or stories from overseas, if that's where most of the news was. Halfway through this segment we would roll the "newsreel." This consisted of three or four minutes of taped stories, each compressed to fifteen or twenty seconds, and was the place to tell what Greenpeace had attempted to stop that day, how Prince Charles had danced with a New Zealand warrior, whether California was going to drop its academic requirements for high school football players, why a dozen whales had beached themselves on the coast of Ireland, who had been convicted of what, who had won the National Spelling Bee, and which volcano was erupting where. If heads of state arrived in Paris, Brussels or Bonn for a meeting, but hadn't actually met yet, the newsreel was where that information went. It was a catchall which allowed us to pack more news into our hour without having to devote the regulation minute-thirty to each story. Some stories deserve much more time than that, but some stories deserve no more than twenty seconds. Most of the stories in the newsreel were hard-news stories, but not always. A report that France had tried unsuccessfully to launch its Ariane rocket might be followed by a report on the successful completion of the annual race to get the year's first bottles of Beaujolais from Paris to London.

We were lucky. We had Don Bowers as senior producer. He'd worked for all three networks, been all over the world, covered everything twice and, as a result, was a first-class newsman who never took anything, himself included, too seriously. Don said later that he was very hesitant at first about working on *Overnight* because of what he considered to be a concentration of the, well, loony-tune element at the network, all on one show. Part of his job, as he saw it, would be to save us from ourselves. One of the sweetest things about Don Bowers is that he actually believes *he's* normal, which is okay with me. Anybody that talented gets to believe whatever he likes. He could think he was the archangel Gabriel, as long as it didn't interfere with his news judgment. Happily, nothing interfered with his news judgment.

Segment Three was called the "Not-Ready-For-Prime-Time News," and for good reason. It was the only place to put a story about Mr. Condom, a man appointed by the government of Thailand to educate people about birth control. Mr. Condom traveled around Thailand, holding birth-control "fairs" at which he got people into the spirit of things by having them blow up condoms as if they were balloons, then invited men into tents for on-the-spot vasectomies. It sounds prurient. It wasn't. It was a perfectly good story about a country's attempt to keep its population down. Any snicker would be in your own mind, not in the story—but granted, it really wasn't ready for *Nightly News* or prime time, if NBC *had* a news broadcast in prime time, which it did not.

The "Mr. Condom" story was a gift from Neil Davis, NBC News bureau chief in Bangkok. An Australian, Neil had come to work for NBC News in 1975 in Vietnam and had been the last Western journalist to leave

Saigon when the American troops withdrew. Neil had shot the film of the North Vietnamese tanks breaking through the gates of the Imperial Palace. Neil had, in fact, shot every war, revolution, riot and massacre in the Far East in recent history. Cameraman, producer and correspondent, Neil Davis was a walking, living legend in that part of the world and the epitome of the "war correspondent." Later a documentary was done on Neil Davis and his dangerous, curious occupation, but there was another side to Neil, and that was what we got on *Overnight.* It was the other side that gave us "Mr. Condom." In September, 1985, Neil Davis, covering what Tom Brokaw accurately called a "tin-horn revolt" in Bangkok, was cut in two by a tank, his execution recorded, ironically, by his own videotape camera, which continued to roll after he fell. In the many obituaries about Neil Davis, everybody talked about Neil Davis's bravery and his years spent on the front lines. I kept remembering his sense of humor, something he'd found an outlet for—on *Overnight.* There will always be somebody around to cover our wars. Who, now, will tell me about "Mr. Condom"?

Another "Not-Ready-For-Prime-Time News" story might be tape of a fight between White House Spokesman Larry Speakes and ABC White House correspondent Sam Donaldson about the legality of taking pictures through the windows of the Oval Office. Actually, it was more of a shouting match on the White House lawn, with Speakes saying Donaldson could point his cameras at the Oval Office windows only when the president was *not* in the office, and Donaldson shouting that he couldn't think why he would *want* to point cameras at the Oval Office window if the president wasn't inside. Speakes shouted that it was private property. Donaldson yelled that this was sure going to come as a surprise to the people of the United States. ABC did not use the tape, but we did because, uncut, it told you something about the White House and those whose job it was to cover it.

When Alexander Haig resigned as secretary of state, he hit the rubber-chicken circuit, asking for and getting $20,000 a speech. After he'd been giving speeches for two months, *Overnight* put together clips from his lectures, clips gathered from local affiliates. Since everybody knows a public speaker must throw a little humor into even the most serious speech, we decided to see how funny Haig was. What resulted was a "Not-Ready-For-Prime-Time News" story in which Alexander Haig proved that as a stand-up comic, he made a terrific secretary of state.

Sports occupied Segment Four. The segment began with sportstalk, a piece of sports news, then we gave the scores on a roll; that is, the scores rolled across the screen while music—anything from Eric Clapton to Mitch Miller—played in the background. That was followed by pictures of the sports highlights of the day, with one of us reading what Pat had written about those highlights. The segment would end with a sports story of the sort you do not see on *NFL Today*—jello wrestling, duck races, blind children playing basketball, the world's slowest marathon runner, opening day at Ascot, Russian ballet classes, chess matches, the competition of classical musicians.

In Segment Five, there was only one story, and generally it was meant to give you background on a continuing news situation, or new information about a part of the world not regularly covered by American television. I recall a six-minute story on the drought in Australia, a drought most people didn't know about unless they made their way to page nineteen of *The New York Times.* Or, if the State of the Union message had taken place the previous night, we might show you how it had been covered in Japan, Germany, England and the Soviet Union. One night it was a long piece on advertising in the People's Republic of China. Another night it was a second look at presidential libraries, their cost, worth and appeal to anyone other than the president whose library it was. And so on.

Segment Six was the place for lighter stuff, including the ever-present animal stories. Herbie loved animal stories, and it was a rare night when there wasn't one in the show, whether it was a story about Iggy the Piggy, a pig learning to adjust to life in a truss, or a story about baby eagles born in captivity and then taught to live in the wild. Segment Six was a change-up pitch, something to make you smile—unless you were the executive producer and given to crying your way through all animal stories. The audience couldn't see *that.*

We began Segment Seven, the final segment each night, by recapping the major stories of the day, then telling the audience about a few items they might have missed, such as the fact that television was about to return to Cambodia, where it had been banned since the Khmer Rouge takeover in 1975, or the fact that a judge in Morristown, New Jersey, had sentenced a man, convicted of sexually molesting two little girls, to spend one night attending an off-Broadway play about the horrors of prison so he would see the error of his ways. (The little girls, at least, did not have to go to the play.) The items were followed by the weather, which on *Overnight* meant showing a map of the United States with little symbols on it for rain, snow, sun, etc.—telling the audience to look for the symbol nearest where they lived to find out what weather to expect the next day. We weren't, you might say, into weather.

After that, there was a piece, usually from an affiliate or an NBC videotape editor or cameraman, designed to close the show on a note of hope—to get people to bed safely.

Mostly, these were picture stories—images of a thunderstorm passing over a lake in the Rockies, from the first ominous rumble to the sun breaking out to show water drops resting on a wildflower; a piece of a documentary on Jacques D'Amboise, the dancer who took children off the streets of New York and showed them the music in their bodies, making them see that anyone could dance, that dancing was too important to be left to dancers; a small town where, on Sundays, the town band still played in the town square and people still brought fried chicken, bread-and-butter sandwiches, lemonade and blankets—everything necessary to spend a Sunday in the park with their families.

Family counted to Herb Dudnick, who said you could get another job but not another family. He thought it was important that those of us who worked on the show see ours; therefore, we were encouraged to bring our wives or husbands or children to the show whenever we liked—and we took off to be with our families when we needed to. According to Herb, nobody was paid enough to work from three in the afternoon until three in the morning unless you were having fun at it—and you couldn't have fun if there was trouble at home. There's television and there's the real world, said Herbie. We lost him to the real world.

The show had been on the air more than a year, and it had been hard on Herbie and his family; he worked longer hours than any of us, and Renee, his wife, worked on the show, too, as a researcher. They were exhausted. So, when NBC News asked Herbie to produce its election coverage for 1984—a job requiring almost a year of preparation—Herbie accepted. He was replaced on *Overnight* by Deborah Johnson, who was new to the program and was, I believe, the first woman to be named executive producer of a daily network news program. Before she came to television, she'd been one of the people to begin a magazine called *Mother Jones.* Some of us worried that when Herbie left, the show would fall apart. It didn't.

We might have known it sooner because Lloyd Dobyns had already left the show to anchor *Monitor,* NBC's tenth attempt at a news magazine. He had been replaced by Bill Schechner, a witty, compassionate man with curly black hair, a drooping mustache, sad eyes and a Talmudic way of looking at eighteen sides of everything. If you were casting *Welcome Back, Kotter,* Bill Schechner would make as much sense as Gabe Kaplan. It was, as I said, a writer's program, and Bill was a very fine writer. Before *Overnight,* he'd worked as an NBC correspondent based in Atlanta, and at first he was hesitant to come to *Overnight* because it would mean moving him, his wife and small daughter to New York, an expensive place to live—what if the show were to be canceled? I assured him there was nothing to worry about. There was no danger this show would be canceled. Our bosses kept telling us so. It is a measure of Bill's character that he still speaks to me.

The transition from Lloyd to Bill was almost smooth, and would have been completely smooth except for the business about the chairs. When it was known that Lloyd was leaving *Overnight,* Tom Pettit, executive vice president of NBC News and a smart, funny friend, said that off the top of his head he thought it would be a good idea for me to move to the chair and desk where Lloyd had been sitting, putting Bill in the chair and at the desk where I had been sitting. Very often off-the-top-of-the-head ideas can be said to be like dandruff—small and flaky. This one was. I told him it was silly. He said to do it anyway. What bothered me was the implication that one chair was somehow better or "higher" than the other. Since it had not been that way with Lloyd and me, it made no sense, which made it perfect for television.

For three nights after the switch, I spilled coffee all over my script because the coffee was where it should be, but I was not. On the fourth night I moved back to my old chair. Billy had no say in the matter because, in television, justice does not count as much as seniority. On the air that night, I explained this business of musical chairs and how it had come about, and said if the executives didn't like what I'd done, they could come do the show themselves and spill their own coffee. Nobody in the executive suite said a word.

Bill was a terrific partner. I loved working with him, and his success on *Overnight* proved that any of us could leave and, when replaced by the right person, the show would keep on being just what it had been before, whatever that was. Herbie was also a fine teacher, and what he taught us we kept. What wasn't broken, we didn't try to fix.

Naturally, we made mistakes. There was the time Bill and I talked dirty on the air. In August, 1983, NASA scheduled a night launch of the space shuttle. It would, in fact, go up while we were on the air, and was too good an opportunity to pass up; we dipped into

NBC's pockets and found enough money to cover the launch live. Bill stayed in New York. I went to the Cape—again, seniority counts. It was a real treat for me; I'd never covered a space shot, and when the shuttle went up, so did my heart, right into my throat, where it stayed. When the noise of the launch died away, Bill asked me on television about that sound, and what it had felt like. Did it, he wanted to know, make my diaphragm rattle? All aglow from the launch, I didn't hear the double entendre Bill didn't intend, anyway, and answered that it gave new meaning to the phrase, "the earth moved." (Another reason I don't anchor *Nightly News.*)

All television news programs have what is known as a "hold" shelf. It is nothing more than a collection of stories that can air tonight, tomorrow night or be held until a night when there is a hole in the program. A story about sand castles can run anytime, with the right lead-in. So can a story about a man who makes player pianos. When you air something from the "hold" shelf, you're supposed to check and make sure the story is still good, that it's not dated—that there's no snow in a story you're airing in July. One night we forgot to check, and what happened is proof of why you shouldn't forget. We believed this was a story that could not possibly be dated; there was nothing in the story to suggest time and nothing in the story that could possibly have changed. So we aired it without checking. The following day, the station that had sent us the story called. We were right; the story was still fresh, but the reporter who'd covered it—and who was seen in the story—had died six weeks ago. They just thought we'd like to know. Wrong.

Another advantage *Overnight* had was the fact that

when we were on the air, most of our bosses were home asleep, and a good thing at their age. The competition at the other networks wasn't a concern because we were doing just fine: after six months on the air we had twice the audience NBC had predicted, and besides, we didn't have to worry about ratings because our bosses told us we were doing this program to fight the dreaded Ted Turner and to give our affiliate stations fresh news tape for their early morning and noon news shows. Anyway, we all knew that the real competition on *Overnight* was not another program, but sleep.

That we understood completely. It applied to those of us who worked on the show, as well; we never got enough sleep because the rest of the world refused to sleep when we did. In China, the traditional greeting translates to: "Have you had rice today?" On *Overnight,* the traditional greeting was: "How much sleep did you get?" The man in my life worked days. He and I made up a new rule: when it came to sex, only one of us need be awake at the time.

A bunker mentality developed, and why not? We were spending at least twelve hours a day in rooms with no windows and no companionship but our own. The second week of the show, we added a bar to the office. Getting off work at three in the morning, then going someplace for an after-work drink made you feel sleazy and pretty much described the bars open at that hour. This way, we could sit around after the show, relax, watch a *Mary Tyler Moore* rerun, have a drink together and then go home. If our preproduction meeting each night consisted of watching *The Muppet Show,* our postproduction meeting was our shared drink after work—and watching Mary. Sometimes I think *Nightly News* could benefit from that sort of postproduction meeting. In their case, it might be better if they drank before the program.

The second big topic around the *Overnight* office was food. Very few restaurants near Rockefeller Center delivered after seven at night, there was no time to go out for food and many of us could not manage to remember to order before seven. Herbie made sure that every night, along with the ten-pound pastries you find on all news sets, there were plates of raw vegetables and onion dip. Onion dip can take you only so far. In fact, when Herbie and Don Bowers left *Overnight* for the political unit, Cheryl Gould campaigned for the job of senior producer on a "change-the-dip" platform. She won even though it had to do with her talent and not the dip, which, once she was senior producer, she did not change.

Friday nights *Overnight* sent out for pizza, which is one of the reasons—along with the pastry, onion dip and the homemade cookies Cheryl's mother kept bringing—that some people (especially me) put on weight and most people ended up thinking or talking about food even when we weren't eating it. I recall a production meeting in Deborah Johnson's office. First, Cheryl told us what she had for lunch, which reminded Deborah we had a story about Reagan cutting the budget for the school *lunch* program. My hair came unpinned from the top of my head and fell in my eyes. I asked Cheryl if she had a hairpin. Deborah pointed out that Cheryl, with her Jewish Afro, didn't use a hairpin; she used a toothpick or something. "Wrong," said Cheryl. "I use a chopstick." At that point, another producer, Kathy Field, walked into the room. "Chopsticks? Oh, goody, we're ordering Chinese food tonight, right?" As

I said, food got confused with everything on *Overnight,* and a motion for Chinese food was never out of order.

Food, respect, good and bad taste, wisecracks and, frankly, love got all mixed up in *Overnight,* for those of us who worked on the program. Around the building, some NBC News employees took to referring to the *Overnight* staff as the "moonies," and I suppose by that they meant that we smiled a lot. We did—we got along with each other, the thirty or so of us who put the show together. As Bill once said: when one of us grew, it didn't mean somebody else had to shrink. It's a rare way to work in television—and remains a strong memory to those of us who were lucky enough to be there.

The program had a certain rhythm to it—again, by Herb Dudnick's design. Lighter stories were interspersed with heavier stories in order to give the viewer time to reflect on what had gone before, while allowing him to receive the lighter information with another part of his brain. Bill also pointed out that we tried, in different ways, to break the barrier between us and them—the people on television and the people watching television. One way we tried to do that was with the "essay" at the end of each show, a two-minute hole where the anchor could shoot his or her mouth off on anything at all. We alternated the essay each night and we did not label it commentary; that is, we didn't have the word "commentary" printed across the screen during the essay. We figured our audience was smart enough to separate fact from thought. The essays could be about anything. Here are parts of some of them. Bill, on the subject of baseball and certain essential truths of the 1983 season: "The teams using Astroturf have not done well; the teams using computers have nothing to show for it; the Yankees spent more money than anyone else and still ended up in third place; therefore the game survived." Me, on the subject of a telephone credit card I found in a taxi: "I called the telephone company to tell them I would send them the card so they could send it to the woman who lost it. The telephone company refused to take the lady's name unless I gave them *my* name and address—and phone number. The telephone company got nasty (it was created stupid). I hung up. But if the lady from Ohio who left her credit card in a New York taxi last Wednesday is watching, please know I sent the phone company your card, and if they don't send it on to you, perhaps, after all, they have decided to take my suggestion about what they can do with it."

Sometimes the essays *were* news stories, stories you weren't going to see on television and might not hear about, such as the story of Tim Lane, who spotted a fox caught in a trap near Apache Junction, Arizona. The animal's foot was half-gone from trying to chew his way out of the trap. The animal was in great pain. Tim Lane talked to the fox to calm it, freed it from the trap, then called the authorities who said they would pick up the little fox, amputate its leg and give it to the zoo. Instead, they picked up the little fox, destroyed it and fined Tim Lane for disturbing a trap. Lane said he guessed he would pay the fine but they couldn't make him change his morals. My comment: "No, but they sure can price 'em out of the market."

The essays also gave us a way to talk about what bothered us. The alleged "Hitler Diaries" were released and a poll was taken of West German young people's impressions of Adolf Hitler. Fifty-six percent had strong negative feelings about Hitler. Eight percent had strong positive feelings. Thirty-six percent had mixed feelings. In other words, thirty-six percent of young Germans weren't sure Hitler was wrong. I felt it showed that paying attention to the past was important if we were to stay on the right side of human decency. Bill said it even better. He pointed out that during the war, information about the death camps had leaked out of Germany and to this country. He said that choosing to ignore that information was choosing to ignore a large injustice. There was the true villain (like Hitler), which one rarely meets in a lifetime—but the ordinary bad hats were with us always. Bill said that we pass small injustices on the street, so to speak, and pull our coats tighter around us. He said it was time—in a country with a souring economy and evidence of continuing racial prejudice (he did not mean West Germany)—to remember the words of a Hebrew scholar, Rabbi Hillel, speaking about seeing injustice and ignoring it: "If not me, who? And if not now, when?"

After that, we got a letter from a creep, addressed to "*NBC News Overnight,* Jew York." The man said we'd lied to the public. There had been no Holocaust. It was nothing but a bunch of commie crap and we were nothing but a bunch of pinko traitors to America and all true Americans. On the theory—Reuven's—that it never pays to ignore a fanatic—we read the letter on the air and suggested the man turn off his set; we didn't need viewers *that* much and frankly, would rather not have him as part of our audience.

Finally, we used the essays to say personal things when we chose to, going against standard television wisdom. When Bill returned from vacation on the Jersey shore, he talked about summertimes there in the house his grandfather had built, and how those summers were important to him because they were also seasons of "family," of roots; his, his father's, his grandfather's and now his child's. He said that his grandfather had always defined immortality as being remembered after you're gone—and if that were so, his grandfather had achieved a grand immortality—on a beach.

For me, the most personal thing I ever said on the air had to do with my mother, who had recently died. I said that she'd wanted to go to college but there was no money, that she'd wanted to work but her husband wouldn't let her, that she'd wanted to go into politics but she knew no other women in politics. She'd said it wasn't her time. Instead, she'd pushed me to read, to stretch, even when she didn't agree with what I read or where I stretched. She said it was my time, and so I pointed out on the air that this two minutes at the end of a television show was indeed my time and I wanted to use it to say a public and sincere thank you, from my time to hers, from me to her. It was hard for me to write, harder to say. I'd buried her only two weeks before. It was also hard for me to open up that way on television; it was contrary to everything I'd been taught about television and our role in it. One is not supposed to use the medium for personal statements and one is not supposed to let the audience get that close, but I did not do it for television, I did it for my mom.

Everybody has a mother, or a grandfather or a pet hate or pet love; everybody has feelings, and the result of airing ours was that the audience began to see us as humans and not people on television, *whether or not they liked us.* Jack Paar, writing about late-night television, said that the general theory of television was to put on people who were acceptable as guests in your living room, but statistics showed that many people watched late-night television in their bedrooms—and you had to know the people you let into your bedrooms better than the other kind, even if, later, you regretted it.

To let *Overnight* in, they had to get to know us and we had to let them. That was the real point of the essay at the end of the show, and the benefit of it.

It may have been odd, but it worked. *Overnight* got a lot of mail, and most of it was intelligent and thoughtful. Our viewers talked back to us, said what they liked and didn't like; it became clear that many of the two million or so who watched, watched regularly. We dubbed them the "constant viewers," and knowing they were out there let us be subtle, let us carry on conversations about the news that continued from night to night. They sent us story ideas and told us who they were and why they watched. They kept us honest and they kept us going.

The writing load was heavy, and I was quite capable of slipping, drifting from okay to glib, from fast to flip. Some people said I was snotty. Some people said I was self-indulgent. Some used words like "cutesy." God, that one hurt. Some people said I was biased, that I hated President Reagan. They said they could tell that by watching and listening to me.

They were wrong. I never hated the man, nor felt I picked on him. It was only that Ronald Reagan was president at the time. When Jimmy Carter had been president, I hadn't had a show. It had nothing at all to do with liberal or conservative. It had to do with power, and who had it. The White House had it, and Ronald Reagan was in the White House at the time. It is the obligation of any reporter to question power, to be skeptical—which is different from cynical—and to report more than just what the president said on any given day. If today he says one thing and last week he said another, it's a reporter's job to point that out. If Ronald Reagan saves $40,000 on his personal income taxes because of new tax laws *he* has introduced, there's nothing wrong with describing it as "another example of how government can help a person."

If the United States, with all its might, invades the tiny Caribbean island of Grenada and calls it a great step forward for democracy, there's nothing wrong with pointing out, as Bill did, that Grenada was an independent nation and had a right to make its own mistakes—that's what independence meant. Bill noted that when Grenada had attained its independence, the United States, sensing certain Marxist leanings there, had cut off all aid to that country, thereby driving it to Cuba and the Soviet Union for help.

Some people said it was an "alternative" news program. Others said it was a subversive news program. Some said (and still say) it was a smug, sophomoric circle-jerk, masquerading as a news program. Columbia University, when it gave *Overnight* the DuPont Award, the Pulitzer Prize of television news, said it was "possibly the best written and most intelligent news program, ever." *Time* magazine said it was one of the ten best *television* programs—not just *news* programs—of the year, and said it two years in a row. The second year *Time* said it, we'd already been canceled.

All *Overnight* was, I believe, was a program that put news in a human context, and all we were, I believe, were a couple of citizen reporters or, as one newspaper described us, "the least sexy anchors on television." Another newspaper wondered why Lloyd wore a vest, why Bill took to wearing red suspenders, why I seemed to wear the same black jacket night after night—why didn't we dress like other anchors and what were we wearing from the waist down? I thought they knew—we were on television; we *didn't* exist from the waist down. A lot, in fact, was written about the program, causing Reuven Frank to remark that more people had read about *Overnight* than had seen it.

November 11, 1983, seventeen months after it went on the air, NBC announced *Overnight* would go off the air on December 2nd. NBC said the reason was money. The program wasn't making any, and NBC said its research showed that it wasn't going to make any; there just weren't enough people watching television at that time of night. Never mind this was the first we'd heard we were supposed to make money. In that, we'd been lucky. As long as they told us ratings didn't count, we didn't worry about ratings. Journalists often resent the fact that the quality of their work will be measured by the crowd it draws; there are too many other factors involved besides the quality of the journalists' work. But journalists need paychecks, too, and so the size of the audience, affecting our employment as it does, can come to matter too much, can come to affect decisions, performance, news judgment—and our opinion of ourselves. Sometimes, when journalists come to feel they are hostage to the ratings, they begin to turn in shoddy work, using the need for good ratings as an excuse. On *Overnight,* if we turned in shoddy work, it was because we were shoddy, that's all, and not because we were anxious about ratings.

NBC said it canceled *Overnight* for reasons of money, and I will let that stand. I've heard other people say money wasn't the real reason—that it was something we said; that it was *everything* we said. I know this: I know that no one ever asked me to alter my words and no one ever asked Bill or Lloyd to do so. Nor did they complain. All they did was take us off the air.

No, that's not right. First they put us *on* the air. That *was* something, and it was more important. NBC gave a group of us the chance to do the news program we'd always wanted to do. For one brief moment, they gave the inmates a chance to run the asylum—and that has to count for more. Shutting it off was NBC's prerogative. In announcing the cancellation, Reuven Frank, a man who had much to do with giving *Overnight* its chance and nothing to do with giving *Overnight* its walking papers, said, "It was our finest hour of news, and remains the model for an hour news program, but merely being the best is not enough . . ."

What happened next shocked us all. Between November 11 and December 2, NBC received thousands of letters, telegrams and telephone calls. People sent nasty notes: "Finally, NBC, you have succeeded in castrating the Peacock." People sent encouraging notes: "Would group fasting help?" People sent petitions. People sent *money*. In Washington, New York and Chicago, "Save *Overnight*" committees were formed—and not by us. Salesmen wrote to ask if they might be allowed to sell advertising time on *Overnight,* since NBC obviously didn't know how. There were pickets outside NBC headquarters in New York. One night there was a candlelight march. We were both flattered and embarrassed. It is difficult to take seriously the notion of lighting candles and marching on account of a *TV program.* People wrote and called RCA, which owns NBC. One lady sold her RCA stock. Newspapers wrote stories about all this.

The week before we went off the air, there was a bus drivers' strike in Boston. A television crew videotaping police arresting some protesting strikers kept the camera rolling as one driver was literally thrown into the paddy wagon, shouting all the way, "Fuck the scabs. Long live the union. Save *Overnight*!"

It made us feel better, but it changed nothing, none of it. December 2 came; we broadcast the 367th and final edition of *Overnight.* That night we were self-indulgent on purpose. We were, as Bill put it, huddled around the video campfire to take a look at some of our favorite pictures, some of our favorite stories. For closing credits, Kim McCarthy, one of the young ones for whom *Overnight* had been a chance to learn and shine, had arranged to videotape everybody who worked on the program, then, with a videotape editor, cut their pictures to Bette Midler's "Friends," so constant viewers could put faces to the names of the *Overnight* staff. Just before the show, we opened some more mail. Actually, it wasn't *just* before the show—*just* before the show I was still writing the show. Why should the last night be different from the first?

One viewer, an artist, had designed, had printed and sent us a card. On the outside of the card were the first names of everybody who regularly appeared on the show's credit roll: Linda, Bill, Deborah, Cheryl, Pat, Danny, Cynthia, Gerry, etc. Over that it said, "It was great fun." Inside the card it said, "But it was just one of those things."

Any experienced producer would have balked. Lucky for us, Kim McCarthy was new at it, and, therefore, not the least bit hesitant to tear up the end of the show and start over, just a few hours before air, dropping Midler and recutting everything to Ella Fitzgerald singing Cole Porter. What resulted may have been the best part of the show. Certainly, how it came to be was another small reminder of the partnership a program can have with its audience.

Happily, we had good news to report, our last night on the air. We led with the news that unemployment in America had dropped to the lowest it had been in more than a year, and followed with a story about the Trolley Cafe in Medley, Florida, a restaurant opened and operated by the town itself in order to employ its own citizens who were out of work. The diner was a success. The story was a refutation that television never reports good news, and only a curmudgeon would tell you that one year later, the town closed the diner, and later, sold it to some people from out of town, who said they would try to hire locally, they sure would.

Near the end of the final show, I quoted Mark Twain, speaking of the young missionary who went among the cannibals.

> They listened with the greatest of interest to everything he had to say. And then they ate him.

There were close to two hundred people in the studio that night: us, our friends, our families, reporters from wire services, newspapers and news magazines, crews from local television stations, PBS and CNN.

I work in front of a camera, not an audience. At one point during the program, something I said made people laugh, and all at once I understood why Chevy Chase never minded the bruises that went with the pratfalls, why Bob Hope could not retire, why Johnny Carson—a shy, introverted man—returned each night to talk to strangers, why *Saturday Night Live* was better than *Laugh-In.* What a thing, to make people laugh, *and hear it.* The laughter carries you from the field on its shoulders, and suddenly you want it to keep going, to take you all the way home and stick around for supper. The intoxication of the moment made me know why we must never allow studio audiences to become a part of news broadcasts; there are already enough distractions (ratings, position, paranoia) lurking about, ready to keep a journalist from doing what's right. But, Lord, it was *grand*—the laughter.

Ted Koppel, in closing that night's broadcast of ABC's *Nightline,* spent the last five minutes of *his* show talking about *our* show—and how sorry he and the *Nightline* staff were to see it go. People sent flowers, which is why, on the last show, you *did* see hazy figures in the background with flowers in their hair. *Nightline* sent champagne. *Nightwatch,* at CBS, sent champagne and other goodies, and their anchorpeople came over to commiserate. That same day they'd learned *their* program was being streamlined and moved to Washington, where it could be produced more cheaply. (Streamlined, in this case, meant they were going to be out of work.) ABC's late-night program, *The Last Word,* had already been canceled. The attack of late-night news had ended. Ted Turner had been headed off at the pass. We weren't needed anymore.

We did what was right. We threw one hell of a party after the show, right there in the studio. We had disco music piped into the system. Nestor Torres, one of our floor cameramen, played piano; Nestor is a fine cameraman and one hell of a pianist. We danced. We laughed. And of course, since it was *Overnight,* we ate. We had a catered buffet. The party lasted past dawn.

What we did was try not to cry. What we did was celebrate our success.

If it sounds strange to say a show canceled because of poor ratings was a success, well, maybe so; but it was a success, nevertheless. We learned there was more than one answer to any question. We learned there *was* more than one way to send and receive the news. And we learned we were right: the audience was just as smart as we bet they were. Sure, we could wish for a ratings system that counted people in hotels, hospitals, college dormitories, factories, nursing homes, businesses—all those places outside the home where televisions exist and are watched in what is no longer a nine-to-five America. Or we could wish for a network to realize it needed a nightly, one-hour news program for adults, at a time when most adults are home and able to watch it—say at ten o'clock every night. We could wish for many things, but we didn't have to wish for a chance to try it our way. We'd had it. Bill said it best: it was one hell of a ride.

What follows are three memories of *Overnight,* its audience, its staff, its effect. First, the audience: the night of the final broadcast, PBS, preparing a program about *Overnight,* sent a crew to a bar in a small Iowa town where people had gathered to throw their own "goodbye" party for a show they watched nightly. A construction worker was interviewed, and said, "I like this *Overnight* show because they treat me like a real human being and don't tell me what to think. They don't talk down to me." Well, how about that—the plumber in Albuquerque is alive and well and doing construction work in Iowa. *Awright*!

Next, us: on the last show, instead of a sports feature, we featured Pat Trese, wise old owl, perpetual child, sportswriter, our substitute anchor and personal Jimmy Stewart stand-in. What Pat said that night was:

> For me it all began, as Ted Baxter once said, at a little 50,000-watt NBC radio station in Cleveland, Ohio. I turned twenty-one and got a job writing for the late Tom Manning, the dean of the nation's sportscasters. Tom had started out announcing the starting lineup for the Indians at League Park—with a megaphone. Later, he was second man to Graham McNamee for the first coast-to-coast broadcast of the World Series and the Rose Bowl.
>
> That's the man who taught me to write sportstalk—one of the very best in the business. He taught me some other things about sports, too—that despite what the modern sportstalkers tell you, winning isn't everything. If Billy Martin's job is up for grabs tonight, it's because the Yankees finished third and not first. If amateur athletes are in trouble for using steroids, it's because they've been told there is no other place but first place—and if you don't win the gold medal, you're nothing at all. That was not the message of the man who trained me or of his contemporary and close friend, Grantland Rice—and if their message seems corny in this age of Superdomes and interminable playing seasons and million-dollar deals and labor-management disputes and cocaine busts, it does not seem corny here, not tonight—and not on this team.
>
> For when the one great scorer comes to write against your name, he marks not

> whether you win or lose, but how you played the game. That was the message of Grantland Rice, and there is this to say about *Overnight:* It's the only place I can recite those lines with a straight face.

Then, this: the week after the program ended, a reporter wrote to me, saying he'd been offered a job at a bigger television station than the one where he worked, but he'd been unsure about taking it because the news director who wanted to hire him couldn't seem to explain what it was he wanted the reporter to do. He kept saying things like, "Be different. Look at stuff another way. Think about words, you know what I mean?" The reporter said he wasn't sure he did.

"Oh," said the news director, "you *know* what I mean—*Overnight*ish." The reporter took the job.

We won. It does not matter that we were canceled. It was just one of those things.

# AND NOW FOR SOMETHING COMPLETELY NEW AND DIFFERENT

Whom the gods wish to destroy
they first call promising.
CYRIL CONNOLLY

Once upon a time there was a television show called *Now*. It should have been called *Never*. That's how good it was. This little gem of a program was a pilot for an NBC News magazine—yet another one—and if you missed its one less-than-shining hour in 1977, count yourself lucky. I wish I could, but it would be difficult since, along with correspondent Jack Perkins, I anchored it.

How bad was it? Well, in one segment, Jack and I sat on white pillows that looked like giant marshmallows, and spoke of Journalism. What can I say? During the time I worked on *Now*, reality and I were ships that passed in the night.

The opening story was about reggae music. NBC,

untroubled that by 1977, reggae had been around for some years, said the program was all about what was "in," called it the cutting edge of trendy. In another segment, Yves St. Laurent pranced about, spoke French that went untranslated and dressed rich American women to look life gift-wrapped Russian peasants; we said it was the coming attraction in fashion—when you're sitting on a marshmallow, you're liable to say anything. In still another part of the program, Jack and I stood next to a fortune-telling machine from a carnival. The machine looked like Sybil the Soothsayer from the movie *Network*. Jack and I looked like some of the less intelligent characters from that movie. It was, they told me, completely new and different. It was also awful.

In my office at NBC, I keep a videotape cassette of *Now* on a shelf where I can see it, where I can be reminded, daily, not to let other people do my thinking for me. If I had learned my lesson in 1977, there wouldn't be another cassette next to *Now*. I didn't and there is.

The first time I ever heard the words *Summer Sunday* was in May, 1984. *Overnight* had been off the air for about six months. By this time, NBC had changed the management of the news division—again. In my ten years at NBC News, I have worked for five presidents of the news division, not to mention four presidents of NBC and three chairmen of the board of RCA, the parent company. To me, stability in management is a rumor.

The new president of NBC News was Lawrence K. Grossman, who'd come from PBS, where he'd been instrumental in putting on the air *Vietnam: A Television History*, an excellent series all three networks had managed to turn down. When he got to NBC, the first thing he did was to ask people who worked there what was wrong. We were impressed. The recurring theme in what we told him was that NBC needed more programs. We had about the same number of employees as CBS News and ABC News, but about half the airtime. It translated into too many people with too little to do.

I was one of those people. In May, I was in Los Angeles, interviewing Linda Ronstadt and Nelson Riddle about the return to popularity of a certain kind of music, music by Gershwin, Porter, Mercer—American standard music. It wasn't a story that would, as we say, blow the lid off this town, but it would allow me to spend a few hours on the beach rounding out my burn (a slow burn which may be said to have begun with the cancellation of *Overnight*).

Larry Grossman called. He said there was this new and completely different program in the works, called *Summer Sunday, USA*. In television, new and different is our favorite old standby.

Larry said it would air for nine weeks during the summer, on Sunday evenings, opposite *60 Minutes*. (Was it a death wish?) Larry said it would be experimental and we shouldn't worry about ratings because he wasn't worried, a statement that was beginning to make my feet itch to take me someplace else every time I heard it. He said nobody would compare it to *60 Minutes*. Later, of course, everybody did, and it's amazing the number of NBC executives who seemed shocked when *60 Minutes* went through *Summer Sunday* like Sherman through Georgia.

Grossman said he would like me to coanchor *Summer Sunday* with White House correspondent Andrea Mitchell. Two women anchoring a network newscast?

Yes, and wasn't it time? I said it was and suggested we start with *Nightly News.* Neither Grossman nor anybody else thought that was funny. (Who meant to be funny?) He said *Summer Sunday* would move around, broadcasting each week from a different part of the country. He said we had this truck that would make it possible to broadcast live from anywhere the truck was parked. If you'd like an explanation of how the truck works, there are books to read and engineers to ask. Me, I know it's a miracle and leave it at that.

The truck would be our secret weapon; however, we all forgot that sometimes the secret of a weapon is how it can turn on you. Our trouble was, we had a completely new and different toy—instead of a real *idea* for a program—and we had convinced ourselves that just by being *live,* we would get people into the tent. In one moment, we forgot that live television had been the centerpiece of local TV news for years, that networks had regularly broadcast live reports, and that live television is exciting only when something exciting is happening. And only when the toys work. Some days you eat the bear and some days the bear eats you. *Summer Sunday* was about to be Summer Sausage.

Advance one month to June, 1984. The first edition of *Summer Sunday* was to air on July 1, a scant few weeks away. Steve Friedman, executive producer of the *Today* show, had been named executive producer of *Summer Sunday.* Some people say Steve is a successful television producer because he's never deluded himself into thinking he's an adult. Some say it's because he was born knowing television, the way some people are born with perfect pitch. Some say he's smart and some say he's permanently batshit—but they don't say it to his face very often because Steve keeps a baseball bat and dart gun on his desk, and has been known to use them—at least he's been known to use the dart gun, which is reason enough to watch your tongue. Besides, most truly talented people are, well, strange.

People who work for Steve may get ulcers, but not Steve; he's a carrier. I like him, but then some people say I'm a carrier, too. As for *Summer Sunday,* it was going to be tough on Steve, because he would continue to produce the *Today* show at the same time. Even if the *Today* show could run on autopilot, working two jobs would be punishing—but Steve can work more hours than anybody I know. He says it's because he doesn't really work all those hours; he just shows up. Only once during that summer did Steve visibly suffer from exhaustion, mental and physical. The result was that he completely lost his voice, a real handicap for a man who considers yelling at everybody in the control room his favorite sport.

I never minded Steve lying to me. Bosses lie to employees all the time. I can't get angry. They do it only for reasons of national security, or to protect me for that which I need not worry my pretty little head about. There is one lie he told me, however, that I have numbered and filed away under the heading: "REVENGE—A FUTURES FILE." Steve told me we were going to have lots and lots of fun that summer. One day I'll get him for that one.

Senior producers would be Karen Curry from *Today* and Cheryl Gould from *Overnight.* By mid-June, the show was staffed, mostly with women. Steve likes to hire women and sometimes, when he really likes a woman, he calls her by a masculine nickname to show his approval (I know, I know—but at least he hires women).

Press releases about *Summer Sunday* had already been mailed to the people at newspapers, wire services and magazines who make their living writing about that which most of them have never done—television. In late June, Andrea and I met in New York to have our pictures taken for the publicity photos and newspaper ads. When we got to the photography studio, an earnest young man from NBC's advertising department proudly showed us the layouts for the ads NBC planned to run. Andrea and I would sit—perch, rather—on top of suitcases on top of a map of the United States. Our legs, he explained, would be cutely crossed at the knees, and we would both wear cute, short skirts. Underneath us would be this line: "NBC TOLD LINDA AND ANDREA TO HIT THE ROAD." And oh, yes—we would be smiling. Cute. Would Tom Brokaw perch on a suitcase? Would John Chancellor flash a little knee? Would Edward R. Murrow smile while somebody said, "CBS told Eddie to hit the road"? When NBC had said it wanted a news program anchored by two women, it had not said we were supposed to do *Gidget Goes Network*. Even when their hearts are in the right place, their heads are sometimes slow to follow.

Happily, Andrea and I were able to persuade him to shoot the ad another way, and to restore his belief that all women in our business are bitches.

Besides, we had more compelling things about which to get crazy. It's dandy to have a truck so smart it can send what you show and say from anywhere. It's even better when you have something worthwhile to send.

Unlike *Overnight, Summer Sunday* would have money. You don't buy that kind of high-tech, magic truck at Toys-R-Us. If money would not be a problem, neither would content; for every minute of the one-hour program, there were at least a dozen plans about how to fill it. Because no one wanted to give up his or her idea of what to do in any particular *one* of the fifty-six minutes (in television, an hour is never really an hour), and because nobody wanted to veto an idea belonging to and cherished by someone with the power to hire, fire or hit you, the decision was made to discriminate against none. We would do them all. What was so wrong about putting a twelve-hour program into one hour? Hadn't they said we could spend money? What more did we need? Eleven more hours, said the devil.

Some of the ideas were good ones. The very best, in my opinion, was the idea of trading places. In this segment, by some stroke of blessed simplicity called "Trading Places," a person currently *in* the news would be given a chance to ask questions of reporters who had written about him. Another segment, called "Face-Off," would show two people in the news who disagreed about something having a feisty go at each other—we hoped. The point of the segment was confrontation, which is impossible to guarantee and no good if it's manufactured. Besides, it's *damn near impossible* to manufacture an eight-minute confrontation. Just about the time the adversaries are getting warmed up, it's time to call a halt and get on with the show.

Then there was "Behind the News." In this, a correspondent like Brian Ross was supposed to come on the show and tell how he got that story. Since Brian Ross is an investigative reporter who concentrates on union crimes, organized crime and government crooks, it was going to be downright interesting to hear him explain on national television how he got those stories—and then see how he ever got another one. Nor would I volunteer to start up ol' Brian's bicycle the morning after he'd "told all" to several million people, just so they could feel they were "Behind the News." A few years before that, Brian Ross had been moved into the office next to mine, at which time I had moved my desk to the side of the room opposite the wall between the two of us. I like Brian and I approve of that kind of reporting, but I do not wish to find my name at the end of a sentence which begins: "Also among the dead were . . ."

Finally, there was "The News Quiz." The less said about this crackerjack idea the better, but I went along with it—after so many years working in television, words like "coward" just roll off my back. The original plan for this completely new and different segment was to have several reporters compete, game-show style, to see who knew more about the news of the week. "Marvin Kalb—come on down." When word of the news quiz hit the papers, a joyful noise erupted at the other television news organizations. As I recall, even *Entertainment Tonight* snickered at "The News Quiz." Immediately, everybody we ever knew called to suggest names for the segment. "Beat the Press," "The Ratings Game": those were the least offensive suggestions. At NBC, the feeling of most correspondents was: "If I'd wanted to be Monty Hall, I would have learned to smile." Nobody was smiling.

The idea was altered. The new plan was this. Before each commercial, Andrea or I would ask viewers a question about the news. For the answer, they'd have to wait until after the commercial break. Some thought this might encourage people to stick around through the commercial, if not the program. It helps to remember that the game of Trivial Pursuit was a hot item at that time, which was a good thing, since this idea was nothing if not trivial. On the first program, I got to ask the question: "Which of the three remaining candidates for the Democratic presidential nomination is tallest—Senator Gary Hart, the Reverend Jesse Jackson, or Walter Mondale?" In case you're interested, the answer is Jesse Jackson. And, for what it's worth, Ronald Reagan is taller than all of them. I consider it a high-water mark in my career as a serious journalist.

Notice how I eased into the subject of the first show. "The News Quiz" was nowhere close to being our showstopper. I'll work my way up to that. Another part of the first *Summer Sunday* show was a segment about the economy, reported by Mike Jensen, live, from the floor of the New York Stock Exchange, a fine idea except for one tiny, tiny detail. It was a Sunday evening. Mike Jensen got to stand all alone on an empty floor, knowing that anything he had to say would be lost in the noise of everybody at home saying stuff like, "Why's he standing in that empty room, Martha?"

In another part of the program, we featured a story about the fun having gone out of professional baseball. I introduced the story, then introduced the correspondent, Mike Leonard, who was standing in an empty Wrigley Field, the game having ended several hours before. It didn't matter, since Mike was there *live,* which was fortunate because at that hour, nothing else in Wrigley Field was. I threw it to Mike, who threw it to the tape he'd shot earlier, when a baseball game had taken place. The tape played, then Mike came back on camera to talk and to throw it back to me, live, in Washington, D.C. I finished and threw it to Andrea, who then threw it to a commercial. By golly, you had to be quick to separate their game from ours. Probably the only time I'll pitch in the majors.

The Beach Boys were on the show, live. But they

wouldn't sing. That was a disappointment. We'd asked them to be on the program because James Watt, the former secretary of the interior, had agreed to appear. One year before, Watt had refused to allow the Beach Boys to perform on the Mall in Washington (right where we sat) for the Fourth of July celebration. Watt seemed to think the Beach Boys were a bad influence—to James Watt, kids who liked the Beach Boys were just one step away from listening to Mick Jagger and bad-mouthing their country, so he asked Wayne Newton to sing instead. Now, a year after the contretemps, we thought—I'm being loose with the word "thought"—it would be lively television to have Watt and the Beach Boys on the same program, in the same city, on the same Mall, and only three days away from the Fourth of July. Fireworks, that's what we had in mind.

As bad fortune would have it, the Beach Boys were going to be in Florida that day. No problem. We'd have Watt and the Beach Boys talk to each other through the magic of television, from Washington to Miami, live. As worse fortune would have it, we discovered, too late, that the Beach Boys would not, under any circumstances or through any technology, talk to James Watt, and James Watt had even less to say to them. The result: James Watt talked to George McGovern. The Beach Boys talked to Andrea Mitchell. Nobody won but Wayne Newton.

Technically, the first show was a mess. Microphones sometimes did not work, especially when no one turned them on. From time to time a camera pointed in the opposite direction from its intended target. Cues were missed. Some cues were ignored. A few were never given. I do not blame the technicians, nor do I blame

George Paul, the director, even if the idea to have people behind Andrea and me *was* his idea. It worked this way: Andrea and I sat in deck chairs, roughly near the middle of the Mall in Washington, which is bounded by the Lincoln Memorial at one end and the Capitol at the other. Twenty yards or so behind us was a rope, and behind the rope were people. By that I mean *real* people—television talk, again. It was thought the presence of real people would add a certain Reality. It did. What could be more real than talking to a camera while people behind you wave to Mom, make faces and shoot you the finger? I'm not sure the inclusion of real people behind us was George's idea. I *am* sure he did the best he could, under the circumstances, and if I say it was a mess, technically, I add that, comparatively speaking, the technology fairly shined when I remember how often the editorial content and the two anchors stunk. We made some poor choices, even if we made them for what, at the time, seemed to be good reasons.

The segment responsible for making that edition of *Summer Sunday* an instant classic, however, at least among our colleagues—it was to television news what the Edsel was to the auto industry—was the segment with Hu Na and Rosa Maria, may they rest in peace.

The show aired on July 1, which, by television or government standards, was close enough to the Fourth to warrant taking as our theme the ever-popular if somewhat broad subject of America. As a subheading, we picked, among other things, the topic of immigration. The segment began with a picture story edited by John Long, an NBC videotape editor based in Miami. He took Neil Diamond's song "America," and edited to it pictures, still and moving, from Ellis Island, Hester

Street and Miami, where Jews, Haitians, Cubans and Bahamians were disturbing the status quo of all those other immigrants—British, Spanish, French, Irish—who'd gotten there first. It was a wonderful reminder that we truly are a nation of immigrants, and it reminded in a way words often cannot.

It was to be followed by an interview with Hu Na, a Chinese tennis player who'd defected a year before. Hu Na was in Detroit, and would not or could not come to Washington, but it didn't matter. Television would bring Hu Na to Washington, where she would be interviewed by Andrea. That would be followed by an interview with a refugee from El Salvador who was in this country illegally. She would be called "Rosa Maria," even though it was not her name; the point was that Hu Na could request and get asylum in the United States because she was fleeing a Communist dictatorship—in a Yuppie world, it didn't hurt that she played tennis—while Rosa Maria was denied political asylum because she was fleeing a right-wing dictatorship that the United States government happened to support (also, she had a lousy backhand).

As a comment on practical politics, it was a sound idea. The segment began. "America" played and a mood was created. Andrea, in Washington, introduced Hu Na, in Detroit; then Andrea asked her first question. "How do you like it here in America, Hu Na?"

"Please," said Hu Na.

"I *said,*" said Andrea, "how do you like it here in America?"

"Please," said Hu Na. Andrea repeated the question a third time.

"I don't understand," said Hu Na. This time Andrea raised her voice. It is a long way from the Mall to

Detroit. No help. Now Hu Na said nothing at all. Andrea tried a different question. Same silence. Andrea smoothly explained to the audience that there must be technical difficulties. She was partly right. There *were* technical difficulties. One of them was the fact that Andrea could hear Hu Na only half the time. Another was the fact that nothing was being said at the other end. However, about this time it began to dawn on the rest of us that there was an even bigger difficulty, something else entirely.

Hu Na *could not speak English*, or, if she could, it had left her for the moment (an excuse I wish I'd thought of first). In awe, we began to understand what was going on, right there on national television, before God, woman, man and child.

It was quite simple. A woman who could not hear was interviewing a woman who could not speak. This *was* completely new and different.

Things really began to pick up then. Andrea quickly ended her meaningful dialogue with Hu Na and turned to Rosa Maria, who, since she was sitting next to Andrea, was at least within hearing distance. Now you must know that Rosa Maria was afraid immigration officers would see her face, track her down and send her back to El Salvador to be shot by the dictatorship-that-wasn't (since we were supporting it and we don't support dictators). Rosa Maria wanted to be disguised. It seemed reasonable to us. We bought a wig and a pair of sunglasses, but at the last minute, Rosa Maria decided that wasn't the disguise she wanted. She wanted a hat. Someone ran to a nearby folk festival and returned with a big straw hat, real big, all brim. Instead of using it to cast a shadow upon her face, Rosa Maria elected to put most of her face into the crown, thus giving a fine imitation of a woman wearing a hubcap instead of a head. As Rosa Maria had done this while Andrea was doing her tar-baby routine with Hu Na, it wasn't until Andrea turned to ask her first question of Rosa Maria that she got a look at the woman, hubcapped.

I will always believe Andrea was still too stunned by the Hu Na business to know precisely what she was doing, because Andrea Mitchell is one smart woman—but what she did right then was nothing. That is, she went ahead with the interview, never mentioning the hat, never seeming to notice she was interviewing a hubcap. She probably was too grateful it could speak English to care whether it was a hubcap, illegal alien or cauliflower quiche. Unintentionally, it provided one of television's funniest moments. Later, when we watched the tape, no one laughed louder than Andrea, and we were able to stop her on her way to the ladies' room and take away the razor blade without causing a scene.

The next week, George Lewis and Lloyd Dobyns offered me one hundred dollars if I could find a way to include Rosa Maria's hat as a casual, unmentioned prop somewhere on the set of every edition of *Summer Sunday*. Maybe if they'd offered two hundred dollars I wouldn't have given Andrea their home addresses and offered to sharpen her razor, for free.

After the first program, we held a few truths to be self-evident, if slow to sink in. Our secret weapon was not enough. A truck is not a program. A truck is a truck. We needed more than flashy toys. We needed something to say, and we needed to limit a one-hour program to one hour's worth of programming ideas. Certain completely new and different concepts were allowed to creep away in the dark of night. At the head of that particular parade was "The News Quiz." Somehow, we managed to keep our grief in check. We decided that each program would have a theme, but from now on, we would do our best to whittle themes down to something a bit more clearly defined than "America." Since the location of each show had already been chosen, the theme of each show, by necessity, would be dictated by location, which had been dictated by our superiors, or the capacity of the truck's gas tank. I never asked which.

Our next show would be broadcast from North Carolina. We were determined to keep moving, despite what Tom Shales, television critic for the Washington *Post,* wrote about our first effort.

> Keep on moving, yes, like the flimflam man who has to get out of town in a hurry or face the sheriff and his bloodhounds. Fortunately, this colossally pointless NBC News show comes equipped with a truck for fast getaways. Next Sunday, *Summer* goes to North Carolina. That is, if the caravan isn't met at the border and turned away by civic-minded state police. Ellerbee said, rather curiously, Sunday: "It would be wise to remember that, considering bad news, it is never out of style to at least think about burning the messenger." It sounded as if she were daring people to torch the truck.

Shales went on to say a lot of other *less* complimentary things about our show, but you get the drift. It would have been easier to get angry at him if only he'd been wrong.

What the hell. We went to North Carolina anyway.

This is no business for the faint of heart, and besides, it wasn't so bad in North Carolina. To begin with, they let us in. This time, our theme was "The New South." You can't say things about the New South without saying things about the Old South, and that meant saying things about black people and white people, and what happened in the South when one side got the notion to even the odds some.

Somebody told us it was twenty years since the historic "march" in Selma, Alabama, a march in which white police turned their dogs, horses, nightsticks and water hoses on black people so misinformed as to think they remembered something in the Constitution about equal rights. It seemed a good starting point for our program: twenty years beyond Selma, what had or had not changed? It turned out it was only nineteen years since the Selma march, but it didn't matter, because the story was good even if the math wasn't. Bigotry or its dissolution is never a bad story.

Nineteen years earlier, Richard Valeriani had covered the Selma march for NBC News. Improbably, he was still a correspondent for NBC News. Whether it was the occasional example of managerial wisdom or merely bureaucratic accident didn't matter—Richard Valeriani was alive, available and willing. That he was a good reporter was gravy. We asked him to go back to Selma for *Summer Sunday.* We had pictures of Valeriani from his trip to Selma nineteen years ago. The pictures weren't terribly flattering—Valeriani had had the gall to report what white people were doing to black people in Selma, and so you couldn't see his face too well because of the bandages covering the parts that some of Selma's citizens had tried to rearrange. We thought we'd show the pictures, anyway, and to hell with Valeriani's pretty face.

This time, when Richard Valeriani got to Selma, they put his picture on the front page of the local newspaper. They did not choose the picture in which he was bandaged. This time, the mayor of Selma asked Valeriani to go to dinner with him. The mayor was the same man who'd been mayor nineteen years ago, but *this time* the mayor's reelection was in doubt. His opponent was a black man who'd been a leader in the march; the election was scheduled for just two days after the program went on the air; and the word around town was that this Negro might actually win, so the mayor spent a lot of time telling Valeriani how happy he was to see him, how happy everybody in Selma was to see him. Valeriani reported most of this on *Summer Sunday*. The report included the fact that almost every white person he met wanted to assure him how much things had changed in Selma and how it was time to stop bringing up that march. All that, they said, had happened a very long time ago. Two days later, Selma reelected the mayor, the same mayor they'd had *a very long time ago*.

We got through the second program without too many technical glitches and with a very fine piece by John Long, the videotape editor who had put together the "America" piece. Long and a camera crew had spent a week driving through the South, avoiding cities, concentrating on the rural South, and taking pictures as they went along. Then he'd combined what he'd seen in 1984 with what he'd seen in 1963 and edited the whole thing to "It's Not Easy Being Green," which is not about being green at all, of course, but about being different. It was a compelling piece of work and we led the show with it. However, giving a videotape editor the responsibility of putting together the lead story was too new and different for management. There were complaints. The idea that technicians could also be journalists was not a popular one among my superiors or the technicians' superiors, but I know one thing—watching the image of a black child sitting on a fence somewhere in Alabama, with a face that kept changing while in the background, a voice sang, "When green is all there is to be, then green is good enough for me"—I knew that piece said something and said it more clearly than any script I'd ever written.

While we may have struck a small blow for technicians that Sunday, demon technology struck its own blow the very next week. It happened during "Trading Places," our strongest segment. On the first program, Senator Gary Hart had questioned reporters covering his campaign and raised damn fine questions about how politics is covered these days. On the second program, the Reverend Jesse Jackson had asked reporters covering *his* campaign to explain, if they could, why, when writing about him, the word "candidate" was always preceded by the word "black." Both the question and the answers made you stop and think. That is called good television journalism.

The third program would be broadcast from San Francisco, where the Democratic National Convention was to take place, beginning the next day. This time, the man scheduled to trade places was not a candidate, but Louis Farrakhan, a Black Muslim minister who had made headlines and enemies with his anti-Semitic remarks. What made the story bigger was the apparent friendship between Farrakhan and Jesse Jackson, who had refused to renounce Farrakhan in a way that was satisfactory to his critics. Some black people supported

Farrakhan, other black people did not. He had been criticized on the air and in print by most of the national news organizations, most of which are run by white people. Inside NBC News, we debated the decision to put Farrakhan on "Trading Places." Some thought it made no sense to give airtime to a fanatic; others thought it made no sense to ignore a fanatic. It was more difficult to find someone in authority at NBC News who thought Farrakhan *wasn't* a fanatic. In case it has escaped your notice, it is also difficult at NBC News to find black people in authority, which is also true for the other networks.

Farrakhan was scheduled to question Nat Hentoff of the *Village Voice,* David Nyhan of the Boston *Globe* and Ken Bode of NBC News. None of them is black. I would moderate the questioning, and if I appear to be black on your television set, it probably needs adjusting.

Everything was set. We were in San Francisco. The other reporters were in San Francisco. Farrakhan would arrive on Saturday night, in plenty of time for Sunday's show. Then we got a telephone call. Farrakhan would appear on the show, but he would *not* come to San Francisco. If we wanted him we must settle for Louis Farrakhan in Chicago, asking questions of reporters in San Francisco, linked by live television. ("Please," said Hu Na.)

Farrakhan stayed in Chicago. The segment stayed in our program. Sunday came. The show began with a historical piece by John Hart, one of the most elegant writers in television or, I suspect, out of it. He set the premise that the 1968 Democratic convention in Chicago had been a watershed for the party, that it had begun a process of separation within the party, and that, in 1984, the different groups which, combined, accounted for the strength of the Democrats—the blacks, women, Jews and unions—might now be tearing the party apart. Several reports followed Hart's, then it was time for Farrakhan to trade places. I introduced him, explained that Farrakhan was in Chicago and we were in San Francisco, introduced the reporters, and told Farrakhan to ask his first question. He did.

And I was the only person on the set who could hear him.

Each of the three reporters sitting next to me had been outfitted with a little gizmo that goes in the ear and works, more or less, as an open telephone line over which all parties can hear each other. That is how it is supposed to work. Mine did. Theirs didn't. While people in the control room tried to fix the problem, I explained it to the audience and attempted to repeat what Farrakhan was asking, accomplishing little more than treating the audience to a fine demonstration of why I will never find work as a simultaneous translator at the United Nations. Was this why the U.N. never got anything done, I wondered?

Next, I tried taking the gizmo out of my ear and sticking it, literally, into Nat Hentoff's ear. I'd never written anything about Farrakhan, but Hentoff had, and Farrakhan was taking exception to every bit of it, commas included. That was the purpose of "Trading Places." It would have helped if the gizmo (all right—it's called an I.F.B., which is short for interrupted feedback. Feel better?) hadn't kept falling out of Hentoff's ear, usually during the crucial parts of what was being said. I kept sticking the thing back in his ear, but soon it was clear the control room couldn't fix whatever was wrong, and no matter what I did, and no matter whose ear I assaulted, only one of the four of us was going to be able to hear Farrakhan at any one time. There was Louis Farrakhan, in Chicago, demanding to be told what was fair about the coverage given him, and here were these three reporters in San Francisco demanding the right to defend what they'd written, and all that stood in the way was television.

Later, I decided to see if I could find out how such a thing had come to be. It took a while and the answer turned out to be human and not technical. The technician on the set in San Francisco, whose job it had been to hook up the I.F.B.'s, did not work for *Summer Sunday*. The network saved money by using a different technical crew each week, hired locally, which also accounted for the fact that one stage manager in North Carolina was a theology student who needed some extra cash.

Since the San Francisco technician did not work for *Summer Sunday,* nobody had bothered to explain to him precisely what was supposed to happen during that segment. All he'd been told was to wire up four I.F.B.'s and put them in the ears of three guests, and me. That he'd done, and then the man had decided to do us a favor. He knew I was used to the thing, but he figured it might confuse the other three if they heard voices in their ears. (Did he think Ken Bode wrote for a newspaper?) He thought it would be better if they weren't confused, so he'd shut off their I.F.B.'s, and then he'd taken off his headset and left to do the next thing he'd been told to do, pleased he'd had the sense to do us a favor, *to think,* instead of being just another button pusher, the way they wanted him to be. The moral of the story is this: If all you want is a button pusher, hire another button to do the pushing. Humans can't be trusted not to think.

The mail started arriving about three days after the show. Nobody seemed to believe a big-time outfit like NBC couldn't make the equipment work, therefore what had happened had been deliberately arranged, so as to embarrass Farrakhan. Rabbis wrote to let me know they hated Louis Farrakhan, but now they hated me even more, because this was America and hadn't I ever heard of freedom of speech, or did I think it was reserved for snotty, undeserving, un-American television reporters named Ellerbee? Nice, patriotic people wrote to say they'd never again watch such an unfair network. The most flattering word anybody used to describe me was irresponsible. I was spared the pain of reading most of the letters about me, because most of them were sent to the president of NBC News, the president of NBC, the president of RCA and *the* president; and I've no doubt all those men defended me to the hilt. The pure of heart will believe anything.

Anyway, I should have known the San Francisco show was going to have trouble. Just before the program I went to get made-up, and when I returned to the set, someone had stolen my stuffed duck.

*Summer Sunday* was not totally an exercise in damage control. There were programs where nothing much went wrong—not exactly the same as everything going right—and there were programs where some things continued to go wrong, but in television we are taught to take no prisoners and move on to the next show. Still, there are consequences.

We were in Dallas. It was Sunday again. I swear I don't remember another summer with so many Sundays. This time it was the Republicans' turn to convene, and our subject was the incestuous relationship which had grown up between television and political conventions, a pretty good topic—certainly a better topic than the imminent coronation of Ronald Reagan, a story in which there was no second line.

By that time, *Summer Sunday* was, forgive me, on a *roll.* Each show was stronger than the one before. Some of them were plain good, and we had done our best show the week before, we thought. That show had been broadcast from Max Yasgur's cornfield in upstate New York, the site, fifteen years earlier, of an event called Woodstock, even if the town called Woodstock insisted on being fifty miles from the event. The fifteenth anniversary was the peg, but the point of the program was to look at that time we like to call the "sixties," no matter that a good portion of what happened during that time insisted on happening in the seventies. The question was whether *anything* that had happened back then caused permanent change, or had the whole thing been no more than a cultural hiccup? I turned forty that week, and chose to see the "Woodstock" program as a birthday gift from me to me, because the subject was one which had interested me for years and one I'd wanted to write about.

In 1969, I was living in Eagle Pass, Texas. I had a five-month-old daughter and was pregnant again. In a few months I would be living in a commune in Alaska. For many of us who worked on the "Woodstock" program, the time around the Woodstock concert had been not so much the dawning but the high noon of the Age of Aquarius. We'd felt it was a time of enlightenment, or should be. Maybe it *was* the time of man, as the song said, or maybe it was just the time. Some of the staff of *Summer Sunday* had been at Woodstock. Some had fought in Vietnam. Others had stayed here, to protest. My coanchor, Andrea Mitchell, had worn a gas mask to her college graduation. We'd had the courage, then, of our convictions—or our confusions—and now, fifteen years later, we wanted to know what any of it had meant. I, for one, often wished I didn't know now what I didn't know then.

As we interviewed people of that time, the counter-cultural shock increased. Grace Slick, the outrageous lead singer of the Jefferson Airplane during those days, told us she couldn't stand, these days, being associated with a phenomenon called "hippies." Country Joe McDonald, who'd stood on a stage at Woodstock and sung, "What are we fighting for? Don't ask me. I don't give a damn. The next stop is Vietnam," told us in 1984 that when you get to be in your forties, things start to look different. The Hog Farm commune in Berkeley existed then and exists now, but now it runs an answering service and charges three hundred dollars a month room and board to people who live in the commune. Bobby Seale, the former Black Panther who, in 1969, had sat bound and gagged in a United States courtroom, on trial for conspiracy to disrupt the Democratic convention in Chicago, now worked to develop jobs for young people in Philadelphia—and wrote cookbooks. Richie Havens still sang "Here Comes the Sun," but now he did it for Kodak commercials. Had we quit the dream or had the dream quit us? Arlo Guthrie told us it was too soon to know and too late to tell. I wasn't sure what that meant, but it sounded like the pretty good start of a song. In 1969, I'd had answers. In 1984, I was becoming less sure of the questions. Putting Woodstock into focus was difficult for all of the barely-reconstructed-hippies-turned-establishment on *Summer Sunday*. According to one fellow on the program, "I've matured. You've changed. He's sold out."

Slick.

The worst part was the story we did about kids today. We'd interviewed young people on college campuses in Boston, Oklahoma, New York, Florida and Berkeley. One thought the name Bobby Seale sounded familiar, but she wasn't sure. Another said of Bob Dylan: "That's music, I think." Still another said the only thing she knew about Bobby Kennedy was that he was Jack and Ted's brother. Some students said it was a wild time that should never have happened, that it was important to have goals and direction. Most said it didn't accomplish much, that period, and that whatever had been accomplished was pretty much forgotten by the mid-seventies. A young MBA graduate described it as "a whole generation who didn't want to go into their father's business."

Listening to them, we were objective; we wanted to throw up. God, it was depressing. In 1969, Sirhan Sirhan was on trial for the murder of Bobby Kennedy, James Earl Ray was on trial for the murder of the Reverend Dr. Martin Luther King and the Army was investigating the massacre at My Lai. In the summer of 1984, *Ghostbusters* was breaking all records at the box office, and the two biggest names in the news were tennis's bad boy, John McEnroe, and Vanessa Williams, a defrocked Miss America who'd had her crown removed for the sin of removing her frock and posing nude with another woman. Joan Baez told us those years were a honeymoon. If she was right, then it looked like the honeymoon was over. It said something that on the day of the show, we carpooled from New

York to Max Yasgur's cornfield—in limousines. It said something that the town had changed its zoning laws to make certain another Woodstock never happened again, at least not there. But it also said something that while we were on the air, there was a group of young people behind us, demonstrating; one of them carried a sign that read: "EL SALVADOR IS SPANISH FOR VIETNAM."

Finally, there was the local farmer whose barn had been invaded by hippies smoking a controlled substance in 1969. When questioned about Woodstock, he looked into the camera rather wistfully from his seat on his tractor, and said, "Oh, I don't know. I wish they'd have another one. Kinda livened things up a bit."

Had we sold out? I still don't know the answer but I'd welcome the opportunity to rephrase the question. One thing, though, *was* clear: the "Woodstock" program, involving us all as it did, was the best program we'd done all summer. By the time we hit Dallas, I was starting to feel pretty good about *Summer Sunday*.

Just off the floor of the convention, I ran into an NBC executive, who took time out from a busy schedule to say, "Linda, dear, I'm your friend, and as a friend, I wonder if you know the damage you've done to your career this summer."

I allowed as how I hadn't known that, but I sure did appreciate a friend telling me—*an hour* before I went on the air to damage myself once more. Grateful didn't begin to describe my reaction.

It's a wonderful business, really it is.

All I remember about the Dallas program is the graceful way Tom Brokaw answered an ungraceful question. Because our subject was politics *and* television, I interviewed Tom about the high stakes involved in convention coverage. I asked him how he accounted for the fact that the NBC News convention coverage, anchored by Tom Brokaw, had come in third in a three-horse ratings race? Without a blink or pause, Brokaw answered me.

"Statistical error."

After Dallas, only one show remained, and it would be broadcast from New Orleans, a city which beats the hell out of Dallas on any level you'd care to name, but then, people from Houston may not be counted objective on this subject. I've skipped over programs that were broadcast from Baltimore, Los Angeles, and once again, Washington, D.C. Each of them had its moments, including one in which I interviewed the vice president of NBC Sports, whose job it was to bid for television rights to the 1988 Olympics in Calgary. Representing my very own network, the man had bid 380 million dollars, and lost. I could have come away from the interview unscathed had I stopped right then, but, instead, I asked the man if, in the act of writing down a bid of 380 million dollars, he had taken the time to write out all the zeros. Mike Wallace would not have asked that. It may have had something to do with the remark later, about the damage I'd done myself that summer. (If you're interested—he had *not* written down the zeros.)

New Orleans. The last show. The last Sunday of the summer. We pretended we went there for journalism, which was a lie. We went there for the food, and apart from the food, I carry three memories from that last show.

First, there was the *Natchez*. The show was broadcast from the levee; we were sandwiched between the French Quarter and the Mississippi River. Our subject was water: too much water, not enough water, the quality of water, the sport of water, the poetry of water, and, in one instance, the effect of water on the weather. During that segment, I interviewed a meteorologist. Until a few minutes before I interviewed the meteorologist, I believed I was going to interview a television weatherman. It was my own fault. I'd gotten wrapped up working on some other parts of the show and put off reading about the man I was going to interview. I wasn't worried because I was *certain* at the last meeting (there were so many, God) we had agreed it was going to be a television weatherman, in which case I already knew what I wanted to ask him—How come those bozos couldn't tell me whether it was going to rain, and then shut up? Why couldn't they keep high pressures, low pressures and radar-screen jargon to themselves? Unless there's at least a sixty-forty chance a hurricane is headed for your block, all that stuff is boring, and worse—it takes up time on television I could use to say many important things which *do* count, especially to me. Perhaps solely to me.

He wasn't a television weatherman, however. He was a meteorologist, a professor and a serious person, who had come to inform and no doubt would have—we'll never know for sure. Thirty seconds into his first answer, the *Natchez,* a paddle wheeler roughly the same size as the average street fair in my neighborhood, began to pull away from where it was scenically docked, a couple of dozen yards from our set. I knew it pulled away, because it marked the moment with its whistle. It was a glorious whistle. It thrilled the ear. It also obliterated whatever it was the meteorologist was saying. I like to think the person on the *Natchez* in charge of blowing the whistle was intentionally having a bit of fun with the hotshot TV geeks from New York City. The timing was too perfect to be accidental. It was not until the meteorologist had recovered from the first blast and was halfway into explaining what he'd been trying to say in the first place, that the whistle blew again. It was a very long whistle. It was a very short interview.

All told, it may have been the high point of the summer. What could be more fitting than finally reaching the point where we were no longer being blown out of the water every week by technical difficulties and human flaws, only to be literally blown out of the water by a boat whistle? I was a happy woman. It made my damn day. It may have made my summer. All at once, I saw the beauty and the *justice* of live television, and I knew that the stranger responsible for my pleasure would be, for all time, my favorite whistle blower. Hurray for journalism.

The second memory is of Dan Webster, political producer for *Summer Sunday* and another survivor from *Overnight.* Danny's biggest problem is being too funny ever to be made a vice president in network television, too smart not to know it, and too dumb to find honest work. On the morning of the final Sunday, I was awakened in New Orleans by a call from NBC News in New York. They wanted to know if I knew that Truman Capote had died the day before. I said I did. Well, did I know Truman Capote was from New Orleans? I did. Well, did I know that on the Saturday before the first Sunday show, nine weeks ago, Lillian Hellman had died and she, too, was from New Orleans? Did I know that? I did, on both counts. All right, then. Did I want to change the essay I had written to close the final show, in order to include something pithy about

Truman and Lillian, seeing as how the coincidences involved were so, well, coincidental?

I did not. I believe I stressed the point. I said they should let *Nightly News* report the story. *Nightly News,* I reminded them, had lots of time because they got to go back on the air, the next day. We weren't going to get to do that, I mumbled. New York retreated, but only to regroup. As the day progressed, there were more calls. New York made a last-minute pitch. Danny took the call. "Can't you persuade her to say some little something about poor old Truman Capote, at least?"

"Only if he drowned," said Danny, and hung up.

It was a good summer, after all, because I spent it working with people like Dan Webster, people who cared and who tried, against poor odds and four kinds of silliness every day, to do their jobs as best they could and not forget how to laugh in the meantime. Those people also made me look better than I had a right to, and I owe them all. By the end of that summer, the swelled head I had brought along when I left *Overnight* had shrunk to nearly normal size, helped along by the knowledge I could be awful, right up there with the best of them.

The third and final memory is of what I *did* say at the end of the final *Summer Sunday.* My last words were, "It has been fun. It is now over. And so it goes."

They were the very same words Lloyd Dobyns had used at the end of the final program for *Weekend.* Of course, no one remembered, noticed or cared. Hell, they may have thought I was saying something completely new and different.

# THE I.T.P. FACTOR

It's all right letting yourself go as
long as you can get yourself back.
MICK JAGGER

Jim Bouton has been a lesson to us all. A dozen or so years ago, Bouton wrote a book about his experiences in professional baseball, a witty tale of how he and the other Boys of Summer behaved when they sent their halos to the cleaners and hit the road. When the book was published, Bouton barely escaped with his scalp. He did not escape with his job. Why? The answer is simple. Truth was one thing. What happened on the road was another. You don't write *that* about Mickey Mantle, even if it's true—especially if it's true. Yes, this chapter is about sex, travel and television news, but I've not written *everything* about what (or whom) any of us did in pursuit of holy journalism, and when I have been too precise I've not used names, for reasons that are as obvious to me as they ought to have been to Jim Bouton.

For example, on my way to one of the political conventions in 1976, a young and very healthy production assistant in the seat next to me announced to everyone on the flight her intention to have "a lot of really neat sex" during the convention. Later that same night, I saw the lady in a dark corner of a restaurant, having some "really neat" fun with the producer who had been seated behind us on the airplane. If I named her, I might be safe; she no longer works in television. If I named the fellow, well, I could wipe that silly grin off my face because *he* didn't leave the business. These days, he's a vice president at NBC News. These days, I'm not. Thanks, Bouton, for the warning.

Not everyone who travels plays around on the road. Some do. Some never do. However, it's understandable that husbands, wives and lovers of television news gypsies get a little worried if the gypsy is in, say, Bangkok, the sexual Disneyland of the world, a place where everything is offered to anyone at all times—at little or no cost. But then, not all husbands, wives and lovers are as wise—or practical—as my pal, Suzy. When Suzy married a veteran ABC newsman, a world traveler who'd seen everything twice, she let him know his rooster days were over; after all, Suzy had been on the road herself and knew a thing or two about roosters. As she explained it to him, his license was revoked; but during their wedding ceremony, at the part where they talk about "forsaking all others," she leaned over to her groom.

"Bangkok," whispered Suzy, "doesn't count."

On the theory that Bangkok does indeed count to many people, all I'm going to do here is tell a few stories, like the one about the network field producer and the fall of Saigon.

He operated out of a hotel in Saigon and, not surprisingly, the hotel had a bar. In the final weeks before the Americans pulled out in 1975, the producer somehow persuaded the hotel manager to list all costs having to do with bar girls as "telex" charges on the producer's bill. Under the circumstances, no one back in New York questioned the high cost of sending a telex from a war zone, or the number of them sent during a military retreat—*or* the huge amount of time the producer must have spent writing telexes. The network paid, and while many people who work for television networks have been paid to get screwed, he is the only one I know who was paid to get laid. I wouldn't tell you his name on a bet. It's an example of what made this country great and helped us win the war, right? Besides, all the producer was doing was taking righteous advantage of the I.T.P. Factor.

It's easier to explain what the I.T.P. Factor is than how or where it got started. Many people claim credit for inventing it, but not openly. I.T.P. is short for "Indignities To Person." It works this way. If the network sends you to Paris in May to cover a wine tasting, the I.T.P. Factor is zero. Naturally, the network seldom does anything remotely as wonderful as that. What is more common is that the network sends you to spend Christmas in Afghanistan. When that happens, the I.T.P. Factor is approximately five percent, depending on whether the hut you're sleeping in is also inhabited by goats. This means five percent over and above the actual costs incurred in getting the story will be spent soothing the indignities done to your person. And the network will pay, one way or the other. Sleeping with goats is an indignity to your person—for most of us. So is getting shot at. If they don't miss, the I.T.P. Factor may jump to an automatic thirty percent or more, depending on what they don't miss.

When looked at this way, the "telex" charges reported by the producer in Saigon are nothing more than a fair reflection of the I.T.P. Factor, and, in his case, the company got off cheap. If the pencil pushers see it differently, then that's another reason I cannot remember anybody's name. I wonder if there is a statute of limitations on expense-account vouchers?

Still, one must be careful. Nobody likes to remember the case of a certain field producer who turned a series of expense vouchers for trips made to the same city over a period of time. The trouble was, the receipts from his favorite restaurant there—receipts supposedly spanning a period of weeks—were numbered sequentially. It's an example of an annoying piece of detail someone in the business affairs office at the network might notice and, in this case, did.

Please don't think we're a bunch of cheats or that the company accountants are a bunch of machines who don't understand news and the job of gathering it. We're not, and they do, but they like it best when certain rules are followed and certain phrases are used, even when those certain rules and phrases don't exactly explain how it *really was*—out there in the field.

For instance, in the winter of 1973, WCBS New York assigned me the task of informing its viewing audience how New York City prostitutes were coping with the current cold spell. It happens every time there's a current cold spell, a lack of other news, and a new kid in the newsroom. I didn't know all that in 1973. I took the assignment. Finally, I found a prostitute willing to talk on camera. Because she could have been earning money during the time she was talking to us, I gave her twenty dollars for her trouble. We filmed. The story aired. I put in for the twenty dollars I'd paid her for her time. CBS refused to pay me, and clipped a haughty little note to my expense voucher, letting me know CBS did *not pay for news stories.* (Not then.) I explained in a second note that I hadn't paid for a news story; I'd paid for her time because it seemed to me to be the fair thing to do. She didn't have to talk to a television crew; she could have earned the money honestly. CBS sent me another nasty note, but this time an accountant who must have been a human being in another life took it on himself to call me. He thought someone should tell me, in case I didn't know, that while CBS did not pay for stories, it did pay for dinners. I caught on. The third time the voucher was turned in, it contained this item: "Dinner with whore—$20." I got my money.

It's all in how you phrase it, and the best example ever is the story about the time Jack Perkins moved from Hong Kong to the United States. In my trade, this story is legend, and if it's not true, it ought to be. I choose to believe it's true. Jack, a correspondent for NBC News, had been stationed in the Far East for several years. NBC decided it was time for him to come home. Jack cabled the New York accounting office: "Assume you will pay to move my family, furniture and junk from Hong Kong to California." New York cabled back that it would indeed pay for that, thus making NBC the only network ever to agree to pay for shipping a full-size Chinese junk across the Pacific. You just gotta phrase it right.

I never came close to Jack's junk, but in 1976, I did my best. NBC sent me, and hundreds of others, to New

York to cover the Democratic convention. The first night, I stayed at the New York Hilton. The next day I moved to another hotel—it doesn't matter why. After the convention ended, I returned to Washington, D.C. Two weeks later, the New York Hilton sent me a bill, a second notice, one of those which begins: "We're certain this has slipped by you, being the busy person you are, and if you've already sent us a check, please disregard this letter . . ."

The bill was for $27,647.89.

A tad high for one night. Even in New York. Even in a Hilton. Even if I *had* ordered a cheeseburger from room service. A frantic call to the hotel finally produced an explanation. It seemed the computer—you just knew a computer was involved here, somehow, didn't you?—had made a small mistake. The computer had accidentally billed me for *all* charges incurred by *all* NBC News employees who stayed at the Hilton during the convention. So sorry. I would be happy to know my real bill was $123.56. (I should have omitted the cheese on the burger.)

At that point, I did the right thing. I wrote out a check to the Hilton for $27,647.89. Then I Xeroxed my check, tore up the original and attached the Xeroxed copy to an NBC expense voucher, which I sent to the NBC accountants along with a note about being happy to help my company whenever it needed my help, but I would appreciate it if they could reimburse me for my trouble just as soon as possible—unless, of course, they needed me to cover next week's payroll. Considering the sense of humor of your average corporate accountant, I suppose I should feel lucky NBC agreed to give me back my $123.56, although I still think it was chintzy of them to bring up the cheese.

In defense of network accountants, sometimes the truth *is* the right way to phrase it. In January, 1981, I was sent to West Point to be one of ten NBC correspondents to cover the return of the Americans held hostage in Iran. It was a big, big deal, but on arrival it became apparent even to the most casual observer that ten correspondents were about eight too many, especially since the military wasn't going to let the media be at the airport when the plane carrying the hostages arrived. They could do that; it was a military airfield. They could also let military camera crews and other military personnel—and their families and friends—be at the airport to take pictures, and did. They were Americans; the media weren't—again. The night before the hostages were to arrive, I explained to the NBC producer in charge that I'd been wandering around the airfield—it wouldn't be closed off until dawn the next morning—and, what do you know, the view from the "old" control tower was wonderful, if you didn't mind the crumbling ladder you had to climb to reach the top and the flies you found when you got there. Nobody used the tower anymore; they'd built a new one about thirty yards away. The plane was scheduled to land, pull up to the area by the new tower, then the hostages would get off the plane—anyone who happened to be in the old tower with a camera would have an unblocked view of the entire event. It was suggested that NBC send a reporter and crew into the old tower about three in the morning, before the base was closed off to the media. All the crew would have to do was wait—and avoid detection. The producer in charge suggested the door to the old tower might be locked. It was suggested that someone seemed to have slipped the lock with a credit card, I don't know how. The producer, like the one in New York who had to deal with the button-maker caper, said I had his full permission to take—or try to take—my crew into the old tower—and that he'd never said that.

We went in at three-thirty in the morning, settled down in the cramped, dirty, abandoned tower room and spent the next four hours killing flies. Meanwhile, back at the NBC base at West Point, desk man Bob McCarthy, having heard the producer say he'd never admit to giving us permission to do what we were doing, collected bail money for the crew and me. Now that's what I call a newsman and a pal. We did not need the bail money; the only close call was when a helicopter circled the old tower, carrying a spotter with glasses.

During most of the seven hours, we lay in heaps on the floor, the camera crew covered by their parkas, the camera covered by my parka and me covered by a piece of Masonite. We tried to imitate debris, and it says nothing for our sartorial splendor that we succeeded so well. We would never have been caught had we not chosen to push our luck. When the plane landed, we crawled down the ladder and walked out onto the runway, camera rolling.

They didn't arrest us; it was too late. The plane was down, the deed was done. The military, after all, had not been able to restrict photographs to those made by itself and its friends. Soldiers escorted us to our car, which was parked by the buses that would carry the former hostages fifteen miles to West Point, and then left us—assuming we would make our way from there.

We did. When the buses, filled with former hostages, pulled out and into parade formation, there was a gap between the second and third bus, a gap that lasted about five seconds before being filled by a car carrying an NBC crew. We were *in* their parade. I drove, Geoff Weinstock kept shooting and we ended up with remarkable images of American faces, crowded together for the whole fifteen miles, banded together to welcome home some of their own. It was the beginning of a national "high": a compulsion to cheer, after months of what seemed to be a national humiliation. People wanted something to shout about. They had it now. I won't forget those faces and neither, I imagine, will the former hostages who saw them from the buses. The people along the road began to tie yellow ribbons on our car as we passed (it went that slowly, the parade) and we were thrilled—for some reason, the public usually isn't that glad to see us. Wasn't it nice of them to cheer a network television crew? Gee whiz. It took us five miles to figure it out and we might not have, even then, if the man hadn't shouted to us, "Way to go, Canada!" Canada?

Geoff Weinstock, the cameraman, caught on first. Geoff and his soundman were the NBC crew out of Boston. The Boston crew does a lot of shooting in Canada; it is the closest NBC crew to that country. Because of that, Geoff had put a Canadian flag decal on the side of his camera. He'd done it a year before, and forgotten about it. But the people on the parade route, seeing the flag on his camera, concluded we were *from* the country that, you will recall, recently had given sanctuary to some Americans at the Canadian embassy in Iran, then successfully smuggled them out of that country. The people who were cheering didn't like us any better than they normally did; they were cheering for Canada that day, not us. And I don't blame them.

We got extraordinary tape of the homecoming, and when I put in for a new parka—mine had been badly ripped in the course of protecting the camera—I phrased it right: "Please replace one parka—fatally wounded in the line of duty. Mission accomplished. Pictures made." What about the indignity to person suffered in spending the night with ten million flies in a rotting tower? What about the I.T.P. Factor? The truly observant should check the quality of the down in the new parka NBC bought me. On the other hand, for that story, I'd have paid money to be there. No matter what the military thinks, I, too, am an American.

A final story about the importance of getting the story and phrasing it right on the expense voucher: in May, 1981, NBC correspondent George Lewis was in Lisbon, covering a European trip of Ronald Reagan's secretary of defense, Caspar Weinberger. Word came the Pope had been shot. At the moment, George was the closest NBC correspondent to Rome and his was the closest NBC camera crew. George called New York. (To call "New York" means to call the main news desk at NBC News headquarters.) New York said for George to go to Rome immediately. He called the airport. There were no more flights that day. George called New York. New York said to charter a plane. George called the airport. The only company with a plane available right then was TAP, the Portuguese national airline, and the plane was a Boeing 727, which NBC could rent for $18,000. George called New York. New York said he should rent the 727. He called TAP: NBC would take the 727.

"Sorry," said TAP. "You can't." George explained that NBC would pay the $18,000. TAP explained that wasn't the problem. The problem was the crew. TAP didn't have a crew available that was checked out on a 727. It did, however, have a crew that was checked out on a Boeing 707, and, lucky for George, TAP also happened to have a spare 707, which it would rent to NBC for a mere *$23,000.* George called New York.

New York huddled with itself, then told George to charter the 707, but get moving, for godsakes. George called TAP.

"Fine," said the airline. "How will you be paying, sir?"

George said he didn't guess they'd take his American Express Card, by any chance? They would not. Cash, they said, would do nicely, as long as they were U.S. dollars. George called New York. What happened next is unclear, but very soon a swarthy man with a suitcase arrived at the hotel and handed George twenty-three thousand U.S. dollars. There are laws about having large amounts of foreign currency in Portugal, but George said it didn't seem the time to bring up the subject. He paid the airline.

By this time, an ABC crew had arranged to share the charter, the bill to be sorted out back in New York. They boarded—eight passengers on a plane meant to carry 144. Naturally, there was a full complement of flight attendants. The attendants outnumbered the passengers. The plane took off. George was asked if he'd like a drink. Slowing down for the first time in two hours, George said gin and tonic would be nice, thank you. The steward served him.

"That will be two dollars, sir." When George finished wiping gin and tonic off his suit, he asked to see the purser, who explained everything.

"It's very simple, sir. You didn't order the charter with the open bar."

"Silly me," said George. "I forgot. And how much would the charter with the open bar cost?"

"Oh, nothing extra at all. But you *do* have to specify ahead of time, sir. It's the rule."

According to George Lewis, the moral of this story is simple. If you're going to spend $23,000 to rent a plane, remember to ask for the one with the free booze. This is true because later, when George filled out his expense voucher, the only item New York refused to believe was the two dollars for the gin and tonic. Next time, George will phrase it right from the beginning.

If all these examples of the craziness of "the road" seem absurd, remember that our job, first and last, is to get the story. Not getting the story will get you fired long before the amount of money spent getting the story will ever raise an eyebrow. No, it's not the real world; it's television.

In the real world, I'm told, grown-ups do not travel with night-lights in their suitcases, at least I hope they don't. However, a number of grown-up reporters who travel with presidential candidates carry night-lights, and for fine reason—silly, but fine. For long periods of time, these people do not spend two nights in a row in the same hotel, town or state, and, as always, it's the little things that cause the most trouble. Like where the bathroom is located. In the middle of the night, this doesn't seem like a little thing. Lloyd Dobyns has never forgotten a certain night in Detroit. He woke up with a strong need to relieve himself and stumbled in the dark to what he believed to be the door to the bathroom. Finding it, he opened it and made his way to the place where he was equally sure the toilet was located, and standing there, butt-naked and smiling in the dark, he relieved his bladder—through the railing and onto the heads of the people still drinking in the lobby bar, some four floors below. He continues to insist the blame belongs to Portman, who designed all those hotels with atrium lobbies. He may be right. These days, however, he packs a night-light to help him find the bathroom in a strange hotel. That is his insurance. Mine is to wear a hat when I drink late at night in the lobby of Portman hotels.

Remembering where they put the bathroom is but one test put to the employee of a television network who is assigned to cover a presidential campaign. As it is not unusual to hit four towns in one day, more than one cameraman on the campaign trail will not go to bed until he is certain that there is a piece of paper on the table next to the bed on which is written vital information. Vital information may be defined as follows: Where am I, and why? Here is what may be written on the paper: "You are in Sacramento. You are covering Jimmy Carter." One sleeps better, knowing such information is readily at hand, believe me.

However, this manner of clear thinking and preparation means nothing if one happens to be overseas, not when New York decides to *make its move.* It's well-known to all reporters that some of the people paid to work the assignment desk in New York are paid for reasons having nothing to do with conscious thought. They are not all trolls; some desk people are smarter and nicer than any reporter. Some. Reuven Frank, during one of his terms as president of NBC News, wrote a memo aimed at the trolls on the New York desk, a memo directing them never, ever to begin a telephone call to an overseas employee with the words: "What time is it over there?" Also, said Reuven, it was not a good idea to wake someone up and then ask him if he'd seen what the wires were reporting. He said there were very few people who, while sleeping, had seen what the wires were reporting. He finished by reminding the people on the desk that no story was ever lost by thirty seconds' thought. It may have been too much to ask.

Let me explain about assignment desks, those who work on those desks, those in charge of them—and the occasional bureau chief. Most of those people are journalists, sound of judgment and clear of eye: they *can* think but their other job is to get everybody moving on a story, fast. When that doesn't happen and the network for which they work happens to get its ass kicked on a particular story, their asses are next in line—always—so they get jumpy, even the best of them. The worst of them get scared. It colors thinking.

Several years ago, there was a fellow in Washington, D.C., who could not relax unless every reporter, producer and crew was somewhere, covering something. The only time he felt good was when the bureau was empty, even if everybody was out covering stupid, useless hearings that would never make news and, therefore, never make air. His system worked until the day an Air Florida jet crashed into the 14th Street Bridge and NBC couldn't get a crew to cover it because all the NBC crews were locked inside hearing rooms, where the rules say you can't leave while the hearing is in session. NBC was eventually able to cover the story, but the man was never quite able to cover his ass. And, *he* was not an assignment editor; *he* was management.

Back to life on the road. At this point, I must admit I've never been assigned to a foreign bureau and have covered only a very few stories overseas, none of which will bring me glory, and for cause. Consider the Royal Wedding in 1981. Prince Charles married Lady Diana. I was there. So were nearly one hundred other NBC

News employees sent to London to help the nearly seventy-five NBC News employees who work there full-time. We didn't want to be caught short on a big story like this one. Besides, TV loves a costume party. I covered the wedding; I just didn't see the wedding. I was too busy covering it outside the church, asking people their opinions about the event. Inside, the event was covered by the BBC, live. Throughout the world, people watched. My family in Texas saw the ceremony. I still haven't. They tell me it was swell.

Probably it was a break for Anglo-American relations, me being outside the church, when you consider what happened the only other time I covered a royal event. That was in 1978, and I worked for *Weekend*. At the time, Reuven Frank was not president of NBC News, but executive producer of *Weekend*. He sent me to London to do a story about the House of Lords and the part it played in modern British government. I was thrilled. I'd never been to England, but had read plenty about the country and, in addition, had a fair command of the language. What could go wrong?

As part of our story, we planned to film the queen arriving to officially open Parliament's new session. It was her duty to do so. It was our pleasure to film it. As well you might imagine, the queen doesn't grab a taxi at the last minute, speed to Parliament, leap out, rush in and shout: "Go."

No, the queen arrives in a storybook coach, preceded by storybook troops and accompanied by all the hoopla the British do better than anyone. Since the BBC would be broadcasting the event live for the British audience, a platform had been erected for the BBC camera. Obviously, the best view to be had was the view from the BBC's platform. Using "Yank" charm and promises that we would never, ever get in their way, I persuaded the BBC crew to allow my camera crew and me to share their platform. They were as nice as they could be about the whole thing, and there never would have been any trouble if I had not, on catching my very first sight of the queen of England, stumbled into the BBC camera and knocked it over, shouting "Here she comes! Here she comes!" I maintain it was an innocent mistake. Anyway, I'm certain the British television audience must have seen the queen arrive at Parliament a million times before. Could one more time matter that much?

It's hard to believe such a small incident had anything to do with me not being allowed inside the church during the Royal Wedding. After all, they got over the Revolution, didn't they? NBC told me I was needed outside the church so I could cover the really important stuff, and my network wouldn't lie to me—not about the really important stuff.

Another time, working for *Weekend,* I went to Mexico, to the oil fields of Tabasco. The name of the story was "What's in It for Juana Morales?" Juana Morales was a Mexican peasant with seven children, an unemployed, unskilled husband—and an oil field in her backyard. In Mexico, the newly discovered oil belonged to the people in the sense that it was a nationalized industry, but it was run by Pemex, the national oil company, and the "people" saw little profit, if any. When the story aired, there also aired what is called a "Producer's Footnote," which was an invention of Reuven's whereby the producer of a story could come on camera and add a little comment of his own. In this case, the producer, Jim Gannon, said while it was widely reported that oil boomtowns like Villahermosa resembled the boomtowns of gold rush days, with wild women, barroom brawls, prostitution and such—well, it just wasn't so. He looked rather disappointed when he said it. I wouldn't dispute Jim for the world, but I suspect he didn't know about the Pemex pilots who'd flown us all over Mexico. They were a couple of swell fellows who swore they knew every single bar in the state of Tabasco, and most bars in Greenwich Village, New York City, where I live. Turned out they were mostly right, but I think Pemex was out of line using a word like "AWOL" just because two of them flew a Pemex plane to New York to make good their boast about the Village. Besides, we eventually returned their plane and their pilots, and without a scratch on either.

Obviously NBC still had faith in me or it wouldn't have sent me to Jamaica, one year after Edward Seaga's election as prime minister of that country, to see if Seaga had been able to improve the island's rotting economy or its almost nonexistent tourist business. I don't care what anybody tells you, it *did* take twelve days to check out all those beaches personally. You can't take a bureaucrat's word on something as important as that. Of course I had help. I had Allison Davis with me. That it took no longer than twelve days was a miracle.

In 1977, I was one of a dozen reporters who accompanied Senator Frank Church to Cuba. We arrived on the first U.S. military plane to land in Cuba in seventeen years, or, as Castro put it, the first to do so legally. Fidel Castro was our tour guide in Cuba. He insisted we visit "Finca Vigia," Hemingway's farm outside Havana, now a museum. Castro pointed out manuscripts, medals, letters, photographs—all kinds of memorabilia lying about, within reach of anyone who might decide to take a souvenir with him. I was impressed because Castro told us hundreds of Cubans came every week to see Hemingway's house. I thought of our own museums, with velvet ropes and such to keep people away from items they might steal. It occurred to me that any system in which people were so trustworthy they could be allowed to wander freely among such items without stealing them probably had something going for it. I wanted to know about that, so I asked Castro if they'd ever had any problems with people filching Hemingway's belongings.

"Certainly not," said Castro, "and we don't intend to. That's why Cubans are allowed only to look into the windows of the house."

Castro also took us to a distillery where, he said, Cubans were making scotch. Castro had decided any island that could make rum could make scotch, and so he ordered this to happen. He insisted we drink some of the Cuban "scotch." We did, and most of us regained full use of our limbs by nightfall. That night we went to a bar in old Havana. The walls of the bar were covered with graffiti. It was the only time I ever saw Bulgarian graffiti. Translated, it read, "WE ARE GRATEFUL TO THE SOVIET UNION FOR ITS FRIENDSHIP." While trying to read slogans about tractors and Che and ridding the world of capitalists and their running dogs, I came on something I took to be a sign of the eventual end of Castro's Cuba. Scratched on the wall, I found this:

VIVA EL FONZ

It was the only time in my life I felt I truly had seen the handwriting on the wall.

Once, NBC offered me the chance to be a full-time

foreign correspondent; I came that close to ordering my trenchcoat, the one with all the hand grenade loops, but the business had changed too much. Once upon a time, the Paris correspondent's job was to know and cover France. Now, the Paris correspondent is usually found in Beirut or Athens or some airport in between. When transmission by satellite began to be routine, the foreign correspondent became the most movable part of the operation. To be stationed in London is to be seldom in London. Correspondents are moved about as if they were so many windup chess pieces, and to New York—it's always just an inch on the map. I remember John Cochran, an NBC correspondent, telling me that in his first six months as a London-based reporter, he was in London three days. I had two small children at the time, and it seemed less than motherly of me to plunk down the kids in a country where they might not speak the language while I hotfooted it for the nearest airport.

Still, those trenchcoats are mighty appealing, and those foreign correspondents sure lead glamorous lives, eating guinea-pig stew in Nicaragua, sipping fancy wine in Cairo, going to chic dinner parties in Moscow, getting hosed down by water cannon in Warsaw. It took a veteran foreign correspondent to show me how really gauche I was. I remember the moment as if it were yesterday. It happened in a videotape editing room in NBC's London bureau. The videotape editor was Derek Wilkinson, but everybody calls him "the Wanker," a peculiarly British term for someone devoted to that special activity for which (it is said) no one need ever look his best. His nickname is not a reflection on his skill as an editor. I believe it has more to do with his attitude. Naturally, we got on well from the start.

It had been a long day. It would be a long night. We had littered the room with empty and half-empty coffee cups and had come to the conclusion it was time to start on the bottle of red wine the Wanker had brought with him. He said he brought the wine in case we encountered headwinds or some other barrier fate might put between us and our goal of getting that sucker on the air before old age took the both of us. Such was the mood in our editing room when we were joined by one of NBC News's European bureau chiefs, a veteran who had been around Europe as much as I had not. She saw our wine bottle and wanted to know what I thought of last year's Nouveau Beaujolais. I explained that I'd given it no thought at all, since I couldn't pronounce it, having only recently begun to expand my horizons beyond wine lists that read:

1. Red
2. White *

* Please order by number.

The first wine I'd ever tasted was Thunderbird. I'd liked it. Well, said the veteran, I could learn. The Wanker said it was doubtful. She offered a quick lesson, taking a cup from the table and pouring some of the Wanker's wine into it. While she didn't actually spit the wine in our faces, she did wince some, but you could see right away she didn't want to insult our taste in wine openly. She said it was an interesting little varietal, probably Algerian in origin, no matter what the label said, but it did need to mature some more. We told the Paris bureau chief we'd try to do better next time, and thanked her for her advice. She left. We went back to work. It crossed our minds to wonder if the wine might have tasted more mature if she hadn't poured it into and drunk it from a cup already half-filled with cold coffee, but we kept our mouths shut. The Wanker and I clearly didn't know shit about fancy wine.

If you're going to be a world-weary journalist, you've got to know the rules of the road and that the rules apply—even if the reporter is only going to take a ten-minute ride to city hall. The first is Weaver's Law, which states: Whenever several reporters share a cab on the way to an assignment, the reporter in the front seat always gets stuck with the fare. Then there is Weaver's Corollary: No matter how many reporters share a cab and no matter who pays, each puts in for the full fare on his expense voucher. I expect both rules will still apply, somehow, the first time they let reporters go along on the space shuttle. In journalism, tradition counts. That, too, is a rule.

Another rule of the road has to do with the hierarchy, and it's the same whether it's television or print. NBC News will get the secretary of defense on the phone faster than, say, KTUU, Anchorage. *The New York Times* will get the Senator's ear faster than the Beeville *Picayune* will. Joel Simms, of Chicago, covered Hubert Humphrey's last try at the presidency for a newly formed newspaper called *Chicago Today.* It had a small readership and no clout. Despite the fact Simms had been covering Humphrey, following his campaign for weeks, he seldom got any time alone with the senator, unlike the reporters from *The New York Times* or The Chicago *Tribune.* Finally, during a campaign stop in upper Michigan, Joel managed to corner Humphrey for a question or two.

"Senator," said Joel, "you don't know me, but I'm from *Chicago Today.*"

"Oh, my, my," said Humphrey, "you sure made good time, didn't you?"

The final rule of the road: People who travel for a television network have to be crazy or get that way fast. This rule explains many things, at least it is the only explanation I can think of for the telephone call Lloyd Dobyns got from Baghdad. As Lloyd tells it, he was fast asleep when the phone rang. At the other end was Pete Simmons, a first-class journalist, world-class producer and no-class Texan. (Texans are permitted to speak that way about other Texans.) He's also Lloyd's best friend. Pete was in Baghdad covering the Iran-Iraq war for ABC News. Pete offered no specific reason for the call, assured Lloyd he had nothing new or important to tell him, and spent the next half-hour proving it. Lloyd, wanting to sleep but not wanting to be rude—yet—tried to make conversation to stay awake. He asked Pete what the funny noises in the background were. Pete said he guessed it was the bombs.

"How nice for you," said Lloyd. "Mind telling me what bombs?"

Well, it seemed there was this air raid taking place at the moment and, after giving it some thought, Pete had decided hiding under the bed in his hotel room would be smarter than running into the street and asking the Iranian Air Force to respect his journalistic goddamned neutrality and stop shooting at him. Anyway, the bed had been closer. Pretty soon it had gotten boring down there, so Pete had pulled the telephone under the bed and, having nothing better to do right then, thought he'd pass the time by calling his old pal Lloyd back in New York, just to see what was new there because in Baghdad there was nothing—absolutely nothing—new: just another perfect day in the Middle East.

Overseas, mental illness can be a real plus. The ability to maintain a sufficiently loose grip on reality is the mark of the veteran foreign correspondent, the true television journalist and the seriously unwell, and accounts for the goldfish NBC shipped to Central America. It's probable that the NBC field producer whose idea it was had spent too many adventure-packed days in what we generally refer to as "war-torn El Salvador," because one morning he decided to airfreight goldfish into the country. When the fish arrived, he stocked the pond in the courtyard of the Camino Real Hotel in San Salvador, home away from home for American reporters covering the current unpleasantness. Two months later, when NBC said it was time for him to come home for a while, he didn't leave until he'd fully trained some of the hotel staff in caring for the creatures, because you never knew when goldfish might come in handy in a civil war. Should you be in the neighborhood, stop by the pond and say hello to the fish. We work for the same company.

And should you need final proof that travel does not broaden the mind as often as it causes brain damage, I offer the story of the Iranian mob and how it came to yell about taxation in America. Consider it not as an aberration but as a textbook case.

One day, during the time when Americans were being held prisoner at the U.S. embassy in Tehran, a group of American reporters watched as Iranians with bullhorns taught the Iranian crowd outside the embassy to chant in English. It had to be in English because the point was to show off for the American TV cameras. Farsi wouldn't play in Des Moines. The "cheerleaders" warmed up the crown with "Down with Carter" (a current hit). So far, so good. They followed that with "Down with America" (an all-time favorite). But then the head cheerleader got carried away. He tried to get the crowd to scream after him, "Down with the imperialist cabinet of the United States." It was too much. There was confusion, babble—trailing into very unfanatic low mumbles.

The American reporters laughed, one American reporter decided to help out the crowd. He would teach them something simple, which is why that evening, on American television, millions of citizens were treated to the baffling sight and sound of an angry Iranian mob in Tehran, chanting in perfect unison: "Down with I.R.S."

Under the Ayatollah Khomeini, Iran enforced Moslem laws against hard liquor, even for the western media. Of course, in 1980, the biggest New Year's Eve party in Tehran, the one with the most food and booze, was the one given by the embassy of Bangladesh, a Moslem nation and a right poor one, too. In a situation where nothing made sense, it made sense.

Later, a determined press corps was able to survive the local temperance laws with the help of Armenian drivers, who drove their network-hired cars across the Turkish border, bought bottles of Johnny Walker, then drove back, first stopping on the Turkish side of the Iranian border to remove the car's gas tank. They drained most of the gas and filled the rest of the tank with bottles. Then they crossed the border, drove a few miles, stopped, took the gas tank out of the car, took the bottles out of the gas tank, then put the gas in the tank and the tank in the car—and drove to Tehran. When the Johnny Walker bottles were emptied the proper way, the press threw the bottles into the air-conditioning shafts of the Intercontinental Hotel, where possibly they remain—a relic of the affection between the western news media and their staunch supporter, the Ayatollah Khomeini.

Covering Iran made all who did it strange. I remember when George Lewis came back to New York after covering, for NBC, the fall of the Shah, the ascent of the Ayatollah, the taking of American hostages and the forced retreat of the American press. Lewis is a smart fellow, and so he was invited to speak at a lunch in New York for a group of editors and publishers. They wanted to know about Iran. George said what he had to say and asked if there were any questions.

The first man who stood up, a man who should have known better since he was in the news business, asked George what he knew about Iran that NBC had never let him say on the air? You must understand that George Lewis has a low tolerance for fools, because what he said was, "Other than the fact the Ayatollah is a fag, there was nothing I couldn't report."

He wasn't fired, but it was close. Real close.

Perhaps I've painted a picture of the television journalist abroad as some half-assed clown, amusing himself and his fraternity bothers with practical jokes, while a zany old world keeps shooting itself in the foot. That's not how it is. People who watch while babies die and ten-year-olds go off to fight in something their parents say is a religious crusade seldom come away thinking war is an adventure. A reporter who has to listen to politicians insist a terrorist bomb is nothing more than an act of patriotism eventually fails to see the humor of the situation. There is no sport in filming the final breath of an African child who couldn't survive on a diet of weeds, and knowing there's nothing to do about it but to keep rolling. Seeing, firsthand, the charred remains of a village that had to be destroyed in order to be saved, will damn near ruin the day of the most callous newsman. The tenth time some self-proclaimed hero of the people tries to make you believe yesterday's lie is today's truth is the time most reporters come to the conclusion that a little reality goes a long way. Getting crazy is the survival technique of choice. Take a look at civilization as practiced in the last quarter of the twentieth century. A good time to laugh, obviously, is when you can, and so most do. It's the little something extra that comes with the trenchcoat. Somebody merely forgot to tell Joel McCrea.

While foreign correspondents have their own troubles—language being one, since there are more than fifty alphabets in the world (happily, more than half of them are in India)—correspondents who travel in the U.S. have their own bothersome details to worry about. For example, Nadine Stewart was hired by NBC News to be a correspondent for our network bureau in Atlanta. Nadine was living in Florida at the time. She packed for Atlanta—a small suitcase only; the rest of her clothes would be shipped to her. When she got to Atlanta, one warm March afternoon, the bureau chief told her there'd been a small change of plans. She was no longer assigned to Atlanta; she was assigned to New York, and the plane left in one hour. Nadine has nothing if not spunk; she raced to the airport, caught her plane and arrived that night to find a New York City shut down by a transit strike and freezing in a freak cold spell. She also arrived in time for the assignment editor to tell her she was scheduled to appear live on the *Today* show at 7:10 the following morning, doing a report from the Brooklyn Bridge, where thousands of New Yorkers could be seen walking to work during the strike. Someone lent her a coat. Someone else told her where the Brooklyn Bridge was, and the next morning at 7:10, there was Nadine, a quick study, giving a good account of what was going on. She finished and you could almost see her sigh in relief; her first network assignment had gone off without a hitch, even if it concerned a topic and location unfamiliar to her. Jane Pauley, on the set at Rockefeller Center, decided to ask Nadine a question on the air.

"Nadine, tell us, just how long is the Brooklyn Bridge?"

How long was the Brooklyn Bridge? God, she'd only just found the thing half an hour before. She'd gone to law school, worked as a reporter and supported herself for years, but she had no idea how long the Brooklyn Bridge was, and so she said the only thing possible.

"Jane, I don't know."

Should you care, the Brooklyn Bridge is 5,989 feet long, counting the ramps at either end. I know because Nadine looked it up that very day and to this very day can be heard working the information into a conversation about almost anything, just for practice. In my business, when you talk about the rules of the road, it's wise to include the rules of the bridge.

Back to sex. I promised sex in this chapter, so I guess it's time to talk about cameramen. There is a myth that cameramen are sexier than ordinary mortals. Last summer, at a birthday party for a friend, a group of women who work in television addressed this matter. Looking around the table, I said I would bet that every woman there, if she were truthful, had a cameraman somewhere in her past. One by one, they began to admit this was so, except for one very serious journalist who sat there stern-faced, silent. We began to tease her. "Come on, confess. We won't tell."

"It's not that," said the serious journalist. "I'm just trying to count."

One night during the 1980 presidential campaign, the candidate's plane arrived in a certain city, the candidate went to bed, and the press corps was free for the evening. As luck would have it, in the same hotel was a convention of women who taught at beauty schools—young women, mostly. The seven or eight television cameramen from the campaign decided to investigate. They went into the ballroom where the women were convening, and they went in with their cameras on their shoulders, mumbling stuff about needing a few pictures for national television. The cameras were not rolling, but a civilian would be unlikely to spot that. Ten minutes later, the cameramen came back, having made arrangements for the evening. Outside the ballroom, the cameras were then passed to the soundmen, who went in to make their own deals. Ten minutes later, the soundmen passed the cameras to producers. When I left, the wire-service reporters were heading for the ballroom, shouldering network television cameras. Don't tell me it doesn't work. I know cameramen who don't carry those things so much as they model them. (I also know many cameramen who take no part in those games, so if your husband or lover is a cameraman, assume he is one of them.)

My final tale of sex on the road is not about cameramen at all. It's about a Jacuzzi, a bottle of wine and a misunderstanding. In 1976, in Kansas City, on the day after the Republican convention, several reporters and producers from at least two networks met at a hotel to nurse hangovers. We were suffering the postcoital depression that comes from figuring out the only thing screwed in the recent past was the country. We were tired. It had been a long summer. Every four years, the summers seem longer than is right. We were not feeling sexy. We were feeling giggly. We heard there was a health club in the hotel. The idea of sitting in a Jacuzzi, sipping wine and soaking our bodies seemed a perfect punctuation mark to the quadrennial heave of the political nominating process.

However, the health club was segregated. There was one Jacuzzi for women, another for men. It just wouldn't do. All we had in mind was hot water and telling each other a bunch of lies, but we had in mind doing it in the company of boys *and* girls. Hell, we were going to wear bathing suits. Still, rules were rules, and as members of the national media, we certainly weren't going to lower ourselves to break the rules of a nice hotel like this one. Not much, we weren't.

We decided on the women's Jacuzzi, gathered our wine and champagne bottles and settled in. We'd no more begun to sip and soak when the hotel manager burst into the Jacuzzi room, red of face, strong of purpose and wanting to tell us something.

"See here. You can't do this!"

Seven voices attacked the poor man at once. It was a stupid rule, we said, and couldn't he see we weren't doing anything so damn wrong, and besides we were dressed and too tired to give a hoot about sex, and why was he going to be a hard-ass about such a silly thing, and weren't we the national bloody press, and had we bothered anybody, we'd like to know?

With all the noise we made, it took the manager a while to get through, but when he did, he said he knew we must be the national press because nobody else would be so woodenheaded and hard-of-hearing. He said he didn't give a goddamn about men and women being in the women's Jacuzzi. All he knew was, we absolutely could *not,* no matter who the hell we thought we were, bring *glass* bottles into *his* health club—which was why he'd brought plastic jugs for us to put the wine in, thank you, and if nobody minded, after two weeks of politicians messing up his hotel, ruining his sleep and screwing with his Karma, he believed he'd join us, if someone would just move over a little—and by the way, if we ran out of wine, the hotel had plenty more.

I understood. The gentleman was merely operating under his own I.T.P. Factor.

# IF YOUR COW WON'T GIVE MILK, SELL HIM

The obscure we see eventually, the
completely apparent takes longer.
EDWARD R. MURROW

In 1978, I threw my television set out a second-story window. When I went to retrieve it, it sported a third-degree crack across the screen—but it still worked. That was when I knew: you cannot kill 'em. Television is forever, or at least televisions are. Lately, I have figured out something else: I am not a television. I am not forever. Especially *in* television. So while I am still working in television news, what have I learned about it?

The first lesson is easy. I've learned I like my work. All things considered, mine is a good job to have. As I've said, the pay is outstanding and you don't have to wear a uniform. For people like me, it's a job that makes sense, because for people like me it is never enough to watch something happen. We want to watch it, then run to tell everybody else what we saw. For a shy person, it is, if nothing else, a way to start a conversation. One day, in the White House press room, a group of reporters sat around talking. The subject of Sam Donaldson came up. Donaldson is the shy fellow who covers the White House for ABC, and he is shy the way George Patton was. Somebody wondered aloud what Sam would have done if he'd been born before there was television news.

"That's easy," said one reporter. "He'd go door-to-door." For Sam, for me, and for others like us, this job saves shoe leather, but I'd wear out a closetful of shoes before I'd try to do my bosses' jobs, even though I greatly enjoy saying they don't know what they're doing, that group of rocket scientists we call television producers and executives.

I do not ever want to produce the evening news. The only newscast I produced all by myself was a horror show. It happened in 1977, and lasted forty-two seconds. NBC, along with the other networks, had recently begun to interrupt prime-time programming twice each night with a fast bite of news. At the time it was called *NBC News Update,* and although it was brief, it was seen by more people than any other news program at NBC, simply because it was in prime time. I was working in Washington at the time, and on that particular night I was the reporter *and* producer in charge of *Update*. NBC must have figured I'd have to work overtime to screw up a forty-two-second newscast. NBC was wrong.

It was a Sunday. Earlier that day, two jumbo jets had collided on a runway on the island of Tenerife, in the Canary Islands. Film of the scene had arrived at NBC after *Nightly News* ended, but in time for *Update*. Without consulting anyone, I chose to devote the full forty-two seconds to showing that film. Usually we'd use four or five short items about different topics. It would have been better if I'd checked to see what prime-time program I was about to interrupt, especially since it turned out to be a made-for-TV movie called *Flight to Holocaust,* the Technicolor saga of a dreadful plane crash.

*Update* went on the air and you couldn't tell where the movie stopped and the news began. Tasteless does not begin to do justice to the moment. It was awful, but by then there was nothing to do but continue, which I did, ending my narration with a poignant line about 576 people whose vacations had ended in death. We cut to a commercial, and there, Lord help me, was Karl Malden, looking sincerely into the camera and telling everybody that the worst thing that could happen to you on your vacation was to lose your traveler's checks. The next day a newspaper columnist suggested I find another line of work.

For a while I thought about going into management; it seemed to me it might be an expedient way to change what I didn't like about television news. In my fantasy, I even had dreams of being able to persuade others in management that there were better ways to gather and present the news; or maybe I could persuade others like me to go into management. As Arlo Guthrie said, "First one, then two of us—pretty soon they'll think it's a movement." (Of course, he also said that if three of us do it, they'll think it's a conspiracy.) I gave up the notion after somebody stole the New York bureau chief's telephone—and he didn't miss it for three days. I couldn't go into management; I was still breathing.

Any changes I want to make in television news will, I

guess, be limited to what I can do in my own stories and on my own show, if I ever have another one. Right now, I have what you might call a "minishow""—five minutes every Friday morning on the *Today* show. It's called "T.G.I.F.," and if the title doesn't tell you what it is, at least it tells you when it is. What it is, is five minutes of stories that have been ignored by other newscasts during the week, stories that range from one about a school offering prizes—radios, TVs, stereos—to encourage students to come to school, to one about France's version of *The Muppet Show,* which is a political satire, to one about a dwarf-throwing contest in Australia. (That one, you will not be surprised to know, was ignored by all shows at all networks.) The stories I use are not stories that will change us—they are stories about us. I get my material from NBC affiliates, overseas news services and the outtakes of other NBC News stories—and yes, I learned that from *Overnight.* Then, the "T.G.I.F." videotape editor, the enormously talented Lynne Hertzog, shuffles them around into some order that makes sense and makes me shine. I enjoy it, and if nobody else wants to do it, I guess it's because nobody else sees the fun—and the benefit—of spending Wednesday evenings screening the Saudi Arabian satellite feed.

When I first went to work doing "T.G.I.F." for the *Today* show—after *Summer Sunday* ended, with a whimper—I pointed out to Steve Friedman, executive producer of *Today,* that every show that had had me as a regular had been canceled. That being the case, I said, I considered the *Today* show, on the air for thirty-three years, to be my greatest challenge.

I'm not sure whether such an outstanding cancellation record as mine is the result of natural talent or pure diligence. If I argue that lousy ratings are often the result of lousy television, how can I say there are exceptions? Good point. I wish now I hadn't made it. Well, how *do* I account for being canceled so often? Simple. I use the Bob Weir theory. Bob Weir is lead singer for the Grateful Dead, the oldest, established, permanent, floating rock band in America. The band goes on and on, year after year, although it has never had a hit record and seldom gets its music played on big radio stations. I asked Weir how he explained the fact that so many people said the members of the Grateful Dead could not sing and play the same song, in the same key, at the same time—or start and finish at the same time, except by accident.

"Well," said Weir, "you can't please everybody."

The Grateful Dead is still working—and so am I. Do I worry about my future in television? No, not since David Brinkley explained it to me years ago.

It was 1976, an election year, and during the summer of that year NBC News broadcast a weekly program about the campaign called, not unreasonably, *Campaign and the Candidates* with David Brinkley. At the time, I'd been employed by NBC News a big six months. I'd never met David Brinkley, even though his office in Washington was just six doors down the hall from mine. Every so often he'd pass me in the hall—and I let him. Brinkley gave the impression he already knew enough people, thank you.

Now we were going to coanchor this program: Ellerbee and Brinkley. Okay, Brinkley and Ellerbee. No problem. After all, I was a network correspondent, a pro. All I had to do was stay calm and not screw up.

The morning of the broadcast I arrived early so David and I would have plenty of time to make friends while we wrote our show together. It would have worked, too, except that I wrote in the newsroom and David wrote, or otherwise occupied his time, in his office, with the door closed. We saw each other for the first time that day as we arranged ourselves on the set, attaching gadgets to our clothes, sticking gadgets in our ears and pretending we had been introduced so we wouldn't have to talk about the fact that we hadn't been introduced. I remember I looked at the clock, and all my cool dissolved.

"Excuse me. I know you do this every day and have done this every day, forever, but you should know it's almost my first time and I am scared shitless. Could we make that—I am scared shitless, sir?" David Brinkley finally looked at me.

"I don't know why you would worry about a thing like that. All they can do is *fire* you." And then we were on the air. "*Good* evening."

At the time, I remember thinking he sounded just like everybody else sounded when they did their Brinkley imitations. It was the last thing I remember until the program ended and several weeks passed without anyone firing me. It took a while to sink in. David was right. They couldn't eat me. They couldn't put me in reporter jail. They couldn't, finally, make me do anything I didn't want to do. All they could do was fire me—and I have two months' worth of canned food at home.

As I said, I'm still here—and so is the canned food. What's more, I have hope for television and me. The unicorn story has renewed my faith.

The circus came to New York City in the spring of 1985, as it does every year: Barnum & Bailey, lions and tigers and elephants—I wonder which poor soul rode the elephant this year—*and* a brand-new, first time ever, one and only, genuine live unicorn. The first night the circus performed, representatives from the American Society for the Prevention of Cruelty to Animals—grown-ups, the lot of 'em—were on hand to observe, and when they were done observing they called the media with the news that it was not a real, live unicorn (this just in). It was a goat with a surgically attached horn, or a horn with a surgically attached goat—but *it was not a unicorn.* Local television stations didn't have to be told twice, not by the whiskers of Edward R. Blinking Murrow, they didn't. Television news was all over that story in a minute. Details *emerged,* one after the other. Bulletin fairly tripped over bulletin in New York City. Sources were *leaned* upon. The bottom would be gotten to, and right smartly. *The investigation would, by God, continue.* Tape at eleven.

Naturally, the A.S.P.C.A. demanded to examine the goat and, naturally, the circus said that was not possible since it was a unicorn and not a goat. The A.S.P.C.A. winked at the audience to this television passion play, and asked the circus where it had found this "unicorn." The circus told the A.S.P.C.A. it really couldn't say; the unicorn just kind of showed up one day.

Things were cooking now. Local television stations hovered, ready, one felt, to interrupt regularly scheduled programming if an "exclusive" could be guaranteed. One night, on the six o'clock news, a reporter interviewed an eight-year-old girl who stated with authority that it could *not* be a unicorn because everyone knew a unicorn was a *horse,* for heaven's sake, and not a goat. How dumb could you get?

A series of interviews with men and women "on the street" followed. Was the child perhaps right? Did it have to be a horse to be a unicorn? Could a goat be one?

Think of it. Full-grown human beings appeared on television to debate how an animal *that did not exist* should look, properly speaking. Finally, as you would expect, the federal government was called to render judgment. Some GS-12 from the Department of Agriculture was made to fly up from Washington and examine the beast. He announced afterward that the animal was in good health and, as best he could tell, reasonably content. It was, however, a goat—*unless you wanted to call it a unicorn.* Now, that is what I call taking a firm stand, and I sure hope that fellow intends to leave Washington and run for the Senate sometime soon, providing no eight-year-old girls take him on in the primary.

During the course of the Great New York Unicorn Scare, the circus took out advertisements in *The New York Times,* advising all citizens that the fogies of this world were once again out to destroy magic, Santa Claus and the Constitution. To no one's surprise, the circus, with its unicorn, quickly became the hottest ticket in town.

Then the circus moved on, its purse overflowing, its reputation renewed, its very case proven once more. Be of good cheer; in an inconstant world, the very point of the circus remains alive and well, and P. T. Barnum remains accurate long past his death—one is *still* born every minute. This way to the egress! Next year they ought to implant headlights on the goat and call it a Camaro. I know television news will rise to the occasion. I learned *that* working in local news.

And I know there will be a place for me in television news as long as there are unicorns, because somebody will have to write about them, somebody who believes in them, and not some grown-up. Will it make any difference if I get old? Has the business progressed enough to allow an aging female who believes in unicorns, truth, justice, rock'n'roll and the American way—not necessarily in that order—to stay on the air? Not too long ago I happened to hear a woman who anchors a local newscast in New York referred to as a "young Linda Ellerbee." Well, I'm glad someone is. Right now, forty-one seems a good fit, and although it may sound pompous, I didn't get to be forty-one in this job without being good at it—and it took getting to be forty-one to be able to say that I am good at what I do and I know it. I've been told I can keep my job, as long as I don't look forty-one. It wasn't put that clearly—it never is—but by now I've come to appreciate the generosity I'm being shown. It's all right if I get old, as long as I don't look old. That, you understand, would indicate a poor attitude on my part. Does it count that I don't *feel* old? No? I see.

It's only television it's only television it's only television. Somebody ought to remember, however, that statistically the bulk of the American public is growing old right along with me. When you speak of *The Big Chill* generation, the word to remember is "big."

If I go, I'll keep what I've learned. The same is true if I stay. The main thing I've learned is that dreck is dreck, and no amount of fancy polish will make it anything else. The medium is not the message; the medium is the medium. What goes in one end comes out the other. I learned *that* from Reuven Frank.

It's up to those of us who work in the business to be honest reporters—and to learn our craft, to make sure that we know how to write, that we produce television and not radio, and that we leave a little something for the audience to do. I learned *that* on *Weekend.* We at our end have to put in the best we have to offer because at the other end is a viewer who deserves the best—and knows the difference. That viewer is our audience, even if it's an audience of one, which it's not.

The viewer has an obligation, too. If the president says that South Africa has "eliminated the segregation that we once had in our country"—as he did in the summer of 1985—and the media report that this simply is not the case, then the viewer must understand that what's going on is not a bunch of reporters being unfair and negative toward the president. The viewer has to know it means the free press is on the job. If the viewer is watching television and the president makes a statement like the one about South Africa—and goes unchallenged by reporters—well, that's why God created an on/off switch on the television set. Any other way of looking at it will produce nothing but garbage television, every time. I learned *that* from *Overnight.*

And—while doing all this—if we forget to be human beings and forget that the viewers and the people we work with are also human beings, we will ourselves be garbage. I learned *that* from Herb Dudnick.

As I write this, there are signs of hope concerning TV news and my network. For one, NBC has put on the air a children's news program, and Herb Dudnick is the executive producer. Most of the staff are from *Overnight;* I can't think of a better group of children to put on a children's news program. For one thing, I know they will not treat the viewers—the future plumbers in Albuquerque—like idiots, and whatever the fate of the program, it is a sign NBC is a network that still tries new things. That counts.

I am further encouraged to see that NBC News is still plugging away with its attempts to keep a television magazine on the air, in spite of the efforts of some of those in charge of NBC's prime-time programming. I don't know what the fate of *American Almanac,* hosted by Roger Mudd, will be, either, but NBC says it is fully *committed* to keeping it on the air. I'm sure they've also told Roger that ratings don't matter.

I have hopes for journalism, too. When the United States invaded Grenada and refused to allow any reporters to go along, it seemed at first that the American people agreed with the government. Mostly it seemed that way because nobody *asked* the American people's opinion before the armed forces invaded. When they did, through polls, the public spoke up. Once again the plumber in Albuquerque came through. The public said the government *should have* let the press go along and cover the invasion of Grenada, just as the press had gone along and covered World War II without managing to lose the war for our side. That was very encouraging news to me, because the only other time in recent memory that an invading country refused to allow the world press into the country it was invading was when the Soviet Union invaded Afghanistan.

The Reagan administration had argued that reporters could not be trusted to be fair in their coverage. Senator Jeremiah Denton, a Republican from Alabama, said the networks never gave but one side of the news. He said he had spoken to news executives who had looked him right in the eye and told him the media are running the country. If we are, we're doing a terrible job of it. I think it's important to know that Senator Denton was able to make his remarks *on television,* during hearings to decide if the law should be changed to make it easier for the F.B.I.—the government—to spy on certain groups in this country. Senator Denton wanted the rules changed.

I covered similar hearings some years ago in Washington, and I have a vivid memory of a highly placed official of the C.I.A. shouting to everybody there: "Remember—the First Amendment is *only an amendment.*" The man was right, and here's something else to remember. There have been many instances in which politicians have taken power and muzzled the press. There is no instance where the press has taken power and muzzled the politicians. I learned *that* from David Brinkley. As journalists, it is in our interest to make certain that John Peter Zenger, if he were alive today, would still be acquitted, whether the government liked it or not. I learned *that* from covering politics and the government.

Is there anything left to tell, any nugget of advice to be culled from my years in television news? Yes, but I had help. Bill Schechner had to tell me.

One night, shortly after Bill began working on *Overnight,* I looked up to see him just sitting there, staring at a blank page in his typewriter, blocked. I watched for a while and he stared for a while. Dobyns, who'd quit the program only a week before, wandered in, muttering about having left this favorite ruler in his, now Bill's, desk. Seeing how things were, Dobyns stopped and sat on the edge of my desk. Now, two of us were watching Bill stare at the blank piece of paper. When we got tired of that, Dobyns decided to help the rookie; he'd tell him what he'd learned. He leaned over Bill, and said: "Don't think. Write." Bill continued to stare, unimpressed. By now, Pat Trese had edged over to where we were, and Gerry Polikoff, the director, who wasn't superstitious except about the duck, saw us watching and stopped to see what it was we were watching. Bill went on staring. It was my turn. I gave him Brinkley's best shot.

"Hell, Bill, all they can do is fire you." Bill stared. Gerry thought he knew the truth. He told Bill everything would be okay so long as he didn't wear black-and-white checks and cause the video to bleed all over the goddamned place. Bill stared.

Pat Trese, sensing the possibility of a scene that might include voices raised in panic, looked to the ceiling and said all he knew for sure was, when Judgment Day came, he wanted to be in the press section.

Herb Dudnick, just back from Pluto or wherever it was he kept his brain, took in the whole scene at a glance.

"Bill," he said, "if your cow won't give milk, sell him."

Cheryl Gould, passing by with a pencil in her hair and papers in her hand, stopped cold.

"Milk, Bill? I don't know about milk, but milkshakes would be nice. Milkshakes are always nice."

Bill stared at the paper. Lloyd left to go to his new office—and his new magazine show, so he could enjoy it before it was canceled. Gerry went back to the control room. Pat went back to his wire copy. Herbie went back to Pluto. Cheryl went to the phone to see who would deliver milkshakes at that hour. I watched Bill stare, but he seemed happier about staring now. After a while he looked up, and that's when he told me the only thing I know worth passing on.

"Linda," he said, "it's the truth. Facts add a lot to any story." He stopped staring and started typing.

* * *

Fact: my cow is still giving milk. I won't sell him just yet. On television, I use the phrase, "and so it goes," to end my reports and my shows. I stole it from Lloyd Dobyns, who says he borrowed it from his parents. Others say he stole it from Kurt Vonnegut, but that's wrong because Vonnegut said simply, "So it goes." One fellow wrote to assure me Shakespeare said it first, or maybe it was Moses. It doesn't matter. Steal from one person, it's plagiarism. Steal from more than one, it's research. I research. Besides, what does matter is that very often "and so it goes," is the only sensible thing to say after one has said many things which make no sense—like recounting the day's events.

Anyway, saying "and so it goes," leaves a door open. The implication is that things are still *going*. The tense is present. There are possibilities. Tomorrow it may not go so. Once, when I was anchoring *Overnight,* I got a letter from a little girl. All it said was:

> Dear Miss Ellerbee,
> When I grow up I want to do exactly what you do. Please do it better.

Well, tomorrow there may be better news, and I may report it better. I hope so. Remember Mark Twain's story about the self-important skipper of a coastal schooner that hauled furniture between Nantucket and Boston? Every time he'd see another ship, he'd run to the rail and with his megaphone cry out, "What ship is that? Whence and wherefore?" One day he saw a stately Indiaman sailing by, sail upon sail unfurled into the wind, its bow plowing through the waves, decks laden with cargo and crowded with sailors. The self-important little skipper grabbed his megaphone and yelled, as usual, "What ship is that? Whence and wherefore?"

Rolling back across the sea came the reply, "The *Begum of Bengal*, with spices and silks. One hundred and nineteen days out from Canton, homeward bound. What ship is that? Whence and wherefore?" The now deflated little skipper meekly answered back, "It's only the *Mary Ann*, with nothing in particular."

During those long seconds just before the red light goes on and the stage manager gives me the cue to start talking, and during these last moments before the book goes to be printed, I am only the *Linda Jane*, properly humble, worried that I'm carrying nothing in particular.

The rest of the time I am Linda Ellerbee, under full sail and running before the wind—forty-one years out—and bound for home.

And so it goes.

# FAST FORWARD

"I wrote a book on the assumption my bosses had a sense of humor. What could go wrong?"
LINDA ELLERBEE

If you thought you were done reading a book I thought I was done writing, don't worry; it means you are a normal person and, therefore, as ignorant about book publishing as I am—or was, once. Besides, you're right. *That* book did end with the words "And so it goes." This chapter is *not* part of that book. It's something else, so nobody will blame you if you choose to quit while you're behind.

September, 1985—that's when Putnam's received a three-inch-high stack of papers, stuffed inside a cardboard box and bound, whimsically, by a length of red silk ribbon. I've read how some writers suffer feelings of loss when they stop fiddling, finally, and surrender to the publisher what the publisher paid them to write (and surrender) in the first place. Loss? Not this writer, not since the day Mrs. Alston, who taught fifth grade at River Oaks Elementary, in Houston, Texas, told me all about the Deadline Demon and what he would do to me if I were unable to complete my geography notebook before she completed her letter to my mother. Loss doesn't come close to defining what I felt when, with two full seconds to spare, I handed over that notebook. Try happy to be alive. Try weak with relief. Of course it should have been a warning, but I was ten years old, making too much noise to hear warnings and too many plans to consider the possibility life might turn out to be one near-miss after another.

The Deadline Demon smiled, I bet.

Years have passed and he hasn't eaten me yet, but it's been close once or twice. I recall a time when I thought bookwriting would be easier than newswriting because (one) you got to do it sitting down and (two) book deadlines were over yonder, way over yonder, somewhere beyond that clump of trees. Next thing I knew, the Deadline Demon was breathing down my neck while I was tying red ribbon around a cardboard box. Right then I swore that of all the kinds of damnfool I was sure to be over the next few years, I would not be the kind who had anything to do with bookwriting, ever again.

Like I said, that was September, 1985.

The phone call came in November, 1986.

"Boy, do we have a wonderful idea! We think you ought to write a new chapter—for the paperback edition of the book—a chapter about the crazy stuff that happened after your book was published. You remember, how you lost your job and went on *The Johnny Carson Show* and got famous for fifteen minutes and all the rest? Surely you remember?"

It will come as no surprise to you that this swell idea was proposed by the publisher of the paperback edition.

I answered from what should have been native instinct. In my case, it wasn't included in the original mix because neither of my parents worked in publishing or television. My first clue was the fact that they were married to each other, but I was able to pick up this instinct along the way.

"For free? Write something for free? You mean you want me to write an extra chapter for free? *Are you crazy or what?*"

Well, here it is January, 1987, and if you are, at this moment, reading what I am, at this moment, writing (for free), well, congratulations; likely it means you had sense enough to wait for the paperback. Imagine. $17.95 for a book that doesn't even have the answers printed in the back. Yes, I did lose my job. No, I wasn't fired. I've tried to figure out why the things that happened last summer happened, but I keep getting these headaches. Then one day I came across something John Kenneth Galbraith wrote. Said Mr. Galbraith:

> "It is a far, far better thing to have a firm anchor in nonsense than to put out on the troubled seas of thought."

Now that is what you call a find. Not only did it illuminate what happened last summer, but it was the first truly descriptive job title I've found, concerning my line of work. *A firm anchor in nonsense.* A firm anchorwoman in nonsense.

My book came out in May. My contract with NBC expired in June. Foolishly, I'd hoped the first would affect the second, which it did, but not in the way I'd hoped. Way back in January it became clear that what we had here was an opportunity for the Timing God to have some fun. Sure, I could have delayed publication until the contract situation was resolved one way or another. It was a gamble—if the book bombed; well, NBC didn't seem to be rushing to get me to anchor, write or report anything more than my five minutes of *TGIF,* as it was—but if the book succeeded, maybe NBC would allow me six minutes a week. This may not sound like the most logical way to chart one's professional life, but consider the profession. All along, I said the book was the story of a sane person in an insane business, or the other way around. If you still don't believe me, just pause for a moment to think about the elephants.

Remember how I wrote that local television news is the place where you ride the elephants? After the book came out, I got a wonderful letter from a television reporter, except I lost the letter so I can't tell you his name, which is too bad because he is a wise man. He wrote that he'd ridden the elephant, too, ridden it, in order to please his station and the circus, right over the bridge connecting the United States with Canada, near Buffalo. He said that when he and Jumbo got to the other side, the Canadian Customs officer looked up at him—way up at him—and shouted, "Are you bringing anything into Canada?"

There was only one conclusion to be drawn, he wrote. And that was this: After so many years of watching television, people no longer notice the elephants.

So, when I wrote this stuff about television, and people who write about the stuff people write about television wrote kind words about the stuff I wrote, I sort of hoped that my employer at NBC might laugh—or at least pause for one moment and breathe a sigh of gratitude, not for what I did write but for what I did *not* write in my book. But after so many years *in* television, nobody was noticing the elephants anymore, either.

Who knows? All I can say for sure is, nobody in management ever mentioned the book to me, except for the conversation that started because I had to tell the president of NBC News who-I-thought-I-was-to-think-I-could-make-fun-of-the-Vice-President-of-the-United-States. As fortune would have it, I got the answer wrong.

This is the place where I want to write: It wasn't my fault. Blame Steve Friedman. I even like the way the sentence looks, but lies always look better, and it *was* my fault. Steve, who is executive producer of the *Today* show and, as I've mentioned, a few bubbles off plumb, heard about The Sesquicentennial. The state of Texas was about to mark its 150th anniversary in the restrained, impeccable good taste one associates with that state—*and Good Morning, America* (on ABC) had announced it would broadcast its entire show on that holiest of days—from that holiest of shrines—The Alamo.

It was Friday morning. I was sitting in Steve's office, playing with his stuffed pirhana, the one on his desk, running my fingers over its sharp little teeth, while behind his desk, Steve fired rubber-tipped darts from a miniature shotgun at a contraption that stands maybe four feet high and looks a bit like one of those old revolving clotheslines. Indeed, it does revolve and as it goes round it presents the intrepid hunter with five flying ducks, off and on, as moving targets will do, even cardboard ones. Someone who works for Steve gave this *thing* to him, hoping he would like shooting at little cardboard ducks so much he would stop shooting at the staff. Steve liked his new toy but never loved it until the day he taped a photograph of one of NBC's many vice-presidents over one of the cardboard ducks. That morning I noticed and commented on the fact that his aim seemed to have improved.

"Motivation. Works every time."

We talked about Texas and ABC and what, if anything, the *Today* show ought to do. Steve shot the vice-president in the nose, which always cheered him up and after a minute he smiled at me.

"I got it! Let the mountain go to Mohammed! We'll carry coals to Newcastle!"

Sometimes I wonder what it would be like to work among the sound of mind or—after so many years working in television—if I'd be allowed to. Does working in television make people crazy or is it only crazy people who work in television? I always thought I was a sane person, but I worry because I'm coming to see mental illness as viable choice—attractive, even—and worse, I've become fluent in speaking and understanding the language of the twisted, which is how I knew what Steve was saying when he was talking about coal and Mohammed.

"Okay, I'll go to Texas. Five days. Five minutes each day, plus live wraparounds. But only if I don't have to report about *or say the word* 'sesquicentennial.' Let Bryan say it. If he can. We'll call the series *TGIT*—Thank God it's Texas."

A word about Texas and its Sesquicentennial. Texas was not celebrating the 150th anniversary of its becoming a state, Texas was celebrating the 150th anniversary of its becoming a *country*, which it did from 1836, when Texas declared itself independent of Mexico, until 1846, when Texas declared itself dependent on the

United States of America, although few Texans put it that way.

The first story aired on Monday and right after that was when people in my own hometown started saying how I was a communist or worse and why was I on television in the first place, especially why was I on with that nice Jane Pauley, who wasn't a Texan, herself, but certainly would not have done what I did because she was a lady. Some of my own kin didn't speak to me for days and, as bad fortune would have it, they weren't the ones I used to hope would never say another word to me back when there was no chance of that happening. The next thing was that people who were not related to me wrote about me in the newspaper. One said I should be ashamed of myself; I had been in New York City too long and ought to go back, and soon.

My story on the *Today* show was all about the Alamo and, in the interest of what we like to call accuracy, I included some facts. Bill Schechner was right. They added a lot to the story. One fact was that historians now had evidence which proved Davy Crockett did not die in battle at the Alamo, as we'd been told (my favorite painting of that glorious, if imaginary, moment used to hang in the shrine, itself, and showed Ole Davy swinging his gun at a bunch of those lily-livered, sneaky, no-account Meskins, except Ole Davy was painted to look like John Wayne, from when the Duke played Ole Davy in the movie about our sacred shrine), but was taken prisoner and executed, four days later. Another fact had to do with those liberty-loving Texans who'd accepted free land from Mexico (it *was* part of Mexico, you know) and thereby agreed to keep calling that land "Mexico," and not "Texas" or "Baja Oklahoma" or even "New Mexico." Then, there was the historical footnote that had to do with the rights for which those brave lads fought, one of which was the right to own slaves. Owning slaves was against the law in Mexico. No wonder they wanted to call it "Texas."

I included in the story an interview with a history professor, a Mexican-American history professor who'd grown up in San Antonio and who talked about how it had been when he was a kid and they brought all the school children to the Alamo so the children could hear how the freedom-loving, right-thinking, God-fearing Texans had been massacred by Santa Anna and the rest of the greasers. He put it more politely, but that was the gist of what we were taught, all of us, Anglo *and* Chicano, who grew up in Texas. My story concluded with the suggestion that perhaps it was time to forgive Santa Anna for the crime of defending his country against some raggedy-ass foreigners who were determined to burgle a piece of it in order to start building Neiman-Marcus stores and raising crooked politicians just as fast as they could. I said that more politely, too, but it didn't matter. Prettying up the words couldn't hide the terrible crime I'd committed. I'd sinned real bad. I'd done a thing no real Texan would do unless some communist-atheist-socialist-Nazi-humanist drugged him, or something like that. I'd gone on national television, live, in front of God, the Nielsens, that nice Jane Pauley and everybody and *I'd let facts interfere with a good story.*

I had no defense. They were right. I admit it and I don't even mind not being able to go back to the Alamo ever again because, if you ask me, since they took down the painting of John Wayne wearing a coonskin cap and swinging "Ole Betsy" at the hired Meskin extras, well, it hasn't been the same. Some people just don't understand about shrines.

ABC didn't make the mistake I did. I know because I watched, while working myself up to make another mistake, the one that had to do with George Bush. That was on Friday, and by Friday I was ready to eat my final taco, telephone my last relative, exit my last freeway and fly home to the peace and quiet of New York City, and would have if *Nightly News* hadn't suddenly discovered Texas and its Sesquicentennial—right there in *The New York Times*.

"Say, Linda, did you know that Bush is going to spend the day in Texas because Texas is celebrating its Sesquicentennial and George is from Texas (no, he's not; he just went there for the politics). Why don't you do a story about the Vice-President and the Sesquicentennial? We'll close the show with it. Don't worry. Let it run long—say, 1:45?"

It was an unremarkable little story. (I still find it difficult to be remarkable in one minute and forty-five seconds.) To jazz it up some, I resorted to a not-at-all-new piece of business I'd stolen from Tom Pettit years before, when we both covered political campaigns, only Pettit always did it better. It worked like this: Bush flew around the state and everyplace he spoke, he said the same sentence, word for word.

"I'm proud to be in Texas on this great, great day." Something like that.

I edited the story so that he was seen saying each word of the sentence in a different town. It wasn't malice. It was a way to illustrate the business of politics and to do so without taking extra seconds. It was, I thought, plain reporting, which is what I thought they paid me to do. The story ran. *Nightly News* called me in Houston to say everybody liked the story and I could come back now. So I did.

Monday morning, when I got to work, there was a

message for me to call the president of NBC News. Hey, I thought, finally I've made an impression. Now we can start to figure out what I can do around here for the next three years. I called, was told to come to his office, went to his office, was told to wait outside, waited, and eventually was told I could go in.

He had this gadget. He pushed a button when you walked in and the door would shut behind you, all by its ownself. I would hear the door closing and, every time, I'd swing around to see who was behind me, shutting the door. It used to make me crazy, which, I suppose, was not unintentional.

He pushed. It shut. I swung. Then, having been made crazy, I sat down and he got up from behind his desk to walk around and sit in one of the chairs in front of the desk, just like me, as if we were both a couple of parolees allowed to hang out in the warden's office on account of being so docile and all.

"Linda," he said, "Linda, just who do you think you are to make fun of the Vice-President of the United States of America?"

I thought for a moment. "A journalist?"

Wrong answer. I could see that.

"A citizen?"

Silence.

"Oh, hell, *we are talking about George Bush,* aren't we?"

That, it seems, was part of my problem. I wasn't a serious journalist. How serious did they want me to be? As serious as everybody else, although, naturally, I should continue to do my work in my own distinctive style—as long as it matched everybody else's own distinctive style. He said everybody else understood what that meant. Why couldn't I? (I don't know. It's this mental block I have against gobbledegook.)

Seeking to surround myself with stronger soldiers, I told him, "Look, in our trade there's always been room for the odd-sounding note. Andy Rooney. David Brinkley. Hughes Rudd. Charlie Osgood. . . ."

He said he didn't much like their work, either.

Oh.

Was there one story, one single story or program I'd done in the last ten years at NBC that he'd liked?

He paused too long.

"I liked your book. I thought it was well-written. If you could write like that for television, we wouldn't be having this conversation."

That was the only time anybody in management at NBC News ever mentioned this book to me and it didn't seem the right occasion to point out that a lot of the stuff in the book had been lifted verbatim from what I'd said on the air. All I could think of at the moment was how I wasn't ever going to get my tie pin with the little peacock on it.

Companies like to give you things. Things are cheaper than money. A few months earlier, I'd passed the ten-year mark and NBC had given me a knife with a little peacock on it. I wondered about a company that would employ me for ten years, then arm me, but keep quiet; I wanted the tie pin with the little peacock on it and there were only nine and one-half years to go.

Surely someone was joking. I didn't want to leave NBC. I knew what was wrong; NBC merely had no program suitable for me, but I assumed that would change any day. Then I read in the newspaper that NBC planned to begin a completely new and different, late-night, off-beat, irreverent news program—and in order to do so, NBC had hired a consultant from *Newsweek* to explain what a program like that ought to be. I began to take a hint. And still, leaving NBC didn't seem real to me. After so many years spent making camp, then moving on, always moving on, like some American Bedouin, then finally settling down with one tribe for ten and one-half years; well, I'd gotten out of the habit of seeing how fast I could pack. Even when NBC offered to let me stay for only a 40% cut in pay, I figured we could work something out. Even when NBC told the newspapers how generous it had been to offer me 40% less than I'd been making, I figured it was still just good, clean fun, especially when the book became a best seller and CBS asked me to anchor its morning news and ABC asked me to anchor *Our World,* its new prime time news program, and newspapers were getting crazy running stories about me and the book, saying things about how I was going to be a permanent substitute for Johnny Carson, and all of a sudden they were going to make a movie out of the book and Marsha Mason was going to play me, and Yale University offered me a chair (maybe I looked tired), and *Ms. Magazine* wanted to put me on its cover, and *Redbook* wanted me to write a cover story, and *Penthouse* wanted me to write a column, and Putnam's wanted me to write a second book, and *The Grateful Dead Newsletter* swore it would pay me fifty dollars a week, cash, to write the truth—and they probably didn't even have the fifty dollars cash—*now you'd think NBC would stop kidding around and keep me, right?*

Wrong.

It had to be the light bulbs.

Let me explain. There used to be this old joke. NBC was owned by RCA, so when somebody wanted to say NBC wasn't as good as CBS they'd say it was because RCA made televisions while CBS made *television.*

Well, in 1986, RCA was bought by General Electric, so I figure that if people who made televisions couldn't understand television, how can you expect people who make light bulbs to understand television?

The offer of a 40% cut in pay stood. Sadly, it was an offer I could refuse.

June, 1986. Friday morning. 8:08. The final *TGIF* aired. I said goodbye, said I was leaving, thanked all the people at NBC who'd taught me so much, even the executives, said it had been great fun, but just one of those things, said every exit was an entry somewhere, said "and so it goes," and then I did. Steve Friedman gave me his stuffed pirhana.

I got myself another little, yellow, stuffed duck and these days, if you look hard, you can spot that little duck somewhere near me on the set of *Our World.* If you want to know where to find *Our World,* just look for it on ABC, Thursday nights at eight. It's up against *The Cosby Show* on NBC, which happens to be the most popular show in the history of television, but never mind. My new bosses say they're interested in quality so ratings don't matter—this time—and I know my *new* bosses wouldn't lie. So, me and my duck, we're smiling.

I like it here at *Our World.* This a place where they pay you to live in the past. What I mean is, *Our World* is about time. Each week, we take an hour and turn it into a time machine, on television. For instance, our first broadcast aired on September 25th, 1986, but it was all about the summer of 1969. The Moon landing. Woodstock. Manson. *True Grit. Easy Rider.* Chappaquidick. Vietnam. *Laugh-in.* Hurricane Camille. *Hair.* Nixon. *Alice's Restaurant.* The trick is to combine film, videotape, interviews with witnesses, music and other sounds of the time with our own words into a kaleidoscope of the way we were, then. Each piece of the puzzle drives the other pieces, and so on. Non-fiction entertainment, that's how Rolfe Tessem explained it to me and he produced the first show, along with Vince Stafford, who's now lost somewhere in the spring of 1975, while Rolfe is watching leaves fall in the autumn of 1949. Me, I'm in a permanent time warp. I've gone back to those summers when we couldn't go swimming because we might get polio, seen *West Side Story* open on Broadway once more, watched the Beatles break up, gotten to know Rosie and her rivets, cried again over Kent State, stood outside Central High School in Little Rock with nine black students who came face to face with 370 armed troops and won, sat in the Oval Office while Nixon fired Archibald Cox, cheered from the stands while Billie Jean King beat Bobby Riggs, watched all those girls scream when Elvis Presley first performed on *The Ed Sullivan Show,* stood listening to Harry Truman campaign against Dewey from the back of a train, shivered as Neil Armstrong stepped onto the moon—and I love it. Time traveling. I can't think why nobody thought of this before. Besides, how many writers get a chance to rewrite history, their way?

I've got a new partner. His name is Ray Gandolf and he looks like your average television anchorman about as much as I look like Connie Chung, but he's smart, a thoughtful writer and a big, bearded bear of a man who did not get what lines he has from frowning. Also, he likes women, which might have something to do with the fact that he's married to a strong, pretty woman named Blanche and they have five daughters. Five. If that's not enough, he also likes Billie Holiday, vulgar jokes and tequila—what more need one say?

Av Westin is the grown-up in charge of us all. Lucky me, I got myself a boss who reads and writes and thinks, even. Those are the best kind—and he has not asked me to change my hair, my words or my attitude, not yet; he does *The New York Times* crossword puzzle on Sundays (so we work Sundays—so what's new and different?) and I tell him I don't mind that he does his with a pencil because lots of people do that, especially people his age. Besides, he likes anchovies and never, ever steps on my lines and almost never makes me talk to strangers, so I'm happy.

"But," you ask, "is he crazy, too?"

I smile before I answer.

"He works in television."

Oh.

In the final chapter of the book I thought I'd finished writing, I mentioned that I was hopeful because NBC once more was putting a news magazine on the air. And that's just what NBC did. It wasn't bad, either. They called it *1986,* which turned out to be an appropriate title because NBC canceled the program in December of that year.

Recently, I was asked if I found ABC to be much different from NBC. And did I miss NBC? Yes and no to both questions. People in this business move around so much that wherever you are, it feels more familiar than strange. I may not know where the bathroom is, but I'm working with a film editor I worked with at NBC in 1977. As for Stanhope Gould, well, I missed him by a week or so. He's still playing one step behind or ahead of the posse, I forget which, but the result is that Stanhope left ABC to go to work for KRON in San

Francisco the month I left NBC to go to work for ABC. Maybe I'll catch him next time around.

It's the same in other ways, too. Not very long ago, someone on *Good Morning, America* called to discuss three possible changes in *TGIF* (yes, it followed me here and I kept it). I asked what changes he had in mind.

"Well, first, would you mind cutting two minutes from it?"

"Yes. I would." (It only runs four minutes.)

"Okay. Number Two. Does it have to end with that music thanking God it's Friday. What if Christians think we're being sacrilegious?"

"Yes, it does, unless you can suggest someone else we might thank."

"Okay, okay. Now, this is the last one. Does it absolutely have to air on *Friday?*"

See what I mean. Feels like I never left home, except for certain people at NBC that I miss, but like those working in television who haven't written books about television, their number dwindles down to a precious few. As I write this extra chapter, sometimes I think about the people who were part of this book and my life at NBC.

Lloyd Dobyns left NBC News. The company did not offer to renew his contract. He's in North Carolina, writing fiction, raising Christmas trees and complaining, I expect.

Herb Dudnick left NBC News. He is now news director at KRON San Francisco, and Stanhope Gould's boss. There's always a place for a man who values the complete person and the incomplete sentence, instead of the other way around.

Pat Trese is gone, too. I don't know what Pat's

doing, but whatever it is, I know he's doing it with considerable style and telling bad jokes the whole time.

Danny Webster left. He's at a television station in Albuquerque, running things, wearing funny hats, teaching people, except for the plumber, who already knows.

Reuven Frank didn't leave NBC News. After 36 years, NBC left Reuven Frank. Something to do with light bulbs, I imagine. I remember when he said that sometimes merely being the best isn't enough. Maybe not, but it's all Reuven ever knew how to be.

And it is enough.

When I told Reuven I was going to write about his leaving NBC, he said, "Just don't call it the end of an era," so I won't, because Cheryl Gould and Allison Davis and Steve Friedman and George Lewis and John Long and so many others are still there and, anyway, if you've seen one end of an era you've seen them all.

ABC is talking about an hour program that would follow Ted Koppel's *Nightline* on Friday nights. ABC asked me would I like to put such a thing together? Maybe a little news (on a reel?). Some sports (on a roll?). Maybe some of this, some of that (a thing and a thing?). Would I be interested?

"Interested? Interested? (Hello, is Pat there?) Interested, you ask? A piece of cake (Herbie, don't hang up yet.). Listen, we'll use stills, too. Every week, the best still news photographs of the week, edited to music, the way Reuven did long before *Weekend,* and we'll put together those news/music videos we learned how to do on *Summer Sunday* (Operator, how many Long Johns did you say there are in Miami?). Foreign news. Lots of foreign news. Satellites have opened everything up now. We can buy that stuff cheap. And we'll translate it ourselves *(Allo, Cheryl—avez vous les escargots?)*. And local stations. We'll use stories from local stations around the country. The way we did on *Overnight.* They got good people out there beyond the Hudson (Maybe Danny can hire the plumber!). And lots of multi-layered editing, the way we do it on *Our World* (Rolfe, I was wondering—got any plans for Friday night?). And we'll end the show with a segment like *TGIF.* News on a skewer. And . . . well, I have a couple of ideas I haven't mentioned to anybody yet, but we get some Shetland ponies . . . who knows? Look, we'll get on and we'll get off on time. What else is there?"

The people at ABC say we should call the whole program *TGIF.* I say that would be perfect because it *is* a good name (if the Christians don't mind) and besides, it certainly explains why they are executives. Any normal person would figure out that a show following *Nightline* goes on at midnight, which is Saturday, not Friday, but that's okay. We will call it *TGIF* and if anybody asks why, we'll say, "Because it's on Saturday." No. I got it. Better yet. We'll say, *"Because it's on television."*

And so it goes and goes and goes and goes and goes and goes and goes and goes and . . .